B E S T   O F
CLASS

Building a Customer Service Organization

Ken Shelton, Editor

Executive Excellence Publishing
1344 East 1120 South
Provo, Utah 84606
phone: (801) 375-4060
fax: (801) 377-5960
web: www.eep.com
e-mail: custserv@eep.com

Ordering Information:
Individual Sales: Executive Excellence Publishing products are available through most bookstores. They also can be ordered directly from Executive Excellence at the address above.

Quantity Sales: Executive Excellence Publishing products are available at special quantity discounts when purchased in bulk by corporations, associations, libraries, and others, or for college textbook/course adoptions. Please write to the address above or call Executive Excellence Publishing Book Sales Division at 1-800-304-9782.

Orders for U.S. and Canadian trade bookstores and wholesalers: Executive Excellence Publishing books and audio tapes are available to the trade through LPC Group/Login Trade. Please contact LPC at 1436 West Randolph Street, Chicago, IL 60607, or call 1-800-626-4330.

ISBN 1-890009-23-7

Printed in the United States of America
10 9 8 7 6 5 4 3 2 1

Contents

Section 4: Case Studies 163

Section 5: Special Cases 213

Introduction

**By Ken Shelton, Editor in Chief,
Executive Excellence Publishing**

*F*or 15 years, we have published in *Executive Excellence* magazine the best thinking on customer service in the spirit of shared gains and mutual benefits, civility and loyalty, contribution and commitment.

Only recently, however, when we began selecting and organizing the best of these articles did I rediscover the breadth and depth of this thinking. The articles seemed to self-select naturally into five different sections: service philosophy, service excellence, process quality, case studies, and special cases.

This collection of thought makes a compelling case for customer-focused strategies and also makes another fine contribution to the *Executive Excellence* "Classics series" of books—an important addition to the library of any organization serious about staying in business.

Rather than preview the content of the 55 chapters in this book, I prefer to make a central point. The main point made by the many contributors to this book is that best-of-class service starts with a different ethic or philosophy and may also require a different strategy, structure, system, style, process, or personnel.

What is certain is that the thinly disguised "serve-us" ethic, where the provider is the principal beneficiary of the service rendered, must give way to an ethic of win-win service rendered in the best interests of all stakeholders. Still, in the service arena, we will continue to see the best and worst examples.

Worst case. Court games and corporate service games, once played with certain protocol and are now commonly pursued with ego and alcohol. Intent players, hoping to win applause or purse, often snub time-honored traditions, throw tantrums and lash out a line judges, even alas on the hallowed lawns of Wimbledon and the halls of Harvard. Junior executives learn to think more in terms of me than we, ace than deuce, as they master top spins, rifle serves, self-service, underhanded jabs, backhand returns, offensive strategies, defensive lobs, and overhead slams. There's no such thing as "love" for the 30- and 40-somethings, only advantage and disadvantage. Indeed, service games, as played in the public courts are in a sorry state: sloppy amateurs, professing some knowledge or experience, seek to lower to do away with the nets, design their own rackets, and erase the lines, or at least appoint permissive judges.

Best case. Great service companies are managed differently, and those differences add up to service breakthroughs—and break points— in service encounters where the customer comes in contact with a service provider and the supporting cast. The best service providers, both individuals and organizations, show us anew the wisdom of caring for customers as people, not just plastic. And they do it not in the condescending style of corporate elitists but in the simple language of— we care about the same things you care about: value, speed, quality, ease of use, ease of purchase, ease of maintenance.

When I first met one of the all-time great service professionals, Herb Kelleher, CEO of Southwest Airlines, I was impressed most with the man's humility, which allowed him to be on the same team with his internal and external customers and other stakeholders. All too often, ego, pride, perception and position come between the service provider and the paying customer. When that happens, game playing takes precedence over service performance.

My hope is that this stellar collection of leading-edge thinking on customer service might influence your service philosophy and performance, resulting in more mutual benefit.

Section 1

Service Philosophy

Chapter 1

Serving the One

By Stephen R. Covey,
Co-Chairman of FranklinCovey Co.

Giving yourself completely to the one individual who needs you at the moment is the key to great servant leadership and front-line customer service.

A friend of mine, an actor, was once in a theater in New York City watching a friend of his, a fellow actor, perform a play. My friend could see that his colleague wasn't connecting with the audience, and so he worked his way into the orchestra pit with the intent of giving his friend a message.

Knowing the play very well, my friend knew exactly where his actor friend would be on the stage at different times. He knew that in one scene his friend would stand just a foot away from the orchestra pit, and he hoped to deliver his message in that brief window of opportunity. So, when his friend stood on that spot, he raised his head up, caught the eye of his friend, and said three words: "Talk to me."

His friend instantly got the message: that he was talking to a glazed-over audience that he couldn't see at all—it was just a great amorphous mass out there. When his friend said, "talk to me," he knew that meant to deal with the person, a real individual with feelings and perceptions, someone who matters. Instantly, he began acting to individuals, even though he couldn't see most of them because of the strong stage lights. But he could see some faces, and he essentially talked to the one. Soon, he captured the audience. He connected, because the key to the many is the one.

You Don't Even Know My Name

Once when I was teaching at a university, a student approached me after class at the end of the semester to thank me for the content I had delivered. It was a huge class of about 550 students. He said, "I admire what you've done in this field, and respect your knowledge, Mr. Covey, but you don't even know my name."

That confirmed to me the old truth: "I don't care how much you know until I know how much you care."

Recently I was teaching a large group of business managers and was going through a series of slides. I continually asked the technical assistant, "Now let's see this slide; now, let's see the next slide." I later received a letter from one of the audience members who said, "I listened all afternoon. Not once did you say please or thank you."

I thought that I was kindly in my voice. I didn't bark out orders; nevertheless, I failed to say the magic words, and the message to that person was not the content—it was a feeling that I lacked common courtesy and respect.

Such feedbacks suggests that the personal touch matters with 90 percent of people, and it empowers the rest.

A friend of mine, who is a prominent professional athlete, teaches a class of four-year-old children at church during the off-season. He loves these kids. He knows them by name; he calls them by name. He affirms their value and worth. He focuses on the one, because each child is important to him. He takes a special interest in them and takes time to greet them. As a result, they wouldn't miss his class for anything. They want to climb all over him and sit in his lap.

Our customers are not much different than these children. They want to be called by name. They want to feel that the company representative really cares about them. That makes a huge difference; in fact, it's often the deal maker or breaker. *With people, the little things are the big things.*

Why Serving the One Works

Why is this principle—*the key to the many is the one*—so important? Why does it open hearts and minds and doors? I think it's because the deepest hunger of the human soul is to be recognized, valued, appreciated, and understood. When you acknowledge the presence of others, and adapt your presentation in an effort to reach them, in effect you say to them, "You matter. You're a person of worth. You have intrinsic merit, and I'm not comparing you with anyone. You are precious. And if you allow me into your mind to leave a message, I know that I'm on sacred ground." I think that's what it means.

As a customer, I can usually tell if front-line service providers are "totally present" during the few seconds we interact, as they take my order or deal with my request. If they're totally present, I sense that they really care.

Caring about the one works because it's a paradigm focused on people, not things; it's focused on relationships, not schedules; it's focused on effectiveness, not efficiency; it's focused on personal leadership, not resource management.

What a difference it makes to work in a caring culture. For instance, Jenny, my 18-year-old daughter, once worked in the customer service area of our company. At the end of her six-week training period, she said to me, "Dad, I feel sad to come to the end of this six weeks." I said, "Why?" She said, "I will miss the other team members so much." I said, "Why?" She said, "We are a team. If there's ever a mistake, it's a team mistake, and everyone comes to support. Our team leaders are servant leaders, not bosses. And their care for us models how we should care for our customers."

She continued, "Even though I'm only on the phone and never meet any of these people, I've cultivated relationships with many customers who call me back as a friend, who write me letters. Some of them I've only talked with once—and yet when they call in to make an order, they ask me what I would recommend." She learned that there is a direct correlation between how she is treated as a member of the service team and how she treats customers—and how they treat her.

Three Ways to Get It

So, how do you get this concern for the individual customer? I see three ways: *hire it, train it,* or *cultivate it* in the culture.

1. Hire it. When evaluating prospective employees, a major airline brings candidates into a room and asks each person to make a presentation. Everyone thinks that company officials are evaluating the person making the presentation. But they're really evaluating, through hidden video cameras, the people in the audience who are watching the presentations. If they are attentive, supportive, and seem to care, they know they're getting someone who naturally has that ability or disposition to care about others. If someone is totally self-absorbed or bored before or after making his or her presentation, having no sense of rapport with the person who's up there struggling, then that's a strong negative signal.

2. Train it. In another organization, executives want to identify those people who are naturally team players. They do this by giving each team a particular task with a tight deadline. The task is of sufficient complexity and difficulty that the expertise of other people is needed. They have to work as a team to get it done. What they find is that natural tendencies and inclinations surface rapidly. Those who are not team players immediately try to take control. They ignore some people; they put down others; they are discourteous; but they are very task oriented. Others are very relationship oriented, but they have no sense of the task. They never accomplish anything.

Now, the big surprise is that the evaluators of the person's team skills are the members of the team. People are aghast when they discover this at the end and realize, "My gosh, look how I treated those people."

3. Cultivate it. You might hire it and train it, but to me the most powerful way to cultivate the service ethic is to develop strong social norms in the culture itself. When your employees begin to see that "this is how we treat each other," then your company will have a sustainable competitive advantage.

The cultivation of the spirit of servant leadership will teach everyone to be kind, respectful, and caring, even though some people aren't naturally that way.

Once I visited with the director of Human Resources of a prominent hotel firm (Ritz Carlton). I asked this woman, "Has this culture of respect—treating each other as you do customers with the motto "ladies and gentlemen serving ladies and gentlemen"—influenced your personal and your family life?"

She said to me, "Absolutely. It's like night and day. I was raised in a very difficult situation. I was abused and battered as a foster child. I went back and forth between different homes and situations. And I developed a survival mind set. I was angry and cynical on the inside, but used human relations techniques on the surface in an effort to be nice to people in the company and the customers. But I had a well of anger right under the surface. After work, if someone rubbed me wrong, I took my frustrations out on them."

I reminded her, "Unexpressed feelings never die—they're just buried alive and come forth later in uglier ways."

She said, "My negative feelings came forth constantly on my loved ones . . . until I started working here."

I asked, "How is it different?"

She said, "Being in this company is almost like having a second family and childhood. I constantly get my modeling from this organization. Now, I see and treat my children differently. I'm more interested in creating a wonderful feeling and atmosphere at home than I am in getting a particular job done."

Another man from the same organization, but different hotel, said essentially the same thing. He said, "You know, this is such an attractive culture to me—it's been such a family to me—that when I go on vacation, I prefer to stay in the lobby and watch the hotel employees interact with customers. I just love the niceness with which people treat each other."

So much of this civility and courtesy has eroded away to cynicism and manipulation in our society. Even at the more exclusive hotels and resorts, I don't think you can expect genuine civility. Money can't guarantee it. In fact, wealth might foster an elitist attitude among service providers who merely manipulate guests with human relations skills for the sake of getting tips.

On a recent flight, I observed a pregnant woman as she entered the plane carrying a child in one arm and a large bag in the other. Two flight attendants stood nearby, talking to each other, as this woman come through. I stood up and said, "Let me help you." The flight attendants continued to watch as we struggled to get stuff into the storage bin. Maybe service is not part of their job description, but if it's their job spirit, they will help. But I suspect that's the same way they are treated inside the company—their complaints are ignored.

Once I took one of my sons skiing for his very first time. He was terrified of the ski lift. I had to encourage him to try, and told him, "Don't worry, I'll ask them to slow it down."

As we approached the lift, I asked the operator, "Could you please slow it down—this is his first time."

He frowned—in fact, he looked disgusted—and said, "Well, okay."

From that moment on, my son lost interest in skiing.

When you're vulnerable, you can be hurt by the slightest inclination or nuance in someone's voice. Kids have a sixth sense for that stuff. And often they're damaged by the cynicism of others. They pick up those vibes instantly. So, that was the end of his skiing that day. I had to go through that process again.

My guess is that the lift operator received the same treatment when he went to his supervisor and said, "Can I get this day off to attend a family reunion?" His supervisor probably snapped and said, "Who do you think you are? You're scheduled to work here that day." And then that supervisor probably got treated the same way by an arbitrary and capricious boss.

The older I get the more clearly I see the connection between the way employees are treated and how they treat customers. It's like a chain reaction.

Of course, we need not run around like reactive beings. We can learn not to be offended. We can cultivate our security from within, based on integrity to fundamental principles, so that we can love when we're not loved, be kind when people aren't kind to us, and patient when they're impatient with us.

The capacity to turn the other cheek, go the extra mile, and be a servant leader comes from a deep vision of what we're trying to accomplish. We see what we seek. If we seek a great thing, we tend to see greatness inside people if they're part of it. And we seek feedback from people who have the courage to share. We don't kill the messenger who brings us feedback. Rather, we show appreciation and have the humility to apologize and say, "I need to improve and make amends." Such behavior gives us the ability to want to be more civil to the next person.

Chapter 2

Choosing Service Over Self-Interest

By Peter Block,
Founding Partner, Designed Learning

*S*tewardship can replace self-interest as the basis for holding and using power.

Stewardship means to hold in trust the well-being of some larger entity—our organization, our community, the earth itself. To hold something of value in trust calls for placing service ahead of control, to no longer expect leaders to be in charge and out in front.

There is pride in leadership—it evokes images of direction. There is humility in stewardship—it evokes images of service. Service is central to stewardship.

A Model of Stewardship

The idea of service through stewardship has been with us forever. Corporate stewardship has come to mean financial responsibility for both the institution and the community. Stewardship, though, goes beyond financial accountability and beyond being accountable for our talents. Stewardship is also concerned with the use of power. One intent of stewardship is to replace self-interest with service as the basis for holding and using power.

It is not surprising we should look to religious models for ways of thinking about the right use of power. Our best religious leaders have flourished through the ages in part because they have understood how to exercise accountability and activism in service to their followers. Mahatma Gandhi is one of the best examples of integrating religious and political stewardship. Ghandi identified three elements making up his brand of service-based power, which he called trusteeship. Granted, Gandhi sets a rather high standard, but his principles expand our understanding of stewardship's political meaning.

1. Power is granted from those below. The community creates the chance for a person to be in a position of power. Power is bestowed upon us by those we lead. We do not claim power; it is not passed on to us by others in power; we have no inherent right to power, whether by birthright, talent, or even achievement. If we serve those who put us in our position, then the recipients of our service and trusteeship are the core workers, the community, and the ones we become accountable to. We may be appointed by a board, or an executive, but they are given their authority as much by the people doing the work as by any other set of owners.

2. Our contribution is our humanity. The obligation of accepting a position of power is to be, above all else, a good human being. Not to be a good leader, not so much to maintain order and fight back chaos, not to know what is best for others—these are the qualities of being a good parent. If you are a boss, the people working for you definitely have expectations of you to be their good parent, but this is not stewardship.

Stewardship is the willingness to work on ourselves first, to stay in intimate contact with those around us, to own our doubts and limitations, and make them part of our dialogue with others. Our humanness is defined more by our vulnerability than our strengths. This is different from leading from the heart, walking our talk, or articulating a vision.

3. What is true is known to each of us. Trust comes out of pursuing what is true. What is true lies within each of us. Stewardship is founded on the belief that others have the knowledge and the answers within themselves. We do not have to teach other adults how to behave.

Our survival depends on our taking the idea of service to constituents and making it concrete in our governance systems. The quality and customer service movements have the right idea, but they implement the service ethic through patriarchal governance strategies. Service-based governance strategies mean the redistribution of power, privilege, purpose, and wealth. All the team building, improvement teams, and skills training in the world will not create service if the institutional questions of choice and equity never change. Organizations have a hard time taking advantage of their own successful experiments. It would force them to redistribute power and ultimately privilege.

Teaching Revolution to the Ruling Class

We serve when we build capability in others by supporting ownership and choice at every level. We cannot continue to govern through patriarchy and say we just want to be of service. When we act to create compliance in others, we are choosing self-interest over service, no matter what words we use to describe our actions. Service-givers who maintain dominance aren't really giving service. Stewardship has to address directly the redistribution of power, and the redesign of fundamental management practices—not for management's own sake, but in service of the redistribution of felt ownership and felt responsibility.

We are, in fact, talking about a revolution. Revolution means a turning, changing, revolving direction. It means a significant change, obvious to the casual observer, even to customers. Evolutionary change is more comfortable. Evolutionary change means everything is planned, under control, and reasonably predictable. The problem with evolutionary change is that it is virtually unnoticeable to the participants. You have to look back over generations to see any difference. If you want to make changes that go unrecognized, pick an evolutionary path. Patriarchy's attempts to change itself have been traditionally evolutionary, the choice of self-interest.

The revolution is for organizations to become the place where our personal values and economics intersect, reforming our organizations so that our spirit is answered, and our ability to serve customers in the broadest sense is guaranteed. Stewardship is the strategy that embodies this goal. Stewardship enables the use of power with grace.

What is unique about this revolution—and gives us hope—is that it is being initiated by the ruling class, the managerial class. Stewardship is a revolution initiated and designed by those in power.

Stewardship gives order to the widespread distribution of power. It is to trust that good things can happen without our needing to control them. It is to accept what is real without having to color it, or fix it, or soften it. It takes a certain faith in ourselves and others not to make control the centerpiece of our transaction with the world. We have come to believe that control is essential to our survival, safety, and even our success. Stewardship is the choice to unravel this connection between control, safety, and success.

The Inside Work

In any reform effort, the hardest change is the inside work, the emotional work. Creating partnership in a work setting is a shift in beliefs and in the way we make contact with those in power and with those we have power over.

Our first instinct is to want to engineer change and to focus on what is outside of us, on what is concrete, visible, and measurable—structure, roles, responsibilities, systems, strategies, and management. The engineering work, the redesign effort of reform is essential, but it is not enough. There is artwork to be done, internal reevaluation of our own wants, longings, and expectations. If there is no transformation inside each of us, all the structural change will have no impact.

The heart of the internal work is to sort through our way of relating to people and resolving our wishes for dependency and for dominance. Dependency is the belief that my safety, my self-esteem, and my freedom are in the hands of other people. When we go to work, no matter how tough we think we have become, we look to our bosses and others above us and hand to them the power to determine, once again, how valued we are, how secure we can be, how much freedom we have. It is this willingness to place our survival in others' hands that fuels the engine of patriarchy.

Experiencing the depth of our own longing for others to provide us safety and freedom is the absolute first step in creating organizations that are based on partnership, empowerment, and responsibility. The wish for safety surfaces in our expectations and disappointments in people who have some power over us. Since we all have someone above us, we all are looking for a little bit of safety. Our willingness to reevaluate our expectations is the first step in implementing stewardship. Renegotiating this internal transaction is the emotional work of stewardship. Until we take back control from those above, we will not be able to extend it to those below.

The coin of dependency has an opposite side—dominance. Dominance fulfills the wish to be in control—to be the all-knowing, omniscient, loving parent or strong leader—giving people structure, clarity, something to lean on and react to.

Renegotiating the Social Contract

The expectations of dependency are that others will provide safety, freedom, and self-esteem. The expectations we have of dominance are that we are entitled to compliance, loyalty, and gratitude. These unstated emotional wants are evoked and agreed to each time we join an institution. The institution wants compliance and loyalty, and in return we want them to provide us with safety and self-esteem. Our wish for safety leads to our willingness to yield sovereignty. The institution's belief that it needs loyalty (compliance) leads it to promise safety and protection. But this contract can no longer be fulfilled. Our organizations can't offer the safety they once did. And marketplace demands require something more than compliance.

Renegotiating the old contract begins by accepting the power of these unstated emotional wants. Once accepted, we can stop being controlled by them. Choosing stewardship is the choice to say no to others' desire for you to claim control and in exchange offer them protection. Choosing stewardship is our choice to be accountable while supporting freedom in ourselves and others. This is a risky choice and comes packaged in anxiety. This choice for accountability and freedom is the essence of the entrepreneurial spirit. It forms the basis for the social contract essential to ownership and responsibility. It confronts self-interest and is the alternative to entitlement.

Creating a social contract based on partnership and empowerment is the difficult emotional work of stewardship. This means saying no to others' wishes for protection and relinquishing our claims for control. At the moment we look to others to protect and take care of us, we also hand over to them some semblance of sovereignty and control over what we do. This is where bosses get their hunting rights. We ask bosses to be our guardians, giving them rights to make decisions about our lives.

Similarly, when we decide to take care of and protect others who work for us or with us, we are claiming sovereignty, even in our generosity. That is why caretaking of adults is no gift. When we claim sovereignty, we release the other from any requirement of ownership, responsibility, and emotional accountability. If ownership and responsibility are what we want, and also what the business requires, then sovereignty, in the form of caretaking, needs to be extracted from our relationships. It is this yielding and claiming transaction that we spend our lives re-forming.

Extracting sovereignty from our relationships often means we start saying no. Saying no to unfulfillable expectations is difficult. If people wish of us to support their effort, watch them less closely, give them advice—the answer can be yes. To the extent, though, that these wants are symbolic of their wishes for security, self-esteem, and freedom, the answer must be no—even though they may experience our response as an act of abandonment or betrayal. They may feel that since we once offered them that protection and self-esteem, how could we now withhold it? The reason we do not offer security, self-esteem, and freedom to others is because it is not ours to give. Theirs to claim, yes. Ours to give, no. The fact that we once made an unfulfillable offer, because we thought we needed their compliance and we thought it was an act of kindness, is no reason to maintain the illusion.

Moving from parent to partner comes down to a series of conversations about purpose, ownership, and responsibility. The boss says in effect, "I want you to share in the felt ownership of this franchise. I plan to share with you the power and privilege of ownership, as long as it is used in service of the larger unit. This is the partnership agreement that I want to manage by." This conversation accompanies the definition of the stewardship contract, which defines the playing field.

Promising Safety Is No Gift

When you hear the claim that employees have been betrayed when they are no longer offered long-term job security, remember that while it is a painful experience, it is a questionable claim. This caretaking contract is the antithesis of ownership and responsibility. We are each in our own way afraid of the dark. Hidden bargains are destined to disappoint, and when they disappoint, it is so late and the feelings run so deep, that they make the relationship difficult to repair. They also make the illegitimacy of our own expectations difficult to own.

There is no easy way out of this. Allowing our dependency to continue is to forsake ourselves. We then have to endure the guilt of an unlived life. Yet claiming our freedom and making choices betrays others' wishes for us. Parents, teachers, bosses, friends, and children all have expectations of us that we do not meet. To claim stewardship, to claim our freedom even as an act of service, is a destabilizing act. This unsteadiness is going to happen because the safety-control-compliance compact doesn't work.

As people explore their unstated emotional wants, they begin to realize that, exaggerated as they might seem, they represent real desires. Patriarchal contracts feed on this longing. They become the mechanisms by which we control each other and hold ourselves back from living out our own vision. It is because we want others to provide us safety and self-esteem that we are willing to live out the vision created by others and deny our own. Patriarchy becomes a refuge for our reluctance to choose adventure and pursue our own purpose.

When we give up the search for others to provide us safety and self-esteem, we need to replace it with something. In essence, we are redefining our ambition. We are letting go of advancement and pleasing bosses as the measure of our success. Perhaps not voluntarily, but in most places, there is just no place to go. Our organizations are flattening as fast as they can. Also, the effort we make with advancement in mind is not terribly functional. Our career progression is about as much in our own hands as our choice of parents and birth order. What has the potential to replace our desire to move ever upward is our desire to create culture we can believe in.

When we tell subordinates we can no longer take care of them and no longer choose to control them, we also need something positive to offer. What we are offering is real choice in defining and creating an organization that has purpose and meaning for them—a partnership in designing a governance system that fosters ownership and responsibility among those doing the core work. The basic exchange is to offer people more choice in return for a promise. Make sure that both a real choice and a real promise are in the equation. The choice is about having control over the way the work gets done and managed. The promise is about results.

Chapter 3

Being Customer- Need Driven

By Darby Checketts,
President, Cornerstone Professional Development

*M*ere customer service is not enough. We must astonish our customers with the comprehensive nature of our support strategies.

Of all the productivity and quality improvement campaigns that come and to go, only one will last. It is the rediscovery of the most time-honored principle of business success: Find a need and fill it. To be customer-need driven is the key to staying competitive in the increasingly dynamic future we all face. Such an achievement requires a commitment that extends from an organization's strategic center throughout every office and factory to every supplier and customer. Such a culture of service requires that each worker consider him or herself connected in an unbroken chain of customers that visibly leads to the end customer. The strength of each link lies in its value-added in the overall process of meeting and exceeding customer needs. Otherwise, it is all too easy to confuse filling a job with filling a need.

Chain of Customers

In modern organizations, the old "chain of command" persists. When organizations grow large, when bureaucracy creeps in, and when leaders expect battlefield allegiance, the focus turns inward. The true customer is too distant. The boss becomes the one who is served. Competition is the enemy. Energies are misdirected—taking the form of beating competition, pleasing the boss, or playing office politics.

Only when the focus becomes service are energies redirected positively to support colleagues who serve and please customers. Such a scenario means that leaders place service above self-interest.

The new metaphor is the chain of customers where joint contributors with interdependent roles pull in one direction to move their products and services closer to the end customer. The focus is clear and straight. A spirit of reciprocity is demonstrated by the timely exchange of vital information among those who are interdependently linked.

The chain of customers suggests that we need to concern ourselves less with who serves us and focus our energies more on whom we serve. When we think less of the rewards we will get and more of the service that is needed, the service becomes more complete and the unsought rewards even more sweet. More than serving the customer's need, we service the customer's loyalty.

Picture individuals linked side-by-side in a chain of customers, where each team member seeks to serve rather than be served. If each is concerned about the next person in line, there will be someone concerned about each link in the chain. The strength of each is added to the next. The combined strength is unbreakable. Ultimately, the end customer's satisfaction will bring the chain full circle, and the team will experience the fulfillment of mission. The leader's stewardship is to value every link in the chain and be sure the chain is unbroken.

What do your customers need from you to assure their own success? How will you maintain the chain to keep it unbroken? How will you get connected to your customers? To get connected to your customers, follow four steps.

1. Know your customers. Know your internal customers and your end users. Next time you meet, sincerely say, "Please tell me a little more about what you do each day and how my function affects your performance?"

2. Rename whatever you do using the word "customer." For example, if you are a sales representative, you might rename your job "customer need filler." If you are an administrative assistant, you might rename your job "customer information coordinator."

3. Redesign your work output as if it were for sale. How would you do the work and package the end product if you had to convince someone to pay you directly for what you produce? To recognize the economic interdependencies, ask yourself: How does what I do contribute to the solution my customers need? Is there anything I do for which there is no clear purpose? If I were buying my own services or products, where would I expect the quality to be better, the cost lower, and the service more prompt?

4. Study and anticipate your customers' needs. Be prepared to act before asked. In any business, everyone is there for only one reason— to get quality product into the hands of eager customers. Some may possess special skills, but all are there to see that products are sold and customers served. When selling and serving are impeded, resolving the crisis becomes the priority of each employee.

Being Customer-Need Driven

To be customer-need driven does not mean to be process driven, nor customer driven. To be primarily process driven is to become too mechanical. It must be remembered that the so-called process is not sacred; it is a dynamic internal means of satisfying the customer's requirements. If the process drives the people and does not yield to the people, sooner or later both internal and external customers may perceive that the process, while technically correct, is not practically relevant. Therefore, we must move from a mindset of "Did we follow the process?" to "Did we fill the right needs in the process?"

To be just customer driven implies blind obedience to the customer. We have all been schooled in the axiom, "The customer is always right." In fact, the customer is not always right. Sometimes the customer does not even know what he or she actually needs. For example, many of us, as customers, have embarked on a new car purchase and, in effect, said to the salesperson, "I want to spend less than $20,000," only to drive home in a $22,300 automobile. The want was low price, the ultimate need was good value.

While the customer is not always right, the customer is always in the right. While you and I, in serving the customer, may know more about the range of possible solutions, the customer is always the prime expert on the symptoms of the underlying needs. Thus, there is an all-important opportunity for mutual education: First, we must carefully listen to the customer to understand the relevant symptoms that suggest the true needs. Then, the customer is more likely to listen to our explanation of the ingenious solutions we have devised to address those needs and perhaps, needs unforeseen by the customer.

To begin the journey toward being customer-need driven, consider these initial three steps: 1) Recognize a true customer need when you see one; 2) Identify more needs that translate to more business for you and a more complete service for the customer; and 3) Undertake all that you do with the customer in mind.

1. Recognize true customer needs. As you begin recognizing your customers' true needs, your customers will be astonished that you can and will join them in thinking through the problem. They will return to do business again and will ask for you by name.

2. Identify more customer needs. Customer needs come to our attention in four fundamental ways: 1) the customer explicitly tells us of his or her need; 2) we observe that the customer needs something; 3) we ask the customer what (or what else) he or she needs; 4) our intuition suggests that the customer may need something. It is surprising how often we stop short at level one: the customer tells us of a need (or want) . . . we provide the obvious solution . . . and, important opportunities may be overlooked. As we seek more input from the customer and use our intuition to foresee potential customer needs, great benefits accrue to all who are involved.

We have entered a new age when mere customer service is not enough. We have entered an age when we must literally astonish our customers with the comprehensive nature of our customer support strategies. Service providers must possess the awareness and the skill that will make them indispensable in the production and delivery of customer value.

Beyond responding to customers' needs, we might anticipate their needs, expand on their needs by identifying additional opportunities for service, and intuitively determine future needs. Seek to see what may not be obvious to others. This is the opportunity to establish a leadership posture in the eyes of the customer and among your competitors.

Is the customer the central figure in your stated mission? Is cultivating customer loyalty viewed as powerful leverage on profitability and growth? Is the day-to-day emphasis on filling needs or doing jobs? Is the information the customer needs readily accessible or does it require technical interpretation and have to pass through certain channels? Are all customer support systems ADEQUATE physically, RESPONSIVE to the customer, and TECHNOLOGICALLY advanced? Does each member of your team know what *world class* looks like, sounds like, and feels like to the customer? Is training a dispensable luxury or a fundamental strategy for long-term success? Do you know exactly what causes your customers to keep coming back? Do you meticulously measure your performance against these factors?

Finally, what is at the heart of this focus on customers? Genuine customer care is the enlightened recognition of the vital economic interdependencies that exist among us all. Genuine satisfaction of customer needs is the tangible opportunity to finish the work day knowing that we make a difference.

Chapter 4

Getting to the Heart of Service

**By Joseph Grenny,
Co-Founder, The Praxis Group**

*T*he quality of our service is inextricably linked to how we see and feel about the people we serve.

Lily Tomlin, in the Broadway play, *The Search for Signs of Intelligent Life on Earth*, sighed, "I worry whoever invented the term *quality control* thought if they didn't control it it would get out of hand."

A burning question today is, "How to get quality service in hand?" More specifically, "Why do some individuals and companies provide minimal service while others bend over backwards for you?"

Our quest for answers to these questions has made us susceptible to quick-fix fads and formulas that are more style than substance. Happily, many substantive answers are right under our noses, in the values we hold near and dear to our hearts!

Sincere service requires a strength of character that we often overlook in our focus on externals. It requires the strength to see each individual with whom we work or meet as a unique human being with needs, goals, and concerns as vital to them as ours are to us. Quality service begins with this vision and ends with putting our values into action, dealing with others as we would like them to deal with us.

Poor service is often the result of impersonalizing other people. It is an easy trap to fall into, particularly as we try to meet frantic schedules, process people in mass, or work in a culture that sees customers as chattel to be channeled efficiently. Remember: what counts is effectiveness with people, efficiency with things.

When we focus on efficiency with people, we miss many opportunities for service; in fact, our "service" may become more harmful than helpful. A horrifying example of this was reported once on the front page of the *Wall Street Journal*. The article detailed the "sweat shop" condition of many medical testing labs. The push for efficiency has resulted in false negative rates for many cancer tests, ranging from 20 to 40 percent! One particular test, the Pap smear, is designed to detect cervical cancers that account for about 7,000 deaths per year. Most of these deaths are avoidable with proper early testing. Somewhere along the line, many medical technicians forgot that they serve people.

Although few of us are employed so directly with people's health and welfare, most of us have some direct impact on people's emotions, expectations, or feelings. Creating and nurturing a deep and abiding awareness of this connection is a key to establishing deeper commitment from ourselves and others to excellent service.

Three Levels of Service

Martin Buber, the philosopher, describes two levels of relationships we can have with others: *"I-It,"* meaning a relationship between me and an object, and *"I-Thou,"* referring to more intimate human relationships. I would like to add a middle level, "I-You" and suggest that these three levels—*I-It, I-You,* and *I-Thou*—represent a continuum of how we see and treat other people. The implication is that the way we perceive other people drives the way we relate to them.

I-It. If I see you as an object, I will try to control, intimidate, use, and treat you as I do objects. I have needs; you don't. My time is of the essence; yours is without essence. My existence is paramount; you cease to exist when you exit my purview. I have had a hard day; for you, one day is like another. I am a person; you are an object.

I-It relationships are characterized by language and conversation that is planned, manipulative, or collusive. At this level, one is essentially self-centered. I see others as resources to be used, stepping stones to be trodden upon. I describe people by labeling or name-calling. People are things to me. My behavior towards others is guided by careful analysis of potential consequences. I respond to my moods or whims when I have the freedom to do so. This shallow relationship requires no intimacy, commitment, or sacrifice. The focus is always on me and my ends.

Granted, *I-It* can be a great short-term approach, proving successful in material acquisition, negotiation, and competition, but it will always mean paying a price in long-term satisfaction.

I-You. Most of our relationships are at the *I-You* level. Communication at this level is characterized as spontaneous, respectful, and friendly. Our approaches to others are more genuine, and our demeanor shows consistency whether in or out of another's presence. Our behavior is guided by integrity, commitment, and sympathy. Our desire is to preserve and cultivate a harmonious relationship or affiliation. Present aims and desires are often subordinated to preserve the relationship. These relationships are generally accompanied by a good team feeling.

The weakness of *I-You* relationships shows in times of stress or distress. An organization that espouses commitment to and respect for employees will generally have *I-You* relationships with its people and experience loyalty from those who have faith in the organization's integrity to these values. The real test will come during perilous times when the decision to affirm or abort the relationship hinges on pure commitment. If my desires for approval, affiliation, and cooperation from you are not fulfilled over time, the relationship will still pitch into crisis or evaporate.

The "refining fire" often exposes the real level of a relationship. It either bonds people in ways that pay rich dividends, or it breaks them. An organization that violates its values in times of crisis will not rebuild the broken relationships for years to come. Its once rosy culture will develop a cancer that only deep therapy can heal.

I-Thou. When we serve with pure motives, drawing on the highest in us, when we truly see others as human beings, we establish *"I-Thou"* relationships. *"Thou,"* the old English intimate form of *"you,"* connotes humanity, dignity, and closeness. Such relationships naturally result in quality service, since we value another as a friend. When I care about the one I serve, my character will not allow me to deceive, subvert, or ignore. I willingly serve and sacrifice and derive real satisfaction from doing so. Such service feeds on itself because its fruits are sweet.

As we grow in character, we become more capable of cultivating *I-Thou* relationships. These are characterized by a relaxed, productive, and cooperative climate where differences are valued; where selfless service breeds mutual trust and synergy; where the ends and goals of both parties are pursued with mutual vigor and commitment.

In *I-Thou* relationships, my behavior towards you is governed by my commitment to correct principles and to your growth as an individual. I respond to you not for reward, nor simply out of regard, but rather out of reverence. I sense your independent worth as a person, and my belief in my principles would never allow me to violate that great worth.

I hasten to add that *I-Thou* relationships aren't permissive. My sensitivity to your needs may prompt me to be courageous, even confrontive. But my motives will be clear to you over time.

Most of us know the difference between seeing other people as objects and as friends. At one end of the continuum, we relate to them, or use them, as means to our ends. At the other end, we see them as human beings, and relate to them as individuals trying to achieve their own ends. And many of us have experienced a dramatic change of heart when our perception of another shifts instantly from one end to the other.

I suggest that the sudden shift occurred because you quickly drew on the positive values that come into play in a human relationship rather than those negative ones we can exercise with an unknown entity, a fly in the soup of our life, something that we can extract and expel. This connection to values immediately taps into the depth of commitment and concern that most of us feel toward those we care for.

Connecting for Quality Service

Quality service requires this connection to positive, deeply held human values. In some instances, we may fall short, but happily the more we work at serving sincerely, from our hearts, the more capacity we develop to serve people well, even when they are difficult.

• Start with the next person you encounter. Consciously try to see this person as important, someone possessing feelings and concerns as you do. As this small exercise becomes a habit, you will find increasing strength to do it with more people, even those who at first blush seem inhuman. Your behavior toward them will change automatically. They will sense your sincerity, and the benefits will be many and varied.

• Recognize the level of relationship you are currently experiencing. A good way to judge is to examine the motives that guide your behavior toward others.

• Clarify your governing principles. Do you believe in equity, compassion, justice, service? Write a statement of those things you will not violate. These will become the criteria for decision making in all facets of your life. When values are clear, decision making is easier.

• Commit as a person or organization to hold your actions accountable to these principles. Make restitution for the times you fall short.

Individuals and organizations that subscribe to shallow service require constant external motivation, image enhancement, and superficial public relations. And because their service attaches no root into their deeply held values, its longevity is limited to the duration of the cheerleading or "smile training."

Organizations that cultivate the character roots of quality service show staying power. They ride the waves of short-term "programs" staged by their competition. They know that when economic storms descend, quick-fix, cosmetic approaches will dissolve, betraying what others are and how they feel about their customers and employees.

Chapter 5

Ten Commandments of Customer Service

By Robert L. Lorber, Darlene Jameson, and Beverly Battaglia, Lorber Kamai Associates

What do Nordstrom, American Express, Disney, McDonald's, Federal Express, and IBM have in common? They all know that customer satisfaction pays.

The Service Age is here! Two-thirds of the United States GNP comes from service-related industries. With crowded markets, global competition, similar pricing, and little perceived difference of product quality by the customer, smart companies are attempting to differentiate their products and services from their competition. This is more difficult to accomplish, as customers are now more selective, better educated, and thus, have increased their service expectations.

Today's customer expects satisfaction and will settle for nothing less than having this expectation met. A Forum Corporation survey states that of 80 percent of a company's customers who are satisfied with their product, 60 percent will purchase that product from them again.

Often, customer service, rather than price or quality, is the deciding factor in a customer's satisfaction. However, recent reports show that the concern for both price and quality have increased. In short, companies will have to try even harder to provide perceptive customers with both a quality product and exceptional service to maintain the competitive edge.

What is the cost of mediocre service? According to the White House Office of Consumer Affairs, 96 percent of unhappy customers do not complain. Rather than complain, 90 percent just go somewhere else. Thus, only six percent of your customers give you a chance to improve your service in order to keep them. Unfortunately, these unhappy customers tell at least nine other people of their experience. Given that it is easier and five times cheaper to keep existing customers than recruiting new ones, customer satisfaction is not only profitable, it is mandatory for the survival of businesses.

The Ten Commandments

Outstanding service companies do more than philosophize about good customer service; they follow the 10 commandments of exceptional customer service.

1. Turn your organization upside down. Instead of the usual pyramid organization (where the frontline people are at the bottom, supporting corporate hierarchy at the top, and customers aren't even included), turn it upside down—putting customers at the top of your organization chart. Everyone else must work for them, and the corporation must support those employees who are closest to the customer. If you look at the customer in this way, you will take a new view of employment practices, training, compensation, and customer satisfaction.

2. Increase service accountability. Hold everyone accountable for providing the highest level of customer satisfaction. Include customer service responsibilities in job descriptions and review how employees are doing in this regard.

3. Identify every customer/employee "touch point." Each time customers and employees touch, you have an opportunity to win or lose with service. The best service companies know this. The Disney organization puts their new employees through extensive orientation and training on dealing with park guests. All employees, ticket takers to street sweepers, are considered to be hosts and hostesses and are taught how to answer questions, provide assistance, and deal with unhappy people. Walt Disney knew the value of these touch points.

4. Compare what your customers expect, want, and need with what they get. Talk to customers, survey them, listen to them. Measure service at every "touch point." Measure speed of response, error-free transactions, and client satisfaction. Quantify these survey results and graph them so that people can see how they are doing. Respond personally to specific concerns. Post positive and negative comments to give employees feedback on their performance.

5. Make service everybody's business. Involve your employees in setting new goals for service and determining methods of exceeding customer expectations. When people are involved in setting the objectives and standards, they have a greater commitment to meet them. For example, one Southern California home builder eliminated 90 percent of the items to be fixed by taking the time to train his staff in customer service and involve subcontractors in the buyer's walk-through inspection. One subcontractor said that it was an eye-opening experience—he had never looked at his work from a customer's point of view!

6. Empower your people. Give every "touch point" employee the authority, responsibility, and support to fix customer concerns and problems, and create ways to improve service. Provide all employees with information, training, resources, and freedom to use their creativity to satisfy customer needs and expectations.

7. "Over" communicate. Provide frequent feedback to every employee about their current service performance levels. This can be done verbally, visually, or in writing. Most employees need specific, objective information about their performance to improve it. Feedback enables them to maintain or improve good performance and change poor performance. Share satisfied customer stories.

8. Pay attention to your internal customers. Some departments provide support services to other employees and thus, have internal customers. Demand the same high level of service from those support departments as you do from those who work directly with the customer. All too often, internal service departments are viewed as unsupportive, uncooperative, selfish, and barriers to getting things done.

9. Pay attention to details. Look at even the smallest opportunities to improve the customers' perceptions of your service. Good customer service demonstrates a caring, concerned, and helpful attitude as perceived by the customer. When you find out what kinds of services your customers like and appreciate, figure out a way to provide them.

10. Recognize your high performers. Share the good news with everyone. Small improvements, when recognized and rewarded, grow into big ones. Providing positive consequences after performance achievement can increase or maintain that desired performance. Remember the old adage of "different strokes for different folks." The better you know your employees and what reinforces them, the more effective your recognition will be.

While most of these 10 commandments may be "common sense," they are not yet common practice. When you build these concepts into your business, you will differentiate your organization from others.

Chapter 6

Customer Value

By Karl Albrecht,
Chairman, Karl Albrecht & Associates

*B*eyond the archaic conventional wisdom regarding products and services lies the coveted promised land of customer value. The arbitrary distinction implied by the terms *product* and *service* may turn out to be one of the biggest thinking mistakes ever made by business leaders. The vocabulary of business centers on the notion that some companies sell products while others sell services. Presumably, under this distinction, some sell both. And, supposedly, those that sell products are supposed to think about service, too.

Unfortunately, the definition of service has been distorted by conventional thinking. Traditionally, service has been construed to mean some sort of person-to-person interaction that's supposed to make the customer happy after the sale of a product. Customer service, traditionally defined, amounted to a necessary evil, a labor cost incurred if the customer was dissatisfied with the product and wanted to return it or have it made right.

This kind of archaic thinking leaves out an enormous range of value-creating businesses that have no "product." Health care, for instance, is a service with no product at its core, as are entertainment, travel, and hospitality. In fact, over half of the money spent in any first-world economy buys nothing tangible. And yet much of business thinking still clings to the obsolete mind-set that "real business" is all about making and selling products. Services are considered secondary and derivative.

The distinction between manufacturing and serving is now arbitrary and obsolete. In the modern sense, all work is service work. Why should bolting a bumper onto an automobile be thought of as any differently than delivering a parcel, cooking a meal, answering a telephone, programming a computer, or performing brain surgery?

The skills and outcomes are different, but both have the purpose of meeting needs, solving problems, and adding value for people. Both require knowledge, tools, and technology. Both happen in specialized environments. And ultimately, both are services.

The new lexicon of business goes beyond manufacturing and service industries, beyond product and customer service, beyond hardware and software. The new defining precept is customer value.

What is customer value? It's the "mindware" created by the hardware and software you provide. It's the customer's perception of specific need fulfillment. It's the end condition that the customer considers worthy of his or her approval. This may seem a bit broad, but it enables us to think of customer value in comprehensive terms. This can cover everything from a tangible piece of merchandise to a pure experience. In either case, the value is not in the thing or experience we deliver; the value is in the result perceived by the customer.

Sometimes a physical, deliverable item is far more important in the customer's mind than anything accompanying it. Other times there is no deliverable, or the deliverable plays a very minor role. Regardless, it is the total perception of value on the part of the customer that counts.

After decades of defining customer value mostly in terms of merchandise characteristics, and largely going on intuition with regard to subjective results, we're having to learn how to discover the rules of value that exist in the customer's mind. It's dangerous to operate on intuition, guesswork, and assumptions in designing the customer value package we offer. We must use methods of inquiry to discover how the customer defines value in his or her own life and world. And we must take those truths seriously in developing a business strategy.

Finding the Invisible Truth

After 20 years of working with organizations, I've reluctantly arrived at a fairly basic axiom: The longer you've been in business, the greater the probability you don't understand what's going on in the minds of your customers.

There is a certain arrogance of tenure that blocks many leaders from innocent-minded inquiry into their customers' attitudes. Ignorance or misconceptions about the psyche of the customer can lead people down the wrong road. For example, too many quality initiatives start by measuring and counting tangible work products and processes, without any evidence that improving them would contribute to the ultimate success of the business.

The quality movement in all major countries is headed inexorably in one direction: customer focus. Any quality-improvement effort that does not contribute to adding value for customers is misdirected. And how can we create customer value in a way that's cost-effective and profitable if we don't know what the customer values?

Having insights into the customer's thinking requires the ability to perceive the "invisible truth." You can look at market statistics all day without seeing it. You can run demographic studies and shred the data in 50 directions without discovering it. The way you find the invisible truth is to listen directly to your customers as they talk about their worlds, their problems, their needs, and their interests. The more innocent and open-minded you are about hearing what they say, the greater the chance you'll discover one or more elements of their experience that present a special opportunity for your enterprise to create superior value. This is the real objective of customer research, finding that invisible truth.

If we're going to make our strategy-development approach customer-focused, we must find the invisible truth—the customer's perceptions of value—and then identify the customer value model, a set of critical criteria that constitute the customer's perception of value in their experience of doing business with us.

Hierarchy of Customer Value

Think of customer value as forming a four-level hierarchy.

1. Basic—the fundamental components of your customer value package required just to be in business.

2. Expected—what your customers consider "normal" for you and your competitors.

3. Desired—added-value features that customers know about and would like to have but don't necessarily expect because of the current level of performance of your competitors.

4. Unanticipated—added-value features that go well beyond the learned expectations and desires the customer brings to the experience of doing business with you. These "surprise" features can set you apart from your competitors and win you the loyalty of customers.

Mastering the first two levels of the customer value hierarchy is necessary just to compete on an equal footing. This does not make your offering particularly attractive in the customer's mind. You must get beyond "customer satisfaction" and move to the *Desired* or *Unanticipated* levels of value to make a difference. On the other hand, features at the *Desired* and *Unanticipated* levels do little good if other features at the *Basic* and *Expected* levels are poorly done. The hierarchy of customer value is progressive and cumulative: each level builds upon the levels below it.

Companies that offer superior customer value are those whose leaders have learned what their customers really value, and who constantly push their organizations to achieve that value.

The company whose salespeople show you that they understand your customer value model are in a better position to win your business.

If you have an accurate fix on how your customers are defining value, you can then make sure your organization delivers that value.

When I had eye surgery, I was asked by the surgical nurse just before being wheeled into the operating room, "Now, which eye is it?" There may have been a good reason behind that question, but it didn't make me feel very confident. The complex nature of hospital organizations virtually guarantees opportunities for things to go wrong, for people to miscommunicate, and for the ball to be dropped or lost between departments. The customer's perception of trust, teamwork, and continuity doesn't come by accident. It must be earned and managed.

It's remarkable how many executives discover, through open-minded and creative customer research, that their most firmly held beliefs about their customers' thinking processes are off the mark. One of the most strategically effective things the leaders of any enterprise can do is to set aside their established beliefs about customer value and take the question directly to the customers. By listening in an open-minded, innocent way, it is possible to discover the invisible truth that can make an enormous strategic difference.

The Only Thing that Matters

The only thing that matters in the new world of quality is delivering customer value: doing things well to win and keep the customer's business.

Old distinctions between "product" and "service" no longer make sense. The "quality" and "service" issues are now one and the same. We used to think of "service" as something peripheral to a physical product—somebody being nice to somebody during or after the sale. Now we must go beyond "product" and "service" to a new concept, total customer value: all of the things and interactions that form a complete experience that wins the customer's heart, mind, and patronage.

In customer-value terms, we can define quality as a measure of the extent to which a thing or experience meets a need, solves a problem, or adds value. Because a total quality effort should focus on both internal and external customers, customer value should be the starting point of all quality improvement efforts. Why improve any process if it doesn't ultimately meet a need, solve a problem, or add value?

Too many quality programs are oriented around tools, techniques, and processes, rather than around customer value and outcomes. Too few focus on strategic needs. Effective leaders realize that "quality" is not some extra program all by itself, but rather is intrinsic to achieving the business mission—part of the organization's basic value system and way of thinking.

The quality movement will focus more on understanding customer value, defining it in operational terms and learning to measure it objectively and subjectively. We must learn to discover, discern, identify, or extract the unique customer-value model that dominates the choice behavior of each customer or stakeholder whose approval we must earn if we are to succeed in our mission. That becomes the critical measure of quality.

Customer Value Package

We need to pay more attention to our customer-value package, meaning the design and structure of the total experience we deliver to the customer. Few executives focus the design of their customer-value packages squarely on the critical quality attributes of their customer-value models. Most operate without any explicit customer-value model at all. They do business based on historical assumptions and uneducated guesses about what the customer is trying to buy.

We can systematically describe and analyze the customer-value package by subdividing it into seven key components:

• *Environmental.* The physical setting in which the customer experiences the delivery of the products, for example, the inside of a retail store, a hotel, a post office, a hospital, the cabin of an airplane, or the slopes of a ski resort.

• *Aesthetic.* Any sensory experience that affects the perception of value, such as the flavor of food, the visual appeal of retail environment, any experience of pain or discomfort, temperature, humidity, background music, sound level or the ambience of a facility.

• *Interpersonal.* The customers' experience of human interaction with those who deliver what they seek; examples are telephone conversations, face-to-face encounters with salespeople, bodily contact such as health care and the demeanor of a person who delivers or repairs an item.

• *Deliverable.* Anything the customer takes custody of, even temporarily, such as a piece of merchandise, a food tray on an airplane, bank statements, and other documents or medications.

• *Procedural.* What a person has to go through to function as a customer, such as filling out forms, providing information, visiting various facilities, making payments, or waiting in lines.

• *Informational.* The information a person needs to function as a customer, such as signs that tell which way to go, financial figures on a statement, instruction for installing or using a piece of equipment, pricing schedules, or knowing what to expect during and after a medical treatment.

• *Financial.* What the customer pays for the total experience, as well as the nature of the financial interaction, such as price of fee structures, billing methods, refunds or rebates, discount terms, guarantees or collateral value such as volume bonuses.

Virtually every organization has these seven key components in its customer-value package, including internal departments that serve organizational customers. Each of the seven elements contributes in some way to the customer's overall perception of value received. Each deserves careful analysis and continuous attention to identify opportunities for improvement.

The ultimate purpose of any quality improvement effort should be to maximize the appeal of the customer-value packages offered at all levels to all customers, both external and internal, within the framework of a cost-effective way of doing business.

Chapter 7

Put Your People First

**By John Parker Stewart,
Chairman, Stewart Systems, Inc.**

*L*eaders who take a back seat and use ideas coming from the bottom up will improve the bottom line over the long term.

The traditional view of leadership is to be out in front. The organization chart puts senior management on top. This mind-set often creates an attitude that the high-ranking people are clearly in the driver's seat and have all the answers. As a result, this can stifle desperation messages, cries for help, warnings, and impending disasters that those closest to the "action" can see but have stopped trying to communicate upward through a nonresponsive maze.

Our challenge is to change the attitude that the only one with the "best" or "right" idea is the executive in the business, the general in the military, the teacher in the classroom, or the parent in the home.

Our research indicates that the best ideas don't come from the smartest or senior person in the company. IBM, Bell Labs, 3M, HP, GE and others have found that ideas often originate where least expected: the fork-lift driver in the factory, the private in the military, the student in the classroom, or the child in the home.

For those who have ears to hear, the message is clear: To remain competitive in an incredibly complex global market, we must put our people first. We must build environments that encourage ideas from all levels, locations, and functions—and then we must listen, truly listen to our people! This requires a new attitude, commitment, and management style.

The Best Companies Do It

Corporations that have experienced considerable success in adopting this belief include Hewlett-Packard, Federal Express, Nordstrom Department Stores, Marriott Hotels, and Motorola. They put their people first: their needs, their suggestions, and their ideas. They consider their people as "knowledge workers"—each with a huge potential for contributing to the bottom line with ideas. They know that heavy-handed authority style should be avoided like a plague.

Any employer can buy a person's hands and feet for minimum wage. All you've done, though, is buy token effort and minimum contribution. What we need goes far beyond their hands and feet. We need their hearts and heads as well.

Industry leaders focus on earning their peoples' hearts. This goes beyond providing a pay-check. Often pay is less important than increased responsibility, frequent feedback on job performance, a supportive supervisor, and being given a chance to contribute.

Leading firms have been doing this for years. Nordstrom treats its sales clerks as the most important employees in the company. (And you know what? They are!)

Marriott believes in creating a superior work environment. One of the keys is to listen to people. Bill Marriot puts it this way, "If I stop listening to his people, they stop talking—and then I'm lost." They treat their people as if they're the number one difference, because they are. Marriott believes you have to "know, appreciate and reward your employees." Then you'll become known in the industry as a "preferred employer."

Digital Equipment Company has few rules. One is that "responsibility trickles down to the lowest levels." New hires are encouraged to make decision and set priorities. DEC puts its people first.

Hewlett-Packard doesn't even have a lay-off policy. They believe their business is information: "acquiring it, displaying it, analyzing it, communicating it, storing it, making it manageable." Are their people first? Absolutely—they call it the "HP Way." They achieve common objectives through teamwork, and encourage flexibility and innovation.

Federal Express has one of the highest levels of employee satisfaction of any company. They treat their people as if they're "gold"—they are! The commitment of a Federal Express delivery person is unbelievable. The pay-off is "golden."

Donald Peterson turned Ford around as CEO when he used a management style that revolved around teamwork, employee involvement, and an obsession with quality. He walked through factories asking everyone: "What do you think?" One day, Peterson walked into car designer Jack Telnack's office and asked him if he liked the cars he designed. "Actually, no, I don't," he replied. Peterson told him to ignore management and design a car that he'd love to own. Telnack, came up with the 1983 T-Bird which was a huge success. This lead to the 1986 Taurus and Sable, which became a cornerstone to Ford's recovery. Telnack said, "That one conversation turned everything around."

The Short and the Long of It

Can traditional companies turn around? Yes, but it takes consistent follow through, not just lip service.

A major concern for American corporations is the tremendous pressure they are under in coming up with glowing short-term financial reports! It seems that everyone (Wall Street, the press, financial analysts, stock brokers) puts disproportionate emphasis on the next quarterly results. Yes, that is important—but we can win the battle and lose the war.

Our overall objective should be focused on long-term performance well beyond three to six months. I have seen countless examples of organizations who lost the proper balance and paid the price for their myopic vision: their people were pushed to burnout because of unrealistic schedules; quality turned out to be a joke due to shoddy workmanship; customers were treated with anything but dignity; R&D was neglected; and career pathing through careful training and development for the every precious human resource commodity was short-changed. It naturally caught up with them. They lost the war!

An objective geared to the long-term care and nourishment of our people will influence long-term health and on-going performance. It will reduce labor unrest, improve quality, and enhance competitive readiness. However, it takes more than lip service. It must verge on obsession at every level of the firm to ensure sustained growth and performance.

Put our people first! They become our customers. Their needs, suggestions, ideas, and contributions should be foremost in our minds. Ray Kroc's philosophy (as founder of McDonald's) was "I do all I can to help each McDonald's operator succeed. Because if they succeed—I do!" He's the type of manager who says, "The only reason I am here is to do all I can to help you get the job done. I'll block for you, tackle for you, clear out the interference—so you can succeed! Because if you succeed, then I do!"

Put your people first and watch the dramatic difference in the end result—namely, commitment, quality, and success.

Chapter 8

The Key to Customer Loyalty

**By Leslie H. Wexner,
Chairman, The Limited**

*E*mployee loyalty is key to customer loyalty, and both are the happy consequences of effective leadership.

How people represent their company is a combination of their skills and their own attitudes. If you walk into a store and ask the manager or salesperson if they like it there and the answer is, "I hate it, but the pay is good," I could script them from here to eternity and it would be transparent.

In great enterprises, the attitude of the people who work there is a genuine reflection of how they feel about the company. You can notice an unhappy employee. A company that is only profit-driven is on the wrong path. You can't emphasize profits above everything else and build a company that people are proud to be associated with. It's the wrong message.

We recognize that customers come first, and our aim is to serve them well, with good merchandise, good values, and good service. If our people have values our customers can identify with, they'll be the best ambassadors we could have.

To create a feeling of shared values, we break down our business units to a size that people can relate to. There's a perception in much of American business that bigger is better because of economies of scale. I think in terms of *efficiencies of scale*. I don't believe in having people pay allegiance to a monolithic $10 billion or $20 billion enterprise that employs thousands of people. It's much more effective when a company is broken into units that people can identify with and that can capture their imagination as individuals. In our company, the primary allegiance is to the operating unit, rather than to The Limited, Inc. That's good for our associates, and it's good for the company.

Reflecting Our Values

Good people are the secret of our success. I refuse to hire anyone I don't think is a good person and who doesn't have the ethics and values we believe in. Once they've passed that hurdle, only then do we consider whether they have the skills needed to do the job. The first time you hire someone who's not a good person simply because they have the skills, that's when you begin to corrupt your organization. Being fair, ethical, and open doesn't mean we aren't disciplined and don't insist on high standards of performance. We demand excellence, but we also believe in being fair.

We want all our people to be an extension of the values of the company. They must respect those values; otherwise, they'll just mouth the words. We want all our people to feel that although they may be only one person in a big company, they do individually make a difference. If they have that feeling, it will be reflected in their everyday contacts with our customers and the other people they deal with.

New employees either accept and assimilate those values or they sort themselves out. When I interview someone, the most important thing is that they understand how we think about things, what our values are, and what the job is. I could sell them the job, and they could probably sell me themselves. But if at the end of the day they think our values and our standards are nonsense, then they'll leave.

They'll leave because the white sheep will force out the black sheep. They won't tolerate nonperformance. I believe there's a self-selection process. We're a very hard-working company. We're open, we have integrity, and we share our common values. If someone is really a scoundrel, they'll be uncomfortable here. They won't like the other people.

We call our people "associates," rather than employees, because they really are associated with the success of the business and also because they really are partners in the company. Over 80 percent of them own stock in The Limited (and they don't buy it at a discount). We believe we have a larger percentage of associates who are stockholders than any other major company. My feeling is that if somebody is going to devote that many hours of the day and that many hours of the week to an enterprise, then they should invest in it, too. And I'm proud of the fact that so many of them do just that. And I think that feeling of being an associate and an owner has a good deal to do with how our people relate to our customers.

Treating Customers as Guests

We want our associates to treat our customers as if they were guests in their homes. They can do that by being courteous and friendly and by making them feel at home. We don't ignore them, nor do we try to force them to purchase something they really don't want. Our goal is to make our customers want to come back. Success in retailing is determined by a number of factors, including how good the merchandise is, how it's displayed, and how clean and attractive the store is. But at the top of the list is the attitude of the people who work there.

To foster a healthy attitude, we try to be tolerant of mistakes. I'm suspicious of people who never make mistakes because that may mean they're too timid or cautious. We try to propagate an entrepreneurial style of management that is willing to take risks if they're reasonably balanced with the prospects of reward. I want our people to hit home runs, but I remember that while Babe Ruth was the home run king, he also led the league in strikeouts.

We consider ourselves good merchants; we are structured and disciplined; and we value integrity and honesty. We take a largely tutorial approach to pass on those shared values. I don't think management can consciously instill loyalty among employees. Loyalty is a by-product of a lot of other things. If your people believe you are providing fair, honest, consistent and intelligent leadership, they will be loyal to you. Leadership that is successful over a sustained period and is a demonstration of personal commitment will gain credibility. Real loyalty derives from the creation of good values, persistence in reinforcing those values, and the determination to communicate them. Our associates know we value their partnership. The most important shareholders to us are those who produce the results.

Chapter 9

The Meaning of Service

By Charles E. Watson,
Professor, Miami University

*T*he happiest people succeed in forgetting themselves as they are consumed in the service of something truly worthwhile.

Perhaps the most useful guide we have for living is this: Living is most exciting, worthwhile, and satisfying when our aims are not to please ourselves primarily, but to be in the service of something greater, having genuine merit.

The good life is achieved by serving others in valuable ways. The genuine fulfillment a person derives from his efforts is not something he can find by pursuing it directly. Instead, it finds him.

Service holds enormous possibilities for each of us. Working to serve others or a great cause, first and ahead of self, will not only produce remarkable results and achievements for the benefit of others, it will also change us dramatically.

We can better understand why service leads to a better world and to a better life than the pursuit of being served by considering what selfless service demands of each person. Living to serve demands a radical departure from customary attitudes and habit patterns. It requires boldness to try to put one's self second and something greater, first.

A life of service places three great demands on people, calling them to 1) remove themselves as the central focus of life, 2) make whatever sacrifices are necessary to shoulder their responsibilities and carry the burdens demanded by their cause, and 3) accept responsibility for the development of their own character, realizing that if they chose to live primarily for themselves, they might reach a point when it's impossible to change from that pattern.

The person who serves becomes less self-centered and more concerned with large purposes, attracts followers, works harder, and performs the drudgery of menial details which, when attended to systematically and thoroughly, often spells the difference between mediocre and extraordinary performance. This person becomes an attractive human being who attracts more opportunities than flow to ordinary people. Most importantly, this person is free to concentrate his or her best efforts on doing things that make a difference in the world.

Admired leaders forget themselves; rather than rest on position, they pitch in when they can assist. The incident when General Washington dismounted his horse and, in the mud and alongside his men, moved a stuck wagon, is a well-known illustration. It's why he became so revered, even in his own time.

A Job, a Career, a Calling

When work is seen as a calling, the possibilities for useful service, adventure, and lasting satisfaction are beyond imagination. Viewing the world from a larger perspective and contributing to a larger good can transform ordinary lives into extraordinary adventures.

When he was chairman of the board of Johnson and Higgins of California, Dickinson Ross described a man who started in the insurance business in Pasadena about the turn of the century.

When he started, he believed that his mission was to provide an estate for every individual he worked with. He found only one product that could provide an instant estate for people, and that was life insurance. So he was a missionary. He also made a wonderful living. This man once told me that it wasn't the product that made the difference—it was the privilege he had to respect people and be helpful to them.

When our commitment is focused on the cause being served, our work becomes a calling. It ceases to be just an economic exchange of pay for performance. We enter into an exciting cause that transcends ourselves. We dignify our existence by good works and contributions.

Consider what business brings to the world. Which institution grows and transports food? It isn't the government, the church, or universities. It's business. Business houses, clothes, transports, feeds, entertains, and provides the means to educate us and care for our health.

Material comforts and economic prosperity are not, as a few might assert, evils. Much of what we enjoy in this world comes through somebody's productivity. A world of plenty, not privation, is certainly good for mankind. And business people need never apologize for their role in making this possible.

Picture young Henry Ford, alone in his shop on Bagley Avenue as he visualized the future. He sees his little automobile speeding a doctor to a remote farmhouse to save a life. He sees miles of roads opening up the country for all Americans. He sees people riding to work, to market, to school, to church free from the tyranny of distance. And he sees new jobs, better incomes, and more free time for everybody.

In more recent years, William Walton, cofounder of Holiday Inn, described how the company he presided over saw its purpose. "We saw ourselves—all of us, from the chairman of the board to cleaning people—as a company of people. We were in a crusade to bring to the American traveling public a highway haven, a home away from home to rest and refresh them."

Ask a businessman why he's in business. About 99 percent of them will say, "To make money." Making money is not the driving cause of performance. Making money is the result of performance.

When Nathan Ancell, who helped start Ethan Allen Furniture, would sit with his board to review what had happened the previous 12 months, the first thing he would ask was, "Do we have better people in our company?" Second, "Do we have a better image with the public from what products we have?" Third, "Do we have better productive facilities than we had in the beginning of the year?" Fourth, "Do we have a workforce that is, from a moral and ethical standpoint, more stimulated and motivated than we had in the beginning of the year?" And fifth, "Did we make enough money to do the things that we had to do?" Ethan Allen did not put money first.

"Human nature," Ancell said to me, "is controlled by the law of self-preservation, which leads to a feeling that you should take care of yourself first—take care of feathering your own nest before thinking of taking care of somebody else. But that's why most people fail—because they have their priorities backwards."

We seem unable to escape the plight of having to rediscover old truths. Henry Ford boldly lived by the creed that any business that first thought of earning a fixed dividend was bound to fail. Either profits would come from doing a job well, he believed, or they would not come at all. Ford ably captured the essence of the service ideal when he said, "A business absolutely devoted to service will have only one worry about profits: they will be embarrassingly large."

The Person One Might Become

A person does not find satisfaction in what belongs to him, but by what his life belongs to. The good life is achieved not by serving valuables to one's self. It's reached by serving others in invaluable ways. The remarkable thing about business is that it offers countless opportunities for people to do good—to add to material abundance, to act with sensitivity and compassion, and to advance justice, decency, and human welfare.

Some things begin large and grow small; others start small and become large. A life, and a business, can grow either way. But it is always growing; and that growth will tend toward its holder's dreams and ideals—what one honors. Service alone is the badge of greatness.

The wise man is really not nearly as concerned with trying to live a flawless life as he is with producing something useful with his life.

A tragedy occurs whenever a person gives most of his efforts to what matters the least and gives least to what matters the most. Self-centeredness is boring. A person who is more concerned with an important cause than he is with his sense of self-importance is free to act nobly and courageously and thus make possible what otherwise might never be accomplished.

John Riccardo, a former chairman and CEO of Chrysler, did many courageous things during his last few years as CEO. They involved denying his ego. First, he hired Lee Iacocca. He promised him the CEO position within a couple of years. But in the attempt to secure a loan guarantee, relations with government deteriorated. So, Riccardo accelerated Iacocca's move to the CEO position a year faster than promised. He stepped down, acting in the best interest of Chrysler and giving it a fighting chance for survival.

Every person needs something greater than just a job, something greater than just a career. We all need a powerful calling, a great adventure in which we can invest our lives. We thereby escape the tragedy of littleness. Our interests and abilities broaden. We achieve greater significance. To live a big life, we must serve something large without hesitation or calculation of the gains. This is how we dignify our existence—by being concerned not so much with the question, "How good have I been?" but by boldly living to create an admirable answer to the question, "What good have I done?"

Speaking to business school students at Harvard University, Richard J. Mahoney, president and CEO of Monsanto, said: "If you go finally to meet your Maker, and you're giving an accounting of yourself and you say, 'Well, I got my company's return on a share of equity from 12 percent to 20,' that sounds a little thin to me as a qualification. If you don't do all the things you ought to be doing, then you've squandered your life."

Chapter 10

Selective Service

**By Eugene L. Bryan,
President, Decision Dynamics, Inc.**

You serve best where you perform best. Customer mix is your most important controllable variable and is a primary determinant for the delivery of quality service.

Every business has its own set of strengths and weaknesses. An optimized enterprise is one that has learned how to build on its strengths, neutralize the adverse effects of its weaknesses, and coordinate all activities for best possible, long-term results. In this context, some of the most crucial activities will be found in the areas of sales, marketing, and customer service.

Superior customer service is essential for long-term success. Unless a company's mix of products and customers are carefully targeted to optimally recognize its capabilities, limitations, and all market opportunities, both its level of service and bottomline will be compromised. In short, Managers must be very selective when deciding what markets and which customers they will serve.

The Adverse Effects of Tradition

I very often hear people say, "We have to take every order we can get." In fact, very few companies have such large marketshares that they cannot be selective. With five percent of your potential market, you have plenty of opportunity to pick and choose. The problem really comes from a combination of overly constricted paradigms and passive willingness to be market-driven.

Tradition is a quietly powerful force that too often locks individuals an entire organizations into detrimental comfort zones. It encourages people to think: "This is what we do; this is how we do it; and this is who we do it for." The adverse effect of tradition become severe when it works to stabilize internal activities without recognition of rapid external change.

Driven Versus Driving

"Market driven" implies and often leads to reactive involvement. "The market" knows nothing of your strengths and weaknesses. Whether by ringing-telephones or product offerings based on careful research, organizations that let the marketplace define their direction, will not be aimed at "Destination: Best Possible". To help their company be the best it can be, sales and marketing personnel must take "the wheel" firmly in hand and maneuver through the marketplace with a watchful eye. If their driving is proactively creative, they'll gain the control and financial strength needed to enjoy their chosen share of the market.

By definition, a sub-optimal mix of customers will yield sub-optimal results. If a manufacturing company accepts a combination of orders that leaves some of its value-adding capabilities under-utilized and over-taxes others, customer service will suffer as a result of late deliveries, quality problems, excessive costs, or all of the above.

Similarly, if an engineering, architectural, or law firm takes on a mix of clients that does not match its mix of talents and hours available, its quality of service and level of profits will fall short of optimum.

It's hard to say no, especially when facing under-utilized capacity. But it's even harder to say no to people once they become customers. Without well-founded discipline, proactive sales and marketing, and willingness to forego short-term profits for greater long-term success, traditional practices will soon lead to marginal results if not financial crisis. Companies that draft or otherwise enlist the wrong mix of customers will not be strong performers in highly competitive markets.

Optimal Use of Resources

Best-possible financial results come from the optimal use of resources, which will always include "selective service." A resource is anything that can be used to serve a purpose. By this definition, market opportunities can be considered resources and the mix of customers a company selects is one of the most critical factors in its business equation.

As market demands and internal capabilities change, so will a company's optimum product mix. This means some customers should be dropped and others added with changing circumstances. This sounds like I'm suggesting a disloyal, win/lose policy. That is not true. Customers will always be coming and going. A company's customer mix is a controllable variable. When companies choose to hang onto established customers that don't fit current circumstances, both parties soon will be caught in a lose/lose relationship.

If instead, a company proactively directs its efforts and prices its products and services to attract the customers that best match its capabilities, all of the company's stakeholders will benefit. Its customers, owners, employees, suppliers, and community will be able to enjoy the gains of a lasting five-way win/win relationship.

We have learned many hard lessons about the importance of quality service. It is absolutely essential in our increasingly competitive marketplaces. The companies that deliver the bet service will be those that have selected the best mix of customers to serve.

For most businesses, defining an optimum customer mix is a complex task that requires much more than traditional or activity-based costing. When the variables involved yield much more than traditional or activity-based costing. When the variables involved yield permutations so numerous that they cannot be explored by the simple arithmetic of cost accounting, computer-based optimization technology is required. But even without such technology, constant awareness of the importance of customer mix will allow creative, proactive managers to gain and hold competitive advantage. They will come closer to Destination: Best Possible than their reactive, market-driven competitors.

Section 2:

Service Excellence

Chapter 11

Achieving Service Excellence

By Tom Peters,
Chairman, The Tom Peters Group

Without a stunning, sustainable service advantage, you can take your top-quality product and shove it.

FedEx. USAA. Disney. Nordstrom. Charles Schwab. RitzCarlton, K. Barchetti Shops. Say "exceptional service" and the usual suspects come to mind. And not many others. Rapid product development is setting many firms apart. But the use of consistent, awesome service as a competitiveness mainstay is still. What a missed opportunity!

Auto Industry Example

Consider the huge auto industry. Car quality has gotten so good, says premier industry pollster J.D. Power, that you really have to work to find clunkers. "Quality as defined by few defects," Power adds, "is becoming the price for entry for automotive marketers rather than a competitive advantage." But stand out in the "ownership experience" (service, writ large) and I bet you'd stay at the top of the charts for an age. Look what the tarnished General Motors has done with Saturn. Some research suggests that the briskselling car, launched in October 1990, is now the second most valuable auto nameplate franchise, right behind Lexus. And that from a lowend vehicle! Saturn quality, styling and price are okay, make no mistake. But by design, the Saturn ownership experience is what sets the brand apart. No haggling. No discounts. No rebates. No commission selling. Treat the customer with intelligence and kindness. If Saturn, in its violently competitive marketplace, can use the reinvention of the ownership experience to build Rushmorian brand power almost overnight (in an age in which brand loyalty has been repeatedly given up for dead), why can't you? Why not? Because, in most cases, you haven't really tried!

Service Elements

What if you did try? My experience suggests that the elements of stunning, sustainable service advantage are these:

• *Obsession.* What launched McDonald's into the stratosphere? No question. The late founder Ray Kroc's ability to see "beauty in a hamburger bun." Call it obsession. So, too, for perfectionist Walt Disney. And, today, for Bruce Nordstrom (Nordstrom), Horst Schulze (RitzCarlton) and Carl Sewell (chairman of Sewell Motor with $400 million in sales from several low and highend dealerships—he's the rare car dealer who gets the service bit right).

• *Structure.* "Direct. Flat. Quick. Close." That's the shorthand for winners' strategies for tomorrow, says Andersen Consulting's W. James Fischer. Smart organizations (FedEx, Charles Schwab) are increasingly transparent to their customers; all the internal intermediaries are disappearing (layers, and the "checkers checking checkers" that one exec friend decries), and customers are gaining substantial access to the firm . . . and directly manipulating the firm's databases to their own ends. The flat, open, responsive, malleable enterprise of this sort is an entirely new and revolutionary breed of cat. I'd urge any firm to close the doors of its service department. Instead, how about the Ownership Experience Department, with units responsible for sales, distribution, and developing lifetime client relationships?

• *Systems.* No one matches car dealer Carl Sewell's passion for systems that focus unmistakably on building long-term customer loyalty. "Systems, not smiles" are the key, notes Sewell. Computer systems (parts, service, customer histories, etc.), incentive systems, recruiting programs, signage, a clever scheme (swiped from Chuck E. Cheese) for retrieving just-serviced cars—all of Sewell's systems zero in with laserlike precision on building customer commitment. Operations research pioneer C. West Churchman says the best systems need to be more than sophisticated and focused; they must be "aesthetically pleasing." I like that. The systems used by Southwest Airlines, Charles Schwab, FedEx, and Sewell easily clear the aesthetically pleasing hurdle; they are literally beautiful and elegant in their power to cement the customer's attachment to the provider.

• *People.* It may be systems, not smiles, but Carl Sewell also wins via the fabulous floral displays in his showrooms, the chocolate candy in foil with each service receipt, and the heroic efforts, done almost routinely, on the part of his energetic employees. Research by the Forum Corporation suggests that 70 percent of the customers lost by 13 big service and manufacturing companies had scooted because of price. Parallel research by Professor Robert Peterson at the University of Texas at Austin claims it's an emotional tie ("love," he says), not mere "satisfaction," that brings the customer back. Psychologist James

Hillman, in *Kinds of Power*, suggests that service can go way beyond "exceeding expectations" (one of the current mantras of customer-service gurus): Service can be "superb, graceful, beautiful, divine, wonderful." At first I was put off by that language ("C'mon, get real"), but then I wondered, "Hey, what if you set a hard-headed business strategy of creating a culture that consistently delivers graceful, beautiful service?" I don't think it's a silly idea. I think it's profound.

• **Women.** "We always discuss things, then I'll make up our minds"—that's the way one female respondent put it in a survey about a woman's role in a family's purchasing decisions. The survey, conducted in Australia, found that a woman's input tipped the family's choice in decisions at least 80 percent of the time when purchasing major furnishings, white goods, holiday and travel planning, the purchase of a family home, new bank accounts, car insurance, life insurance, and a home computer. Sure, you'll find an increasing number of women in all sorts of jobs, and even the occasional female autofactory manager. But to suggest that firms really understand what it means to design and deliver products and services for women would be a gross overstatement. Back to cars: I believe that the first automaker that goes beyond lip service to achieve "core competence" in catering to women will create a 10-year (plus) sustainable advantage. This story could easily be repeated in banking, pharmaceuticals, and other large corners of the economy.

• **World View.** "It's all so simple," says a James Clavell character in *Shogun*. "Just change your view of the world." It is that simple. And that hard. It's not just a service obsession, it's a bone-deep understanding that an entire firm can be dramatically reoriented to enhance and beautify the customer's experience of ownership.

• **Bombs Away.** It's ironic, but IBM's tumble in the late 1980s gave great service a bad name. And that offers all of us a great lesson. IBM and service were long synonymous. But when things began to go sour for the computer giant, IBM replaced abiding courtesy with obnoxious muscle, trying to strongarm long-term clients into sticking with its outdated systems. Only an outsider like new CEO Lou Gerstner Jr. could frontally attack IBM's towering arrogance. And he has.

Thus, the need to divebomb, from time to time, your core competence in service (should you build one). It's the ultimate leadership paradox: You've got to ride the horse hard to become an industry standard setter. And that very focus contains the seeds of your destruction—i.e., the high odds of getting blindsided. But before you get blindsided, you've got to get there in the first place. And when it comes to a stunning service edge, most companies have a long, long way to go, and perhaps a matchless opportunity. Stunning service is still the best-kept, hardest-to-copy secret in the business world.

The Katherine Barchetti Story

Sophisticated technology remains a tool to abet more involved interaction with citizens. That's a theme that scrappy Katherine Barchetti, who runs two high-fashion K. Barchetti Shops (*What's working*) in Pittsburgh, clearly understands. Her database allows her to know damn near everything about her 30,000 plus customers—and to measure her employees' effectiveness six different ways every day. The measurement scheme is not the latest in management by intimidation (although Barchetti is a perfectionist), but rather part of a determined effort to turn each employee into a full-blown, fully informed retailer—capable of anticipating each customer's very personal needs.

If today is like most others, Katherine Barchetti, is eating, breathing, and sleeping numbers.

Though her store revenues per square foot are more than three times that of the average retailer, Barchetti isn't worrying about bottom-line results. She's more interested in knowing her customers' spending habits, suit sizes, and mailing addresses. "I think numbers run the world," she says. "If you like what we have but we don't have your size, or don't have enough of them, if we have too many, if we didn't buy the right price point—everything is a number."

But Barchetti's tallying and tracking is really about service, attention to detail, and building relationships with customers. It's about knowing that Mr. Smith enjoys an evening at the symphony and Ms. Jones can shop only during her lunch hour. "People in the fashion industry talk about demographics," says Barchetti. "But I've never seen a relationship between demographics and fashion. People dress psychographically. They buy for their lifestyle."

Barchetti has personalized shopping for all her customers. "I want to make people want to buy from me. Every decision in the company is based on this." She maintains meticulous records on customers' sizes, preferences, and past purchases. She arranges private fittings. She calls customers to tout a new clothing line. The goal is to "make a customer, not a sale," says Barchetti.

Long-time customer John Elash says he loves to buy from Barchetti. Recently a Barchetti sales associate offered to bring clothes to his office because he was short on time. "She's even called me from buying trips in New York to ask my input or tell me about a great suit," says Elash.

Customers aren't the only ones touting Barchetti. She's been called "the best retailer in more than 800 cities," by Robert Sprague, a leading retail analyst, and "amazing" by several staff members.

Sales associates work in ad hoc teams. One will greet the customer while another pulls up his or her record in the database. Meanwhile, a third will wander over with a pair of shoes and a belt. (No one at K. Barchetti Shops work on commission.)

Crescent-shaped work tables large enough to hold a couple of suits with coordinating mix-and-match items are used to assemble the wardrobe. Merchandise is stored in large cabinets within an arm's reach. Table designer Bill Kolano says the sales associate doesn't have to leave the customer's side, "which helps maintain a psychological bond between the customer and the sales rep."

Store manager Anita Berk says she knows everything in some of her regular clients' wardrobes (include Elash's). "I even know their families," she says, adding that family members often call on her for gift suggestions. "We try real hard to please the customer."

"It would be unusual for them to suggest a suit that I already own," says Elash. "I don't know if it's the result of the database or the personal contact (the sales associate has) with the customer."

Service is nothing new to Barchetti. Her career started at the age of 8 selling vegetables door-to-door and making clothes for her seven younger brothers. She organized fashion shows at age 17 and opened her first clothing store with $1,000 at age 21.

Today, her hard work continues: teaching (and funding) cooking classes for inner city youth, cooking for 60 for a fundraising dinner, lecturing at clubs and universities, holding a seat on the board of the Downtown Pittsburgh Partnership, an alliance between private enterprise and the city to promote business development—and, of course, running a $3 million business.

To spread the entrepreneurial word, Barchetti and Berk lead training sessions at employee meetings held "every Monday and Saturday for the rest of our lives," says Barchetti. One meeting focuses on product knowledge: why Barchetti chooses a product, how it relates to current inventory, what percentage of business it comprises. "These are the things we need to know to sell intelligently," says Barchetti. "Our meetings are how we run the company."

The second weekly meeting covers retailing: buying, what's happening in the market, last week's numbers, what competitors are doing this week. "I'll make phone calls in front of staff," says Barchetti, "to let them see me handle good and bad situations," which is important for a small business. For example, sales associates at Nordstrom are allowed to take back anything from the customer, no questions asked. "In a small business we can't afford to do that," she says. She's attempting to make salespeople into retailers with personal judgment and market sense.

At the meetings, employees report on specific merchandise, such as a style of shirt, tie, or belt, that they are responsible for. They manage every aspect of the product: buying, maintaining inventory, coordinating, marketing, selling. If one class of merchandise is ahead on sales for the month, employees will discuss ways to increase sales in another category.

"I don't hire people that need to be managed," she says. "I hire people that can manage themselves and can manage a project for us."

Employees also work on projects such as coordinating the store's annual fashion show, displaying the store's $1.5 million worth of merchandise, or managing inventory. Involving employees allows Barchetti "to clone my grasp of the industry. I now have 22 people selling with my high taste level and my level of knowledge."

Barchetti holds her employees to her standards. "People have to measure up," she says. Sales associates' performance is tracked daily and printouts are available so they always know how they are doing. The measures show where an individual's talent lies, Barchetti says. And if someone doesn't "get it" after two months, she believes they never will.

Occasionally, Barchetti will show her no-nonsense attitude to customers, too. "The most important things are customer complaints," says Barchetti, "but some people are chronic complainers." Barchetti says she won't deal with customers that abuse her employees, won't buy from vendors who are dishonest ("even if we make money"), and won't tolerate employees who "don't get it." She accepts no excuses. "Most retailers will talk about why they didn't make their numbers. I say stop rationalizing and accept responsibility."

She even has her own action plan for achieving service excellence:

1. Know your customer. Katherine Barchetti knows everything about tens of thousands of customers. It's her obsession and her basis for remarkable performance.

2. Engage your customer. Knowing everything about your customer is next to useless if you don't put the information to use. That's the lesson from Katherine Barchetti, who teaches personal responsibility. Customer engagement should be the hallmark of your operation.

3. Treat the customer as an individual. With literally millions of customers, that's precisely what the Katherine Barchetti is trying to do. Her sales associates know their customers' taste.

4. Let your customer lead you. Let them, with assistance, take the lead in telling you about their tastes, their needs. It's a tough lesson, unpalatable to many—but seems to be paying off big-time for our exemplars.

5. While building high customer involvement, build high "people" involvement. Katherine Barchetti is attempting to turn each of her employees into a retailer.

6. Turn expectations on their ear. K. Barchetti has reinvented retailing.

7. Have nerve! Do what it takes meet your customers' needs.

8. Make no excuses. Stop rationalizing and accept responsibility.

Article has been reprinted with permission.

Chapter 12

Service Excellence

**By Price Pritchett,
CEO, Prichett & Associates, Inc.**

*I*f you manage customer relationships and transactions well, you will work around the roadblocks to service excellence.

Dealing with clients and customers is not like working with "things." In solitary work, you're putting parts together, playing with ideas, running a piece of equipment, or wrestling with numbers. But in customer service, you're working with moods, tempers, expectations, and misunderstandings. You're dealing with personalities, with human beings. You have to cope with their headaches, hormones, and personal hangups.

It can be a brutal job. The social effort you have to put forth hour after hour, day after day, represents tremendous emotional labor. You have to meet and greet people, control your attitude, plus make an effort to understand, serve, and satisfy. That's a lot of mental and psychological work, and the emotional cost is much greater when clients and customers are unappreciative, unrealistic, uncooperative, nasty-tempered and demanding, maybe even dishonest and demeaning. Some like to have fun at your expense. Some seem dumb and misinformed.

Facing the same sort of people and problems, month after month, can deaden your heart and dull your senses. Customers may begin to look the same and sound alike. Yet each person feels he or she is special, different, and deserving of your best efforts.

Dealing with this can drain your psychological energy and eventually lead to emotional fatigue. If you ever reach the point of being used up and burned out, your work will show it. You get tired of trying. You move through the motions, and the job gets done, but your heart really isn't in it.

Service quality then begins to slip—and that can lead to a make-or-break situation. Customers measure the quality of the firm by the quality of your service. In their eyes, you are the company. You shape its reputation, bit by bit, all day long.

Without paying customers, nobody has a job. Your company will shrink, wither, and die unless there are people willing to pay for what you do. Customers vote daily on how well you do your job, and they vote with their money. If your competitors serve the paying customers better, you lose the vote.

Seven Potential Roadblocks

Let's examine seven potential roadblocks you may have to maneuver around in search of service excellence.

1. Product quality problems. Customer satisfaction is directly affected by the quality of the product. Product quality problems can leave you with a salvage operation on your hands. The reputation of the company is riding on you. At that moment of truth, outstanding service is the only hope for getting around the product quality roadblock.

2. Fouled-up systems and procedures. Organizations sometimes cripple service excellence because the necessary work guidelines aren't in place, policies are inefficient, or rules are too rigid. Standard operating procedures are not always designed to be "customer friendly." If rules and procedures are getting in the way of customer service, maybe it's time to bend them a little and make some judgment calls. Have the guts to stand up for the customer instead of defending rules that get in the way.

3. Inadequate equipment and supplies. Customer service gets complicated when the organization doesn't provide the necessary equipment and supplies. Frontline effectiveness is restricted if people don't have the gear they need. The organization may be "penny wise and pound foolish" by not equipping people properly for service excellence. Properly supplied, it's possible for one person, acting alone, to deliver monumental customer service. Usually the legends of service excellence are the stories of how one individual took on the challenge of a critical customer problem and, single-handedly, overcame the odds.

4. Work overload. Sometimes clients and customers hit all at once. Lines form. Lights blink as calls start backing up. Pressure mounts as people get restless and impatient. Being overworked and understaffed can really put you in a customer service corner. You can't give people the time they need. You're spread too thin. This situation usually results in buck-passing, unresponsiveness, and superficial problem solving. The challenge is to maintain a good attitude, to show grace under pressure. Keep in mind that if it's a bad situation for you, it's probably a worse situation for the customer.

5. Lack of job know-how. You can't fake service excellence for long. It's not enough to be well-intentioned in your efforts—you need to answer questions and solve problems. Job knowledge is a key requirement for service excellence. If the organization fails to provide the necessary training and coaching, you can't expect people to know how to handle customer needs effectively or to show initiative and assume personal responsibility for learning the technical side of the job.

6. *Co-workers who cop out.* An organization's reputation for customer service, good or bad, is built by everybody who works in the place. It's also true that frontline customer contact employees can't do it all. Your coworkers' efforts have a direct impact on your chances for success in serving clients. That can be a problem, because it's easy for some departments and work groups deep inside the firm to lose sight of the customer. When they fail to support service excellence, you can get caught in the middle. You may end up carrying somebody else's load. Karl Albrecht, author of *Service America*, writes, "If you're not serving the customer, you'd better be serving someone who is."

7. *A corporate culture that doesn't care.* You run into another roadblock when you have to cope with a cult of mediocrity. Some firms routinely produce shoddy products and accept shabby treatment of customers. If the corporate culture reflects low standards—a widespread shortage of organizational pride—it's difficult for you to deliver high quality service consistently. You have to become a missionary, a zealot, a fanatic, if you want to influence the service attitudes of others.

Service excellence involves some degree of damage control. But why try? Why care? Why struggle to take up the slack? Why fight to get around the roadblocks? The hard reality is this: that's your job. Nobody else is in a position to do what you can. When the organization slips up somehow, you can do the most to help it recover. You're the ace in the hole.

Two Winning Strategies

Two winning strategies will help you achieve service excellence.

1. *Manage the relationship.* The first and highest priority in service is to build good relationships with your customers. These three actions will help you build good relationships:

• *Take the initiative.* Make the opening move. Be proactive, not reactive. In every customer encounter, mobilize yourself and be the first to reach out. The best defense is a good offense. Taking initiative enables you to wield early influence, even "shape" the customer's attitudes and behaviors in the desired direction.

• *Be positive.* Once you choose to act, to take the initiative, you must decide how you will behave. You have three options: 1) you can be positive (upbeat, affirming, personable, interested, respectful, and considerate); 2) you can be neutral (indifferent, bland, flat, matter-of-fact, or distant); and 3) you can be negative (unpleasant, mean, angry, rude, defensive, or uncooperative). The payoff is in being positive because it gets the relationship moving in the right direction. When you take the initiative and act positively, you put psychological pressure on the customer to react in a positive fashion. Granted, the customer will not always respond in kind, but the odds are certainly in your favor. Naturally, you want to receive positive treatment from your customers, so set the stage for it. When customers are being rude, negative, and difficult, the odds are you're not the target—you just happen to be within range. So don't take it personally when you come under attack. Remain positive and professional. It's your choice.

• *Make the customer feel special.* Your first two moves—taking the initiative and behaving in a positive manner—get you off to a good start. Making customers feel special is the "extra touch" to make things roll in the right direction. The customers that you make feel special will become special customers. Provide such remarkable service that you literally surprise the customer. Make him or her feel "privileged." Go beyond the call of duty. Give more than the customer expects—in the way you relate and in the way you try. Approach each customer as if he or she were your only customer, as if this were a person you must get to know, satisfy, and keep happy. The only way to manage the behavior of your clients and customers is to manage your own behavior. You can only control yourself. But that's enough, if you do it right.

These guidelines not only help you win new customers, they let you hang on to the ones you already have.

2. Manage the transaction. After setting the stage for a good relationship with the customer, you still have to conduct the business. If you don't manage this business transaction effectively, sooner or later it will damage the relationship. There are three key steps in managing the transaction:

• *Listen and understand.* The opening move amounts to problem identification. So focus in on the customer. Give your undivided attention. Don't jump to conclusions. Don't prejudge. Don't start placing blame. Don't argue or become defensive. Don't even start solving the problem yet. Concentrate on getting in tune with the customer, finding the same wavelength. Make that person's point of view your own for the moment. Show your interest in understanding the situation, according to the customer's logic and perspective. Remember: customer problems always represent a window of opportunity.

• *Be helpful.* Now grab hold and take action. Demonstrate your understanding of the situation. Having a handle on the customer's expectations, wants, needs, and concerns, you can now address the top priorities. Take personal responsibility for satisfying the client. Consider yourself an agent of the customer. Put your heads together and create options. Search for alternatives. Do some problem solving. Keep the focus on resources that can be brought to bear on the situation. You have a better idea of what's available to work with than the customer does. The idea is to fix things. Admit mistakes and apologize when your organization is at fault. Show empathy and appreciation.

• *Deal with the uniqueness of the situation.* Consider how this customer is different. When you spot the unique aspect of a situation, you have an angle on how to handle it. Now you can customize your approach. Try to be creative. Maybe you can grant special favors or bend the rules to make things work better. You will know when you need to flex. You can give in when it makes sense to do so. Sometimes you can't give everything the customer wants. But every time you can give some of the things the customer wants. Contribute what you can. If you do enough right things, the customer will be forgiving of the things you do wrong. In your efforts to manage the transaction successfully, never dodge problems. Use them!

People who have their problems and complaints handled effectively will become your most loyal customers—and probably your most pleasant ones. They will depend on you. You have proven yourself under fire. Customers don't expect you or the organization to always do things perfectly. They can accept some mistakes, and they understand that things occasionally go wrong. How you recover is what counts. When you fall the hardest, you can bounce the highest.

The Magic Touch

Excellent customer service rarely comes from following a rigid list of rules about what to do or say. Don't get so mentally locked in on the drill that you end up serving the rule system instead of serving your customers. Remember what really counts to clients and customers:

• Personalized attention: being treated like an individual with very personal needs and a unique situation
• Positive behavior: respect, consideration, concern, appreciation
• Being understood: their feelings, and point of view
• Helpfulness and results!

Precisely how you go about delivering this isn't all that important to customers. Service excellence means giving what really counts to the customer. If you want to be a pro in the way you deliver customer service, find the behavior that plays to your personal strengths, and you have found your own "magic touch." The idea is to give the customer the best service performance you can. To do that, you have to rely on your best talents. They offer the most promise for a high-powered performance in the way you handle clients and customers.

The key to service excellence, as you deliver it, is to know your personal strengths and play them to the hilt. Don't try to be somebody else. Service excellence, as you provide it, will reflect your individual style, your very own "magic touch."

Chapter 13

Use the Profit Power of Customer Service

By Paul R. Timm,
President, Customer Satisfaction Strategies

As customer service goes, so goes business. Like it or not, customer service is the new competitive battleground.

Customer service horror stories are getting right up there with sports, movies, and real estate at many a cocktail party. The lack of customer satisfaction has reached crisis proportions.

Management's efforts to reduce product defects are now refocusing on efforts to avoid customer defections. The average American company will lose about 20 percent of its customers this year. And most customers defect because of dissatisfaction with the company's service. Service, in the eyes of customers, includes employee concern, communication, and competence.

People are increasingly intolerant of poor or indifferent service. Once, my daughter, Erika, made a small deposit to her savings account at a local credit union. The teller smirked at her small transaction and made her feel unimportant.

Erika came home upset. "I hate that place," she told me. I want to close out my account and go to a bank that wants my business." After finding out what happened, I agreed that she should do business elsewhere. She withdrew her savings from the old account and opened a new one at another bank.

Later that week, Erika and I talked with the manager of the credit union. He was an old friend, and I felt uncomfortable as Erika explained her actions. She told him that she felt she had been treated poorly and then said, "I'm sure this is no big deal to you. I only had $370 in my account."

But it was a big deal to the manager. He said to Erika, "I'm very disappointed in our company. You're 17 years old. We could have had you as a customer for 60 years! And besides, you'll tell other people about our services, and we may not get their business—or the business of your friends, your children, and your grandchildren! You better believe I'm upset. Is there anything I can do to get your business back?"

The manager believed in customer service. He talked about it all the time; he ran training sessions; he encouraged the best in customer relations from all his frontline people.

So why did he lose this customer? Why do companies constantly lose customers? The problem is complex and calls for much more than the cursory "program" to change behaviors.

Facts of the Matter

Getting people to give great service is an enormous management challenge. Consider these facts:

• It costs five times as much to attract a new customer as it does to keep an old one. Ironically, few companies have a systematic strategy for customer retention.

• Unhappy customers tell 11 others about a bad experience. These 11 may tell five others, resulting in 67 people getting the bad word about a company. About 68 percent of customers who quit doing business with an organization do so because of company indifference.

• It takes 12 positive incidents to make up for one negative incident in the eyes of customers. And yet, 95 percent of complaining customers will give you another chance if you resolve their problems promptly. But most organizations have no reliable mechanism for receiving complaints in time to fix them.

• Only 4 percent of unhappy customers bother to complain. For every complaint we hear, 24 others go uncommunicated to the company—but not to other potential customers.

Despite these gloomy facts, customer service improvement also offers an exceptional opportunity for distinguishing your organization and for gaining a significant profit advantage.

By increasing customer retention by a few percentage points, organizations have seen their profits jump 25 to 100 percent. Likewise, companies with successful customer service programs do a better job of retaining employees: there's a direct correlation between the customer-retention rate and work force stability.

What is a manager to do? Why can't the boss simply order people to give good customer service? Because customer service is a complex process. If it were easy, every company would excel at it. But it isn't, and they don't. And therein lies the golden opportunity.

With flatter growth, the constant supply of new customers will no longer be available. Businesses will become increasingly dependent on their repeat customers. Organizations that reduce customer defections will thrive and prosper; others should expect diminished market share and reduced profitability.

Exceeding Customer Expectations

The quick fix does not work. Sending people to smile school does not produce lasting benefits. Only a long-term, ongoing commitment to meeting or exceeding customer expectations can assure a company of loyal repeat buyers.

I call the process of exceeding customer expectations the "E-Plus Strategy." I encourage clients to find their unique "E-Plus" by asking two questions of their customers: 1) What do you expect to receive (both physically and psychologically) from your transactions with this company? and 2) What will you perceive as surpassing those expectations?

Now, how can you find your E-Plus and launch your company's efforts toward cultivating repeat customers—the key to profitability?

Please understand that E-Plus cannot be installed by fiat. It requires an ongoing effort and commitment—a commitment that must start at the very top. The six-step process begins with identifying who our customers are and why they buy.

1. Identify. E-Plus demands ongoing two-way communication with customers and employees. First identify specifically who is buying from you. This may not be as obvious as it seems. Probably 20 percent of your customers account for 80 percent of profits. Job one is to segment your market and be sure that the 20 percent is forever in the minds of all company employees. These are your golden customers. You should know them well. You, also need to identify the motivations of your customers. Why do they buy from you? Are you selected because of product quality or selection, lowest price, location convenience, speed of transaction handling, service after the sale? How do you get this information? Ask! Talk with your customers and ask, "How am I doing?"

2. Measure. Measurement should be an ongoing process that looks in two directions. First, develop ways to measure customer satisfaction. Second, look inward into the organization and measure the behaviors, attitudes, and level of trust among employees.

Periodic "audits" of employee and customer attitudes are critical to success. But don't rely on feedback cards. If you measure only the unsolicited input of a few customers you'll see only the extremes at both ends. And if you average these responses, you'll get a distorted picture. A river may average only three feet deep, but you can quickly get in over your head. A wide range of imaginative, valid, and often simple measures are available. Be flexible and creative. Don't feel locked in to the way things have always been done.

3. Catch. Two things need to be caught by managers: 1) a vision of the power of good customer service; and 2) people doing things right.

Vision involves recognizing the long-term impact of customer retention. If we "reframe" our attitude toward each customer, seeing him or her as tens of thousands of dollars over the long term, we begin to catch the vision of the value of customer retention. The cost of losing even one small customer can have devastating long-term effects.

Our second catch—catching people doing things right—is one of the most powerful management tools. The manager who spends time with frontline employees and with customers has ample opportunity to complement and reinforce employee behaviors. This, of course, calls for the manager getting out of the office and finding out what's happening on the firing line. Management is not a career for the reclusive. Managers of excellent service organizations spend major chunks of their time out with the customers.

4. Grow. The E-Plus strategy requires managers to grow feedback networks and service champions. Service champions are grown by giving employees more power to act as advocates for your customers. As workers demonstrate maturity and good sense, give them additional opportunities. A worthy employee can be told that he or she will no longer need to get management approval before giving a refund or an additional premium to a customer.

While some managers resist giving up control of approvals, studies show that employees invariably use good judgment in such matters and, if anything, can be more careful than the manager. Increased responsibility and authority are seen as rewards by mature employees. People feel better about a job over which they have increasing control. E-Plus happens when employees are seen as working for the customer, not just working for the company.

5. Track. Track what goes on in the organization, especially the occurrence of avoidable snafus, the customer's ever-changing expectations, and the rate of customer retention. Make sure that you're tracking the right things. Some companies track and reward or punish behaviors associated with work hours or complaints received. Then they reward the wrong things. They reward people for spending lots of time (pay by the hour) when they should pay by the job or sale. Instead of encouraging people to suppress complaints, they might do well to encourage complaints so that improvements can be made. Few organizations track customer retention. Ask a bank manager how many new accounts he opened this month and he'll have a figure. Ask him how many customers he retained and he'll give you a blank look. New accounts are easier to count, but the retained customer may be more valuable. Be creative in developing measures of the right things, especially customer retention.

6. A culture that cares. Finally, the E-Plus strategy must be implemented within a company culture that values caring. Managers must realize that employees treat customers essentially the way bosses treat employees; and cultures are grown over a long time as they create success rituals.

A culture begins to be articulated as company members buy into the three R's: restrictions, resolutions, and rituals. Restrictions are the "thou shalt nots" of the culture. In customer relations, for example, a restriction may be that we never make fun of a customer or act sarcastically toward him or her.

Resolutions are the "shalts." For example, a resolution may be that private conversations among employees will stop when a customer approaches. Another may be that employees will use free time to write thank-you notes to customers.

Finally, the rituals may include the celebrations and "hoopla" associated with customer service. Skits, parties, and award ceremonies are types of rituals. Others may include weekly ideas sharing meetings or "field trips" to other businesses to see their good ideas.

Remember: a culture of caring evolves over time; the three R's provide the bones; effective management fleshes it out. But also remember: E-Plus is not E-Z. It takes time and effort, but the rewards will be enormous. So, commit to an E-Plus strategy for customer retention through excellent service.

Chapter 14

Creating a Customer Focus

**By Richard C. Whiteley,
Co-Founder and Vice Chairman,
Forum North America**

*O*nce, seven Forum executives and I went to Japan to learn from the best Japanese companies how they implement Total Quality Control. During this intensive two-week period, we visited eight companies in the manufacturing and service sectors. All were recipients of numerous quality awards, including three Deming Prizes and one Japan Quality Control Prize.

The experience in Japan left us with a profound belief that quality has little to do with trade barriers, culture, cost of capital, sympathetic unions, or a supportive government. While these may be factors, the primary factors are capable management and leadership.

Most improvement initiative failures point to the top of the organization. Senior managers are simply not doing what must be done to transform their companies into customer-driven quality producers—they are not leading the charge, nor are they sustaining it.

The number one reason for turnover of frontline service personnel is that they believe senior management does not empower them to serve their customers well and, thus, to do their jobs well. They perceive too great a gap between what senior managers say about quality and what they actually do about it.

With some notable exceptions, American companies are lagging because they lack clear, consistent, and persistent leadership from the top. And without this leadership, we are wasting human and financial resources at a frightening rate, and gaining little for our efforts.

Four Keys to Quality

After working with fine companies like Motorola, Corning, Westinghouse, and British Airways; after visiting the likes of Toyota,

75

Komatsu, Mitsui, and Nissan; and after completing a research project on leadership, we have found that effective leaders do four things.

1. Create a customer-driven vision. Work with your company or unit to create and communicate a clear statement of purpose linked to the customer. This is often expressed in a vision—a picture of an ambitious, desirable future for the organization.

For instance, the Toronto-based Four Seasons Hotel seeks "to operate the finest hotels in every city in which we're located." Houston's award-winning Methodist Hospital states, "Our permanent commitment is to our patients. We are dedicated to providing the finest medical care in the world and being the best service organization anywhere." Motorola seeks to "make our customers winners by exceeding their expectations." And GM of Canada, earnestly seeking to regain lost market share, focuses on both its customers and its people with "Customer for life, I am GM."

In today's climate of mergers, acquisitions, takeovers, downsizing and delayering, employees have become cynical. Old-fashioned loyalty has been replaced with distrust and in some cases outright fear. But people still want to do a good job, to have pride in themselves and their company, and to be winners.

A thoughtfully crafted vision can provide a rallying point, a direction for employees that has meaning beyond cost and profit. It can be uplifting and motivating. Equally important, the vision gives direction for all members of the organization. It becomes the beacon that draws departments, work units, and individuals in the same direction to a specific point in the future.

2. Support the vision. Once the customer-focused vision is clear, senior management must act as its champion and support it both actively and relentlessly. No token or passive support here. Some examples include:

• Protecting budgets for quality programs when others are being cut. At crunch time, what is really valued survives.

• Assigning strong executives to the key quality positions.

• Personally presiding at ceremonies recognizing quality and service achievements.

• Creating cross-functional teams to ensure that key processes such as compensation, billing, and product development are under control.

• Personally appearing at or even teaching training programs aimed at creating a customer-driven quality culture.

3. Eliminate resistance. Leaders who want to change their organizations from inward-looking, operations-driven, and turf-conscious bureaucracies into powerful market-facing, customer-driven winners are challenged by the prospect of transforming the cultures of those monolithic organizations. And change doesn't come easily, or gracefully. There will be resistance. The leader's job is to eliminate the resistance by creating payoffs for those who change and consequences for those who don't.

Payoffs need not be special monetary incentives. People who adopt the new approach should succeed. They will acquire new knowledge and skills, and in time will achieve positive results. These results should be rewarded by the regular performance management system. No special bonuses or incentives are necessary and, in fact, may be divisive. The company succeeds when its people succeed. A promotion is also a payoff. Are the risk-takers who are leading the charge to the new vision being promoted? If they are, you can bet others will join the charge.

The key to success here is what happens in the time gap between launching the new initiative and realizing the results it is designed to achieve. This is where patience and recognition come into play. It is a fragile time when the new ways of the future are taking root and, like fragile seedlings, must be nurtured. The astute leader will be particularly attentive during this period. He or she will be patient and focus on the process of becoming something new, and not let too much focus on the longer-term results prevent the work unit from getting there. During this period, the leader is a cheerleader who recognizes sincere effort and even welcomes the inevitable failures caused by it.

For some people, however, this change will be challenging. They will resist. And the executive's job is to eliminate the resistance. This requires compassionate confrontation. Confrontation must not be avoided because the fence sitters are ever alert to how the leader deals with resistance. If resisters are not handled, it is a clear signal to the entire organization that supporting the new direction is a matter of individual discretion. It is here that leaders must be tough-minded. It is here that most fail.

4. Live the vision. "There is a declining world market for words. The only thing the world believes is behavior, because we all see it instantaneously. None of us may preach anymore. We must behave."

Today's corporate leaders would do well to heed these words from Max DuPie, Chairman of Herman Miller. Now is the time for action, not talk. Too often we see leaders "mandate and move on," leaving the details and follow up to underlings and fancying themselves great delegators. The magnitude of change required for most companies to become totally customer-focused demands the unfailing attention of a committed and involved leader. It simply can't be delegated. People will look to its leader for cues: what the leader does, they will do; what the leader ignores, they will ignore. To create change, the leader simply has to become a living example of the results he seeks through the change. For example:

- *Bill Marriott, Jr.,* travels over 200,000 miles a year visiting Marriott properties around the world. He has been known to walk directly to the kitchen of a Marriott restaurant unannounced and taste the soup which his customers are being served that particular day to ensure they are getting the quality they deserve.
- *Daniel R. Scoggin,* former CEO of T.G.I. Friday's restaurant chain, was so concerned that each restaurant be totally focused on its customers that he initiated a policy whereby the manager of each restaurant is required to sit in every seat in the restaurant every month. The objective? To simulate the customer's experience for the manager. How else would the manager know if there is a draft in a particular spot, or if a curtain needed cleaning?
- *Robert Crandall,* American Airlines' CEO, conducts 25 to 30 "President's Conferences" every year over the company's 156-city route system. Most employees attend at least one a year, and no conference ever ends until the questions of every employee present have been answered.

By themselves these actions are not world shaking, but they are significant. In highly visible and unmistakable statements of behavior they signal to all who observe the earnestness with which these leaders believe their customer-keeping visions. This signal is the clear and consistent behavior that empowers frontline personnel to make the vision a reality.

In these very challenging, even turbulent, times there is simply no substitute for consistent, involved, and out-front leadership. It is the first and primary ingredient which will enable any organization to sustain past successes and create new opportunities. Perhaps Jack Welch, the legendary CEO of GE, summed it up best when he said: "Good business leaders create a vision, articulate the vision, passionately own the vision, and relentlessly drive it to completion."

Chapter 15

In Customers We Trust

By Chip R. Bell,
Partner, Performance Research Associates

*T*rust your customers, even knowing that some will try to take advantage of you. Show trust, and you will succeed.

Have you ever tried to arrange to have a complimentary dinner delivered on credit to someone in another state? The experience starts with a long-distance call and ends with a "Sorry, we don't take credit cards." You are left wishing L.L. Bean, Land's End, and J. Crew all had food divisions!

But I'm ahead of myself. The saga began innocently enough. It had been a dreary January week for my Minneapolis-based partner. The post-holiday blues had collided with his year-end paperwork to leave him with less than a cheery disposition. "Why not treat him and his wife to a top-of-the-line pizza (he loves pizza) delivered when and the way he wants it!" I thought, still basking in the seasonal spirit of giving—and the more forgiving North Carolina climate.

I telephoned Minneapolis information from my office in Charlotte. With some prodding, the directory assistance operator came up with a list of restaurants in my partner's rural neighborhood. I called the first, started my story, and was quickly told, "Naw, we don't deliver." As I listened to the premature dial tone, I found myself thinking, "I never even got to tell him the. . . and, I'll pay you $100,000 to deliver it part!" Two food establishments later, the no-delivery refrain had changed tunes to "Sorry, that's outside our delivery range." Three establishments after that, I was getting, "Great idea, but we don't take credit cards."

My good Samaritan gesture was starting to become very expensive with seven phone calls and still no pizza. Then, I reached Ben James at Gina Maria's in Excelsior—and, my belief in the spirit of service was quickly renewed.

Ben patiently listened to my goal and string of disappointing, long-distance encounters. "You're calling from North Carolina?" he asked almost in disbelief. "Well," he said with resignation in his voice, "We don't take credit cards either . . . but, I trust you. You just give me your order. I'll call your partner to arrange for a convenient delivery time, and you can just mail me a check." It did not stop there; in fact, Ben called me back 10 minutes later to let me know that he had tried my partner's phone number, gotten no answer, but would keep trying. "He may have to get his pizza tomorrow night, but I won't let you down," he said with a big smile in his voice.

I sat back relieved—and a little in awe. And, I felt moved by the whole experience. What had made this encounter so special? What was it that made me gladly say, "Ben, you've been so helpful I will be adding a 20 percent tip to your check. Would you mail me your menu so I can use your services again?" It was not his responsiveness, his warmth or even his understanding, though they helped. My feeling of being served above and beyond was bound up in his friendly assertion, ". . . but, I trust you."

Customer Trust

The essence of great service is customer trust. Whoa! I can already hear the objections—the stern cautions from the auditors. The doubting Thomas brigade is loading their bottom-line guns for an attack on this naive romantic stuck in yesteryear—when doors were left unlocked and a person's word was his (or her) bond. "We have a new era of sabotage, selfishness, and cynicism," they caustically assert, "and, if all our employees acted like Ben, we would be belly up in one week."

Is the world that mean and crass a place? It makes me wonder just how many—if any—organizations have gone under because they regularly demonstrated their superior service in part by trusting customers. Sure, there are the few who truly get their jollies or impress their friends by ripping off establishments. But, if companies are run in a way to protect them from the small minority, what message is being given to the vast majority?

A highly successful Charlotte-based deli restaurant called Arthur's has the cash register located opposite the serving line. Patrons enter, order over the counter, get their food, eat and then pay on their way out. There is no check; you simply tell the cashier what you ate and pay for it. "Don't you worry about people cheating you?" I asked the owner one day. "Not really," he said. "We know a few do. But, what we loose in shrinkage, we more than make up in regular customers who come here because they like to be trusted." There is typically a 20-minute waiting time just to get in this place at lunch every day!

What is it about trust that makes customers feel valued? In part, it communicates one-half of a partnership reaching out to the other half. And, customers reward partnerships. The smart money is on customer retention—turning transient samplers into long-term partners. Not only is it more expensive to acquire a customer than to keep one, but, the average customer in year five of their relationship with you will spend much more then he or she did in year one or two with you. Customers are loyal to service providers who trust them; they abandon those who treat them with suspicion.

Trusted customers become ex-officio members of your sales and marketing department. Stanley Marcus, founder of Neiman-Marcus in Dallas, enjoys telling the story of the young debutante who returned a $175 evening gown after one evening's rough treatment and wanted her money back. "It was obvious her own reckless behavior had left the dress in shambles. But, I gave her back her money. And in 1935, $175 was a lot of money for a dress." Marcus beams as he relates the punch line, "But, not only did she spend over a $100,000 with me over the next 30 years, she made sure all her wealthy friends did likewise. Trusting her turned out to be a great investment!"

So, why doesn't every service provider think and act like Gina Maria's, Arthur's and Stanley Marcus? It starts with short-term thinking that measures the cost of the transaction rather than the worth of relationship. It is often grounded in a management philosophy that says, "Give 'em an inch and they'll take a mile. If we don't have tough rules and controls, if the customers don't scalp us, our employees will." But consider this: if a manager fails to trust employees, what actions will employees take with customers?

Give yourself a 60-day trust period. Get employees together and let them know you desire to demonstrate more trust to customers. Ask employees to identify areas where there are "We don't trust you" messages telegraphed to customers. Separate those areas where legal or quasi-legal issues prevent you from altering your practice. With the areas left, outline new "trusting" steps you want employees to take. And remember: to get employees to trust customers, you must demonstrate your trust in employees. At the end of the 60-day period, briefly interview a few regular customers to get their reactions.

Three Ways to Show Trust

Here are three ideas to help you demonstrate trust to customers:

1. Consider a service guarantee. Make the guarantee easy to explain (no fine print), simple to administer (no tedious forms), and easy for the customer to collect on (no "we'll mail you a check in 90 days"). Pilot the guarantee for a time, or for a part of your business, and see what you learn.

2. Review your organization's credit policy. Does the policy make customers prove they are not crooks before being trusted? Rewrite them with an eye to demonstrating trust.

3. Trust employees more. Trusting customers starts with trusting employees. Examine your rules and procedures to isolate ones which have a "guilty until proven innocent" theme or tone. Rewrite or weed out the ones which "apply to all in order to catch the few." Take a look at places where the leading theme is "prove it to me first" and then find ways to send a more trusting message.

The magical power of trust is that it begets trust. If you demonstrate trust to customers, they will trust you back. Such trust shapes their perception of you as a service provider. They will perceive you as much "easier to do business with" than other providers. They will be more tolerant, more patient, and more forgiving when mistakes occur, even defending you to other customers. They will also perceive higher quality and a greater value for their service dollar.

But don't expect a trusting environment overnight. Continue to model trust, to involve employees in ways they can model trust, and to ask customers for feedback. Their "I want it fast, convenient, and good" demands are taking much greater priority over "I want the cheapest." They will reward with their repeat business those service providers who treat them with respect, with responsiveness, and most of all, with trust.

Chapter 16

Customer Relations Under Fire

By Robert D. Dewar,
Professor of Organizational Behavior,
Northwestern University

*M*anagers often need to undertake mending missions to retain valuable customers who might otherwise be lost.

Service managers know the importance of quality service; and yet, many service providers fail to see the critical importance of appropriate and quick response when something goes wrong in the service exchange. The quality of the response may well determine the future health of the business. When something goes wrong, remember the *Law of Bad News:* stories about your service failures get juicier and worse every time they are told; and its corollary: you can never win a storytelling contest with a customer.

When your operation makes a mistake in service, customers expect you to do something about it. They will be surprised and delighted if you actually do respond with the appropriate actions to compensate them for their real or perceived loss. Verbal apologies are no longer sufficient. Customers want to know that the cause of the failure was corrected.

Instead of simply accepting service failures, managers need to view failures and other service problems as real opportunities to get "good" stories told about you instead of bad ones. Service providers must be willing and prepared to alter the course of a potentially ugly situation. They must see that the customer and others who hear the "bad" story will be lost to the competition. Therefore, service employees must be prepared through training and empowerment to automatically launch a "rescue mission" which has enough substance and meaning to quickly recoup the customer's goodwill and, consequently, retain the customer's business. Providers who respond inappropriately or give up easily on one customer will probably have repeat bad performances with other customers.

Four Stages of Service

To be prepared for the "mission," service providers must first understand some basic principles. These employees must maintain their composure and think clearly under fire, quickly analyzing the situation and knowing that when a failure occurs, the customer will go through stages of shock, anger, revenge, and acceptance (SARA).

1. Shock. In this first stage, the customer may express surprise: "This can't be happening to me!" "Why would this happen to me?"

2. Anger. Depending on the severity of the service failure and the inconvenience (or loss), the customer usually moves quickly into anger, becomes rude, and sometimes attacks the service provider.

3. Revenge. If the service provider does not respond appropriately, the customer will often leave the encounter still angry and move into revenge—plotting how to get back at your company for the failure, telling "bad" stories, or thinking about "calling the better business bureau or an attorney."

4. Acceptance. Eventually, the customer moves to acceptance: "I'll overlook the failure, but I'll never go back there again." Of course, the customer never really "forgets it" and usually takes every opportunity to warn friends, relatives, and associates to stay away from you by telling the "bad" story about your failure.

Service employees often fail to respond quickly when something goes wrong because they, too, go through their own SARA. They may be shocked that one customer is unhappy and questioning the service that another customer is willing to accept. They may get angry because they take the customer's reactions personally. If service providers are not prepared for the "failure encounter," they may well verbally apologize to the customer, but then make sure that the next cup of coffee is cold (revenge). Or, they may begin to accept too many failures and say, "Boy, what a grouch! We don't need those customers in here."

The intensity and manifestation of employee SARA will vary depending on such factors as the nature of the failure and degree of customer dissatisfaction. Therefore, employees will need special training to recognize and deal with their own reactions to an irate customer. You do not want employees yelling at customers or attempting to correct a customer's manners unless you are in the adult day-care business. In conjunction with training, service providers will also need special motivation (i.e., empowerment and positive reinforcement) to overcome their own SARA. One service company regularly brings its service providers together to share (behind closed doors) their own stories about difficult customers. After each provider tells his or her story, the group votes on which customer qualifies as the biggest "frog." The employee who had to deal with the biggest frog without losing his or her cool gets an award for "professionally kissing" the frog, despite the fact that the frog didn't necessarily turn into a prince or princess. The award encourages professional behavior in a bad situation and prevents a bad encounter with a customer from becoming a horror story about your service.

The response should be very fast to prevent the "bad" stories. Service employees need to catch their mistakes early and begin the "mending mission" quickly, preferably while the customer is still in shock and certainly before the customer has to ask for the correction. Also, a verbal apology is not enough. The response should have some substance so that it makes up for much of the side costs to the customer. For example, the time spent driving a new car to the service center several times for the same problem as well as the inconvenience resulting from not having the car are "real losses." Perhaps providing a loaner vehicle or picking up the car for repair work would be appropriate. More serious service failures may warrant a complimentary oil change or tune-up. An automobile service center should prepare their providers to make these decisions. The service organization will have to ascertain whether or not they are capable of delivering on compensation promises and evaluate the impact it may have on future business.

Elements of Mending Mission

Executives in service organizations need to recognize the critical nature of this mending mission and empower service providers to respond appropriately when a failure occurs. Empowerment programs should include the following elements:

• Employee training programs with evaluation and followup.

• Information systems which give the service provider knowledge of what the organization is capable of doing and tell the provider what "class" of customer they are dealing with and whether or not special treatment and escalation of service are warranted and feasible.

• The organization will have to give the provider the authority to make tough decisions and take immediate action. Effective service responses have to be done under fire and require that service employees have authority.

• Empowerment also means the service provider will have to be held accountable for the results of their actions (e.g., if a desk clerk decides to give a free room to a customer whose reservation was lost, there should be some followup as to whether repeat business results). Everyone wants authority, but few want accountability. Managers must select and train service providers who are willing to be held accountable for their use of authority to ensure customer retention.

• A systematic analysis should be performed on your service operations including an analysis of what the side costs might be to the customer if your service fails. Service providers are often the best people to gauge the appropriate response and compensation. Therefore, they should be involved in this analysis as well as in choosing the appropriate "payout" to customers suffering the side costs of your failure.

Managers involved in the service enterprise must continually ask whether their operations are truly responding to customer needs or whether they are merely paying lip service to the old adage which bestows infallibility upon the customer. If one of your company's primary goals is to increase business, you can be assured it won't happen if you have a bad reputation for service.

Chapter 17

Update Your Service Strategy

By Grace Major,
President, Sigma International, Inc.

*B*ecause of rising customer demands, leaders need to adopt a "take charge" strategy for satisfying customers.

Ten years ago, customers expected mediocre service. They were reluctant to request anything special and hesitant to complain about significant problems. Today, customers expect excellent service. They aggressively demand extras, and believe they ought to complain about any perceived flaw.

An oversimplification? Perhaps. But the balance of power has swung in service interactions. Customers used to feel defensive, now they feel entitled to take offense. This customer "offensive" can wreak havoc with service providers. Many frontline personnel can't deal with customers who demand so much more. If top management doesn't act, they can expect to see customer satisfaction levels drop.

The Customer Offensive

As companies everywhere bend over backwards to "delight" their customers, people learn they can get the responsive, personalized service they prefer. Increasingly, they "win" when they stand up for their rights and are gratified when they ask for special considerations. Naturally, some take advantage of those eager to satisfy them and push for more. We now have some aggressive customers who might be characterized as:

• *Get-It-Nows.* Opportunists and manipulators figure the time is ripe to push service providers for as much as they can get.

• *Exploders.* Frustrated people look upon service personnel as victims upon whom they can safely vent their pent-up anger.

• *Get-Evens*. Service providers who have given extra attention and concessions to their customers want to be gratified when it's their turn to be the customer.

• *Me-Toos*. Those who are irked that others "win" by demanding price breaks and extra goods decide they better enter the fray to collect their fair share.

Our well-intentioned attempts to satisfy customers can result in rewarding those who push for as much as they can get. Frontline employees are encountering customers who are far more demanding and aggressive.

Dealing with customers today can be like torture," says the vice president of operations of a Fortune 500 company. He adds: "It's appalling how aggressive some customers become—they virtually beat up on our service reps."

As customer expectations and demands escalate, executives are finding it's getting harder to please customers. Not surprisingly, satisfaction ratings sometimes suffer. A frustrated director of 1,000 telephone company personnel notes that his group's ratings have fallen "even though we're doing far more for our customers than ever before." Like many others, he is discovering that customer expectations are growing so fast that his organization can hardly catch up.

Last year's customers would have been delighted with improvements that no longer satisfy this year's customers. Because they expect so much more, this year's (and next year's) customers are less inclined to check the "very satisfied" box on a survey.

Focus on Customer Interactions

Now that customers want personalized, respectful attention, contact people are supposed to conduct an interaction—not just do a job—that pleases each customer. "The bar has been raised," says Jim Robertson, manager of the Quality Center at Motorola University.

Service personnel are having a tough time coping with the new breed of demanding customers. They don't know how to manage their interactions and are uncomfortable with anything more than a simple, routine exchange. That's because most service personnel have only been trained how to process a service request, troubleshoot a problem, or do their "technical" tasks. They tend to focus on these technical tasks and to filter out all customer communications that distract them from their "real" job. That's how they were taught, that's the behavior that's modeled around them, and that's been the tradition. Those who sense their failure to interact satisfactorily may resort to avoidance or other counterproductive behaviors. Your organization is vulnerable at every customer contact point.

Hard-driving customers who expect special treatment make the following old ways of providing service inadequate:

• *Just cope.* The ostrich approach that focuses on the technical processes and minimizes communication with customers.

• *Give 'em what they want.* The going-out-of-business approach that capitulates to any customer demand, even to the detriment of other customers.

• *Be nice.* The transactional analysis approach that relies on charm school tactics to encourage the customer to be nice too.

These approaches don't work anymore, unless your business involves only simple, "cookie cutter" customer transactions. Most service environments now require more personalization and more leadership.

What do customers want when they interact with your service personnel? Assess the gap between how customers hope to be treated versus how they are treated. Your customers probably prefer to deal with people who can:

• Clarify their needs, expectations, concerns, and priorities

• Resolve problems related to those priorities

• Respond to complaints constructively

• Determine the best options when the company is unable to give them exactly what they want

• Lead the way to productive conversations and effective work relationships.

Can your people do these things? And can they manage the customers who aggressively demand the impossible? If not, you must train and coach them. You can't just ask them to conduct satisfactory customer interactions; you must enable them.

A popular service strategy has been to instruct frontline personnel to "be responsive." This approach is too passive now. Being able to "take charge" will make their jobs easier and more enjoyable. Many of them realize that they need to develop a strong set of customer management and communication skills.

• Admit that it can be challenging to satisfy customers today. Don't position yourself on the customer's side, against your employees.

• Establish guidelines on what can and can't be given to customers. Support your people when they enforce those guidelines.

• Enable your frontline people to manage the interactions they have with customers. Train them how to do it.

• Train your managers first. They can then serve as role models and coaches.

• Remove barriers that inhibit your people's ability to satisfy customers. Ask your service providers: What limits your ability to satisfy customers?

• Make sure your customer satisfaction surveys are measuring the right things. Do those surveys address what is important to your customers today?

• Recognize people who provide good service. Don't neglect those who manage a demanding customer situation in an optimum way.

As your service environment becomes more challenging, make sure your customer contact people are ready, willing, and able to manage their interactions. Enable them to take charge and lead the way to productive customer interactions and satisfactory solutions.

Chapter 18

Ten Steps to Improved Service

**By Gary M. Heil and Richard Tate,
Associates of Blanchard Training
and Development, Inc.**

*I*mproving the quality of your customer service requires commitment and consistent effort from everyone.

Since creating a product that is unique in the eyes of the customer is becoming increasingly difficult in today's competitive environment, more companies are relying on service to achieve competitive advantage. Outstanding service companies share some basic similarities, but they also customize systems, structures, management styles, and employment practices to suit their strategic goals.

To improve the quality of your service, take the following 10 steps.

1. Make a commitment to service. The return on investment for companies that impress their customers with value-added service can be staggering. These returns are not the result of providing excellent service, but of customers perceiving that a company delivers service that is unique. Achieving quality service takes a serious commitment from every employee to exceed customers' expectations to the point that customers are willing to tell others. Too often, leaders are unwilling to change enough to overcome the forces that perpetuate the status quo. Changing customer requirements, new technologies, decentralized structures, and greater employee flexibility must be viewed as opportunities for improvement and not as intrusions on present business practices.

2. Develop a proactive recovery strategy. The quickest way to improve your service reputation is to improve your recovery process. Customers are impressed by companies that make an empathetic, hassle-free effort to recover when customers perceive that they received less service than they expected. These efforts dramatically communicate to customers that the company cares, that it is sensitive to the customer's business and that it will stand behind its product or service—no matter what. An effective recovery strategy requires that a company go all out to find disgruntled customers. Most companies attempt recovery only after a customer initiates a complaint and then focus 100 percent of the resources allocated for recovery on the 5 percent of the disgruntled customers who ordinarily complain.

3. *Ensure continuous improvement.* Effective service improvement is the cumulative effect of a thousand small improvements made daily. It often requires changing the culture from one that accepts the status quo to one that is excited about change and continuous improvement. Innovating service practices and redefining service delivery must be everyone's job. Start small and demand improvement from everyone. Define success as continually improving in all areas including service, first-time quality, cost reduction, productivity, and development of human resources. ,

4. *Listen to customers.* Listening is the foundation of all good relationships and a prerequisite to business success. But surprisingly few companies systematically listen to customers, suppliers, employees, and competitors. The radical service improvements needed will require better customer information systems. The more we know about a customer's business, the easier we can form strategic partnerships. Because service professionals spend so much time with customers, they must be the primary source for developing and updating the system. Have each customer-contact employee ask one customer per day for one improvement idea; and then share the responses, analyze the information, and make improvement mandatory.

5. *Facilitate change.* Service problems are leadership problems, often resulting from management's unwillingness to change structures, reduce inflexible policies and procedures, set higher service goals for themselves and their work groups, and spend more time on customer-related issues. Service improvement efforts fail more from ineffective management practices than from lack of frontline effort. Yes, the frontline people are often unwilling or unable to take risks necessary to embrace their changed role and enthusiastically deliver service that consistently exceeds customer expectations. But this happens because leaders fail to ensure that: desired service outcomes are well defined; the service delivery process is clearly communicated and perceived to be flexible; guiding principles and core values are established; and everyone understands their role in the show.

6. *Define the playing field.* Frontline employees must understand the rules of play and how to win before they can successfully customize service for the customer. There must be a clearly defined

direction (a goalline that indicates how to score) and predefined parameters (the "rules" or boundaries) that outline the limits of responsibility and decision making. In the past, outlining boundaries has been done primarily by correcting mistakes. Unfortunately, this does not communicate what is desirable, only what is out of bounds. When employees are not secure, they focus on avoiding problems and mistakes and not on creativity and customization. This uncertainty often results in such responses as: "I'd like to help you, but . . . ," "It's not my job," "I just work here," or "It's just our policy." These responses are the natural consequence of a risky service culture created by uncertain boundaries and inconsistent goals.

7. Provide autonomy. Creative, enthusiastic service professionals who routinely make business decisions and improvise when necessary are the foundation of excellent service. Yet, many companies ignore the benefits of engaging the talents of their work force. Too often they ask frontline employees to park their brains at the front door and blindly obey predetermined policies and procedures. Serious service improvement involves people meaningfully in every aspect of service delivery, including service planning, innovation, and process improvement. It means replacing many "rules" with judgment, allowing for greater flexibility in frontline decision making within well-defined parameters. It requires more trust between leaders, employees, and their unions; a greater sharing of information; and an unprecedented commitment to continuous education. The heroes in a customer-focused culture must be highly trained, enthusiastic, frontline service professionals who make hundreds of decisions daily to deliver a customized product faster than every before.

8. Measure performance. Managers must educate everyone to routinely measure all of the responsibilities crucial to success. Cost-reduction measures should be balanced with measures of service, quality, leadership, employee flexibility, and continuous improvement. The most valid measures of service quality are the subjective opinions of customers. Only customers can evaluate service in light of their unique expectations. Consequently, responsibility for measuring and demonstrating continuous service improvement should be focused closer to the service professional. Only when service teams are actively involved in every facet of the service business, including measurement of service quality, can organizations hope to capture the creativity and enthusiasm that is needed to radically enhance service delivery.

9. Hold everyone accountable. When we ask, "Who is responsible for service improvement in your organization?" we are usually given the names of several people whose responsibilities cross many functional areas. When a service problem surfaces, these people point out that the root cause of the problem exists with another group. This "fragmented accountability" is no accountability at all. Until a single person is accountable for service improvement and until serious personal consequences are set for failing to achieve service goals, continuous service improvement is unlikely. Lack of individual accountability allows leaders to avoid focusing on ineffective managerial practices, such as adhering to time-wasting routines, attending endless meetings, failing to set goals that test their talents, and failing to change ineffective reporting and promotional structures. If all employees were held personally accountable for influencing the perception of the customer, customer service would be perceived as a part of the strategic plan instead of a "slogan" or "theme program."

   10. Celebrate success. Every organization must develop a culture of celebrated discontent—a simultaneous feeling of accomplishment and a desire to improve. Too often, though, organizations create an almost schizophrenic "either/or" mentality—celebrate one minute and be emphatically discontent the next. People find these environments confusing and uncomfortable. They begin to discount true celebration as an introduction to the real agenda—usually a push for more productivity. Most cultures have far too few celebrations and few measures focusing on improvement. Organizations must celebrate often, making the celebrations sincere and spontaneous. Those who consistently demonstrate improvement must become the heroes.

   These 10 fundamentals will help create a culture of continuous service improvement. Organizations can no longer assume that what made them successful today will make them successful in the future. They must see the world as it is, not as they wish it to be, learn to like change, and take advantage of the opportunities that change creates. Companies must begin to define success for everyone as continually improving everything—everyday. Nothing less will do.

Chapter 19

Speed: The New Entitlement

By Jack Burke,
President, Sound Marketing, Inc.

*R*egardless of whether customer satisfaction has become an entitlement, there are still measures you can take to readily satisfy your customers.

"Project Outreach" is a holiday tradition within the Burke household. Each year we assist our local church in gathering food, toys, and money for distribution to about 350 "hotel families" in LA's Downtown Skid Row.

Delivery day has always been one of heartfelt joy as we're greeted at the hotel room doors with glistening eyes in hopeful anticipation. Aside from the "do-good" syndrome, there was always hope because each year the faces were new. This was only a transitory stop for a family trying to regroup and recover.

December 1994 was different. First of all, many of the faces were the same as last year. Upward mobility had stalled. Secondly, the attitude had changed. Gone were the warm embraces and grateful greetings. In its place was a silent acceptance of the gift. As I discussed this phenomena with others, the truth unfolded: our gifts had become their entitlement. What a difference a year can make.

No this isn't a treatise on sociology. I tell the story to exemplify how quickly a benefit or a gift can become an entitlement. Customer satisfaction, for instance, was originally a goal to be achieved by businesses who cared about their future. Today it is an entitlement. Customers are no longer impressed with satisfaction; they deem it to be a system-given right of capitalism! Good service and professionalism were once considered value-added benefits in the sales equation. Today they have become entitlement.

Expectations have grown exponentially as these "entitlements" have taken a firm grip on the hearts of consumers. It's not enough to just satisfy a customer's needs. In fact, even complete satisfaction isn't enough anymore. You now have to "WOW!" your clients by totally exceeding their expectations.

I believe that the cart has gotten in front of the horse. We're missing one of the most basic forms of entitlement that has ever developed—the entitlement to "speed". As an article on the front page of the *Wall Street Journal* began, "Time is money. Time waits for no man. The unforgiving minute."

Recently, I left the counter of a restaurant in frustration because five minutes had elapsed without a greeting, a menu, a cup of coffee, or even a near-miss with a waitress. I ended up at McDonald's. I had wanted a more elaborate dinner, but the first restaurant failed to acknowledge my entitlement to speedy service and lost my business.

Major hotel chains are already recognizing this need for speed. Hyatt and others, for instance, are adding convenience-restaurants to service the "eat and run" mentality of today's business travelers. Just look at the coffee carts that abound in lobbies. Even morning room service has become too slow for most travelers.

Once, I would watch in awe as the FAX machine would send a document to its destination. Today I impatiently wait as it slowly takes 30 seconds to process a page. Perceptions change quickly!

Researching a paper once meant an occasional trip to the library. Today that inconvenience is unacceptable! Research means a modem connection to the electronic libraries on the information highway.

This entitlement to speed has gradually spread itself into other technologies that have not had any change in processing speed. The telephone is a perfect example. Speed-dialing aside, it still takes about the same amount of time to make the connection and the spacing between the rings remains static. Yet, if the phone has not been picked up by the second or third ring, I no longer tolerate the wait. Often I'll hang up and redial on the basis that I must have dialed the wrong number. After all, no one would let a telephone go beyond the third ring.

Speed has become an entitlement, and automation has provided the tools to meet the entitlement to speed. The question is: Have we taken time to imagine what this can accomplish and then plan for the implementation?

An Exercise in Imagination

The sales person of tomorrow is driving to the first appointment of the day. The cellular car phone rings with a call from the company's in-house telemarketing sales center: "I notice your afternoon schedule is open. We just got a hot lead, and you're already in the general area. The appointment is set for 2 p.m., I'm faxing you a facts sheet now. Good luck." Our sales person picks up a voice-activated computer appointment notebook and notes the appointment on the daily log. Stopping at a red light, our sales professional glances at the inbound FAX about the new appointment and calls the prospect to confirm the time.

Arriving at the first appointment, our sales person enters the prospect's office with a laptop computer (with a CD-ROM reader of course) and cellular phone. This particular meeting is to review deliveries over the past quarter, confirm current orders, and introduce a new product. Using the laptop, our producer accesses both the delivery and order files for this client. Together they review the information and compare current order levels with the client's projected needs. Revising quantities on order, the sales person utilizes the computer modem to FAX the revised figures to the sales office and to his client for a hard copy confirmation.

Finishing up old business, the sales person inserts a CD-ROM and sits back as a video is played over the computer screen advising the client of a new product offering.

Afterward, while driving to that new appointment, a cellular phone is used to catch up on messages from a personal pager and office voice-mail. Arriving a few minutes early, our sales pro remains in the car for a few minutes and uses the cellular laptop modem to check e-mail.

I hope this doesn't sound too far-fetched, because there are sales professionals operating in this manner today! Unfortunately, many businesses that currently have all of these automation tools at their disposal have not yet scratched the surface of what can actually be done with them.

Meeting the demands to the entitlement of speed, however, is not all high-tech automation. Here are just a few things to review that could be turning off your prospects before you ever get started:

1. Does your switchboard receptionist answer the phones immediately? How often does that phone ring more than three times when you call in?

2. Once answered, how long is the average call placed on hold? Remember, time goes much more slowly when you're waiting. Twenty seconds on hold can easily seem like two minutes to the caller. To help eliminate problems, the operator should check back with the caller every 20 seconds if the call is slow to be processed.

3. Get rid of the automated answering systems. These menu-driven systems often force the caller to endure one or two minutes for the compu-voice to list their options. And, once a selection is chosen you are often branched into another menu. A well-trained, personable telephone receptionist can handle the call in one-tenth the time. Also, if your customers are calling long distance, they may resent paying for the additional line time.

4. Develop a policy on call-backs and adhere to it. Sales personnel should return all calls during every break between appointments. If not possible, a support person should make a call to advise the client/prospect when they can expect to hear from their representative. Internal support people should return every phone message within 30 minutes.

Think back to the last time you left a message with a customer service operation for some product you had purchased. As each hour goes by without a call-back, you become more angry, until you finally reach a decision to never purchase from that company again. Ring a bell?

5. Process all paper (information) daily.

6. Automate your sales staff and train them in both the science and the art of using that automation for greater marketing effectiveness.

Every journey begins with the first step. You won't get your "speed quotient" up overnight. Perfection may be elusive; but the first step is only a second away.

Chapter 20

More Than Satisfaction: Building Customer Loyalty

By Ed Yager,
Founder, Yager Leadership

When a customer needs service, there is only one job description and it applies to everyone: take care of your customers before anything else is done.

Do you know how many of your customers will say about you, "There is no one I would rather do business with?" Will your employees say, "There is no place I would rather work?" Study after study has provided this same information despite all of our efforts the past decade to improve quality and reliability and to reduce prices through better internal control that the difference between those that succeed and those who do not will almost always be determined by interpersonal processes. In fact, 85 percent of customer defections is directly related to indifference or arrogance of service providers or suppliers employees. The overriding complaint impacting those in the political arena the past decade can be described by the public's perceptions of arrogance and indifference, whether by the individual government employee or by the culture of the agency as a whole.

Whether you are dealing with the auto service technician who follows your complaint about a failed camshaft with an interrogation related to what you did to cause it to break, the 911 operator who refuses to answer your complaint because you are emotional or angry, the retailer who feels it is his or her obligation to become angry, or the retailer who feels it is his or her obligation to give you a lecture on the way you have talked to them when you become angry with their poor service, their response is inappropriate. We have identified these rules and principles for service and service planning.

1. Because many more customers could and probably should complain, invest heavily in learning from those few who do. Your real problem is not the complainer, it's the unhappy customer who has not complained and as a result keeps you from learning.

2. *Take notes, create checksheets, and listen—document every detail of every complaint in order to improve your service.* Evaluate the customer's expectations—how do they use the product, what didn't they understand about the instructions? In this way you can eliminate these problems in future transactions.

3. *There is one paramount rule—absolute honesty.* No excuses, no buck passing, no pleas for sympathy, no delay. "We are wrong—we apologize—how can we make it up to you?" is the only appropriate response.

4. *Never, never ignore a customer.* We have all been in situations where the employee forces himself to avoid looking at us or making any recognition or eye contact. If the work load is overwhelming—acknowledge the customer, express understanding for their frustration and look for some solution to reduce the pressure.

5. *Have an "emergency" service process ready.* When the workload is too heavy, have a process for putting the service in place instantly. Add a packer, prewrap or prepackage; work the line to pull difficult, delayable, or quick transactions out of the line, make sure those in line are ready (i.e. is everything priced, are checks approved and written, paperwork held for later—no matter what the corporate office demands, the customer must come first), and never, never allow personnel to do noncustomer related work in front of customers waiting for service. Even custodians can be trained to help with some element of the customer transaction when necessary. Never let the customer get caught in your bottlenecks.

6. *Continuously study, stand back and watch, and then improve the customer service process.* Look for wasted steps, glitches, duplicate effort, and inefficient movement. Spend time at the exit door, every day, talking to customers and asking for their feedback and advice. Don't delegate this to anyone else.

7. *Insist on team work.* When customers need service there is only one job description and it applies to everyone. Take care of that customer before anything else is done. If you find your employees trying to compete a task but the "customer gets in the way," you can bet you are also in the way of the customer by trying to do that task. Change the way or when you do what you do.

8. *Use customer feedback as the primary measure of performance.* Assure satisfaction with time, length of wait, ease of returns, and administrative matters (check cashing, inventory control, out of stocks, etc.). These things matter.

9. *Look at everything through the eyes of the customer—from the parking lot to the telephone system, from store layout to customer treatment.*

Create a flow so your customers can get from what they need to how they can pay you. The major shift in customer thinking is from "for employees only" to "for our customers' convenience."

10. *Empower all employees to service and surprise customers.* Give the tools for check authorization, exception handing, etc. to the service provider and then monitor the process. Don't slow it down with artificial controls and verifications that do not add value. I (and all the customers behind me) just recently waited at a checkout counter for 10 minutes for a supervisor to authorize my check. When she finally arrived she simply initialized the check without ever looking at it or me. What possible value could this add? Learn the Disney lesson—train those sweepers because they will answer as many or more questions as others.

11. *Dump any employee who cannot learn to treat customers, any customer—internally or externally—with the consideration and respect they deserve.* Employees who imitate rocks, and speed bumps, even if technically competent, or those who work hard yet offend every person they talk with, are not adding value, no matter what you might think.

12. *Never criticize an employee in front of a customer* unless you want the rest of your customers to suffer the consequences of the employee's anger or frustration.

13. *Pay people big time for customer service.* Forget nickel and dime incentives but calculate the contribution, set aggressive goals, and pay the employee what he or she is worth. I can't imagine in today's competitive environment a business owner who employs a person to generate volume or profits many times his or her pay and allow him or her to quit because the pay policy does not approve an increase because of some artificial "salary survey," yet it happens hundreds of times daily. The most successful businesses have consistently said they recruit carefully, hire the best, pay 15 to 20 percent above the prevailing wage rates and then demand performance worthy of that trust and compensation.

Nothing is more important in today's environment than the quality of service, the responsiveness to the customer, and the continuous improvement of processes and methods involved in achieving that service. Again from the Disney experience, Walt's advice to his workforce at the opening of Disneyland over 40 years ago was "Do what you do so well that they will want to see it again and show their friends." Great advice for us all.

Chapter 21

Building Customer Focus

**By Brian L. Joiner,
Co-Founder and CEO,
Joiner Associates, Inc.**

*H*elp people understand that their future success is directly tied to their ability to serve and delight customers.

Imagine walking through your organization and asking people, "Who are our organization's most important customers? How does what you do help the company provide value and quality to those customers?"

What results do you think you would get to this informal survey? When each employee answers those questions well, you have a true customer focus.

Why have a customer focus? The answer should be obvious: if we please customers, they will send us money. If we don't, they won't. Another major benefit of a customer focus is being able to identify and eliminate work in our organizations that has little meaning or value to customers. When we routinely deliver high value, customers become loyal "partners."

But achieving a true customer focus is more challenging than it may sound. The difficulty is not that we don't know what to do—nor that we are unaware that a customer focus is important. In a recent survey, we asked executives to name the top three issues facing their company. Nearly 60 percent listed the need to become more customer focused. However, we need to create systems to translate knowledge about customers into strategic direction and daily action. And, creating systems that cause this to happen is management's job.

Though your organization undoubtedly has some people who already have in-depth knowledge about customers, you need to develop customer information that will be helpful to all employees and to create systems that make sure this information is shared and used. A good starting point is for all employees to understand:

• Who your major customers are.

• How your products or services reach customers—the value chain involved in creating and delivering products and services.

• What characteristics are most important to various customers and how each step in the customer chain adds value.

• How your organization works as a system—how their work fits in, how they and their internal customers add value in the eyes of the customer.

Though we want to please our internal customers, we must remember that external customers are the most important judges of quality. Our service to internal customers must be clearly connected to our external customers' needs.

Leading the Charge

As we all know, few employees will be enthusiastic about going the extra mile, making the extra commitment to customers, unless they see us, their leaders, doing the same. The way that top management spends its time, and the questions they ask of each other, are critical in determining the focus.

To create a customer focus, executives must enjoy interacting with customers and helping them solve problems. We must love the products and services that we sell and the customers we sell to. We must constantly talk positively about customers and take immediate action when customer problems appear.

To check whether your actions are helping to build or destroy your customer focus, ask these questions: 1) If I were to act in the best interests of our customer, what would my decision be? 2) How can I better understand our customers' needs? 3) What can I do to help my employees put a customer focus into action? 4) What are the systems by which we achieve a customer focus? Which of those are most in need of attention? How can we continuously improve each of them? These questions provide a framework for assessing and upgrading our customer focus.

Besides asking these questions, executives must also take action. We need to look at the information we already have. And we must have regular meetings with key customers or customer groups, asking questions that provide both specific issues and broad themes: "What do you like about doing business with us?" "What don't you like about doing business with us?"

In these interviews, we must not be defending current services or products. We must listen to what our customers have to say. Often we "know" why something hasn't been fixed, but it's time to open our minds to our customers' views, to challenge our own thinking.

Creating true customer focus takes energy, creativity, and perseverance. The role of executives is particularly crucial, because your attitude and efforts shape the entire organization. In particular, you must have regular contact with customers, ideally through site visits. You will also need to create systems and methods that encourage and maintain employee knowledge and enthusiasm for delighting customers.

A customer focus must be in line with the organization's strategy. Employees must feel that by helping customers, by taking the time to gather and analyze customer information, they are helping the organization achieve its strategic goals. They must understand who the organization's most important customers are. There must be systems for effectively dealing with immediate customer issues such as complaints, claims, refunds, and technical support. Information on customer problems, needs, and expectations must be gathered from a wide variety of sources, analyzed, integrated, communicated and widely acted upon. Management meetings and systems must continually strive to solve causes of service problems in ways that drive higher customer value and lower costs. And, we must not only hear but also act on the voice of the customer, translating what we learn into specific action plans and testing our plans and actions against, "Is this getting us closer to what our customers need and want from us?" If you try to address the problem piecemeal, you will probably fail.

Remember: our employees won't treat our customers any better than we treat our employees. If we respect our employees and help them, they'll respect the customers and help them. But if we blame our employees—look down on them—they'll do the same to our customers.

Chapter 22

Creating Raving Fans

By Ken Blanchard,
Chairman of Blanchard Training and Development

When your employees become raving fans, they will make raving fans of your customers by delivering little extras.

There are three secrets to creating Raving Fans: 1) determine what you want to do, 2) discover what the customer wants to do, and 3) deliver plus one percent.

The first two secrets have to do with the vision of perfection you have in relation to serving customers. First decide what you're willing to do, then find out what your customers want within that parameter, and then see if there is a fit. The third secret has to do with implementation—how you coordinate your systems to make a difference.

I often ask people, "How many of you in your companies think customers are important?" Everybody puts their hands up. Then I ask, "How many of you would like to have Raving Fans customers?" Everybody puts their hands up again. The real question is "Who does it systematically, and who treats it as a fad?"

For example, I don't particularly believe in having an employee of the month. It gets to be too routine and predictable. People worry that they can't have people in the same department nominated two months in a row or that there is an employee who has been loyal but who is too new to be recognized.

I believe in employee of the moment. We call it Eagle of the Moment. What this means is that any time anybody exceeds a customer's expectations, whether it's an internal or external customer, it is a time for celebration. What we have done with some of the companies we've worked with is to set up "eagles' nests" so that when people spot an "eagle in flight"—an employee delivering outstanding service—they can call an eagle's nest and use a Polaroid camera to catch the eagle in flight. I have told so many people about eagle behavior, yet hardly any company ever grabs hold and implements it. This is surprising because people come up to me all the time to tell me what a great idea it is.

An example of where this idea was implemented almost immediately was at Saturn Corporation. I went to Tennessee and did a session for their customer-service people. The night before, I got a call from a man named Milt Garret of Garret Consulting, who supports the concept of Raving Fans. Milt had heard I was at Saturn and wanted to tell me the story about what Saturn did with his wife.

His wife, Jane, had been diagnosed with cancer five years ago, and she was able to beat it. Last year when Milt got home from training, Jane said to him, "Tomorrow is a special day. It's the fifth anniversary of my being diagnosed with cancer." He said that he tried to be creative and make it a special day, but somehow he didn't feel he made it special enough. So the next day, a Monday, he went to the Saturn dealership because his wife liked Saturns and wanted one for a long time, but didn't want to pay the expense because their son was still in college.

Milt met the salesman and put money down on the car for Jane. Later that week, when he was on the road he found out from one of his kids that the color of car Jane wanted was white. So he called up the dealer and asked if they had any white Saturns. The man at the dealership said they only had one, so Milt asked if they could save it for him. The salesman asked if he was sure that Jane really wanted it because they were selling eight cars a day, and they couldn't guarantee that it would be there unless he could commit to purchasing it. Milt told him to save the white car for him.

When Milt got home on Saturday, he took Jane out for a ride and told her that he had to stop by Saturn to get some information on a session that he was doing the next day. So he asked Jane to come in with him. As they walked into the showroom, the dealership had moved the white car right into the center of the showroom. Jane went to it like a magnet, opened the door, got in, got out and said, "Milt, isn't this a beautiful car?" She walked around to the front of the car and all of a sudden let out a yell and started crying. Milt ran to her to ask her what was wrong. She pointed to a sign that read, "Congratulations Jane, Five Years Cancer-Free—Here's to Life! From Milt, your salesman, and the Saturn dealership."

What Milt didn't realize was that the Saturn people had moved all of the other customers and sales people outside so that Jane could enjoy the moment with some privacy. When the people outside saw Milt and Jane hug, they started to applaud.

The Saturn people put the principles into practice. When I did the session and talked about this employee of the moment, they immediately put an eagle's nest in and started operating it. Their whole commitment to the customer is pervasive and sincere.

Once a pregnant woman came in and bought a Saturn from this same dealer. She loved the car, but, three months later, she learned that she was going to have twins. The car wasn't big enough, so she called the dealership and told them her situation. They told her that they would give her money back and help her find another car that better met her needs. When Saturn had a reunion in Tennessee, over 10,000 Saturn owners came for the weekend.

The people who are making a difference and who are ready to act on their commitment are ready to go. The real winners don't talk about service, they just do it. If they hear a good idea that can help improve service, they implement it.

The whole concept of deliver plus one percent is not just a theory—it's something you live by. So if you have a good idea, put it into action! Pick the best new idea that can make you that much better and focus on making it a reality.

Section 3:

Process Quality

Chapter 23

Six Keys to Quality Service

**By Keith Bailey and Karen Dunn,
Co-Founders, Sterling Consulting Group**

*B*ecoming customer-focused goes beyond "fixing people" out there—it includes every person and process at all levels.

Organizations committed to becoming more customer-focused can't depend on training alone. Often, reevaluation and redesign are required in six key areas.

1. Top-down commitment. Executives quickly agree that quality service is an important element in business success. The difference is the degree to which they walk their talk when it comes to service excellence. Their actions, not their words, signal to staff what is really valued. The saying, "Fish stinks from the head down" describes how management sets the cultural tone. And there is no faster way for management to hinder quality improvement than by promoting service excellence with their words while expressing mediocrity by their actions.

Effective managers show their commitment to quality service in two ways: 1) taking a roll-up-your-sleeves approach and jumping in when it comes to dealing with customers and finding out what is going on; and 2) modeling excellent service skills when interacting with their employees and with customers.

2. Measurement and feedback. In a workshop, we recommended that a particular company do a customer survey. At this suggestion, a senior manager jumped out of his seat and warned his colleagues, "This is a bad time to survey our customers—they're mad at us right now!" Many companies operate on the false assumption that they know what their customers want. One of the most important steps in improving service excellence is to know, not guess, what your customers want and expect, and how well you are meeting or exceeding their expectations.

Take the pulse of your customer before starting any service improvement program. To get accurate feedback, use such methods as telephone interviews, mail surveys, face-to-face interviews, complaint analyses, lost account surveys, and focus groups. After gathering the data, reroute any appropriate findings back to those surveyed. This confirms that they were heard and serves to detail any changes that are being considered or made.

Gathering feedback from staff is the other significant aspect of discovering where you stand. We often begin our work with clients by conducting a Quality Service Audit. This "cultural x-ray" is an inside look at the customer focus and allows for a detailed analysis built upon specific criteria.

3. *Education and training.* Service education and training both contribute to the staff's awareness of the importance of service. *Service education* is any process that underscores and illuminates how service improvement relates to specific jobs, tasks, and behaviors. It can take the form of newsletters, briefings, meetings, videos, etc. By *service training*, we mean the more formalized, classroom style approach that strives to build skills and awareness in specific areas such as: customer service skills for frontline staff, customer service skills for backroom staff, orientation for new hires, service management skills for all managers, and quality problem solving skills. Maximum effectiveness is gained when education and training are combined.

4. *Customer-friendly systems.* This area can be overwhelming to executives who are becoming customer-focused. Part of the problem lies in the tangled web of procedures, policies, and hardware that make up the systems and act as a blueprint for the way a company does business.

Systems, while obviously indispensable, can help or hurt the customer and staff depending on how they are designed. The two key problems are: 1) Systems that are set up to protect the company from having the employees or customers take advantage of them; and 2) Systems that are an inherited way the company has always done business, and no one questions their validity or effectiveness. Obedience to the procedures and policies often overrides common sense.

The key service-related systems include: sales/ordering systems, supply/logistics systems, accounting/payment systems, after sales service systems, complaint procedures, crisis/contingency systems, and telephone/computer systems. Examining and changing in-focused systems—those that work favorably for the company but unfavorably for the customer—are keys to successful service-improvement. Until the service problems caused by the systems are resolved, any ground to be gained in quality service improvement is limited.

5. *Quality service standards.* Friendliness, courtesy, responsiveness, and accuracy are worthy goals, but how do you achieve them when they mean different things to different people? For example, if you ask 20 people, "What does being friendly mean?" you will likely receive 20 different answers.

The solution is to quantify quality by developing specific, objective, and measurable service standards that translate service qualities into specific behaviors and actions. Standards allow objective evaluation of staff performance and ensure consistency in treatment of customers. Standards might be answering the phone within three rings; returning all customer calls within 24 hours; or filling all orders within 48 hours of receipt.

6. Recognition of service excellence. Three elements create an environment of recognition for service excellence within companies: 1) a formal recognition program (department, division, or company wide) that provides rewards for the individual or team that best fulfills the specified service criteria; 2) informal recognition, the casual everyday acknowledgment of staff that is often expressed by spontaneous gestures; and 3) salary and advancement. If people can't see some personal benefit (the possibility of advancement or an increase in salary) in return for increased sensitivity and service to customers, then the gospel of service just becomes so much hot air. These three elements are essential to ensuring that the service improvement effort sticks.

The quest for quality in every aspect of business is an ongoing process—quality service is never over and done. Companies that consistently deliver excellent service never assume that they have arrived. They continually strive for the edge and create improvements before their customers request them or their competitors introduce them. As one executive put it, "Our job is to make our existing services obsolete before our competitors do."

Chapter 24

The Core Value of Service

By Keshavan Nair,
President of Benjamin/Nair, Inc.

*E*ver since Prahalad and Hamel wrote about core competence, the idea that businesses should excel in activities that are central to their business has become a dominant management theme.

A corporation needs more than core competencies, it needs core values. Competencies describe what is done from a technical point of view; core values describe what is important to the spirit of the people in the corporation. A core value must be applicable to all levels and parts of the organization. A core value is not unique to an organization. Several organizations may have the same core value. It is the level of commitment that makes an organization unique. It is the same with individuals. We subscribe to many of the same values. It is how we live up to them that differentiates us. A core value has to be embedded into the decision making and routines of the corporation. It becomes the basis of statements like "This is who we are" and "These are our expectations of each other." A core value gives heart to the technical proficiency of core competency.

Service should be the overarching core value of a corporation. Service not in the narrow sense to any one constituency, but to all the stakeholders in the business. Service is a core value that can uplift the spirit of every employee by providing a sense of purpose at both the corporate and individual level.

Service as a Core Value

The concept of service as a core value is simple. The organization and the individuals in it, from the CEO to the lowest level employee, see themselves as helping others in one or all of the following: 1) defining goals, objectives and needs; 2) choosing a path to achieve their goals and meet their needs; and 3) taking the journey along the path. The operative concept is helping, being of service to others. The concept is simple, but implementation is not.

Service as a core value is not just a policy; it is deeper and more profound—every individual and the organization as a whole value being of service. When service to others is valued, trust, loyalty and truthfulness flourish. These create efficiencies. "Trust and similar values, loyalty or truth-telling, are examples of what the economist would call *externalities*," writes Nobel Laureate economist Kenneth Arrow in *The Limits of Organization.* "They are goods; they are commodities; they have real, practical, economic value; they increase the efficiency of the system, enabling you to produce more goods or more of whatever values you hold in high esteem."

Service and leadership are intertwined. Take a moment to examine your own life. When somebody helps you toward your goals or meets your needs, you often elevate that individual to a position of leadership. For example, in the area of knowledge, we elevate teachers; in sports, coaches; in work, those who help our careers; and in life experience, elders. If the individual who has been elevated to leadership uses the position to further serve, he or she further reinforces the position of leadership. The same is true for organizations. For example, service to customers usually elevates a business to market leadership. If that leadership position is used to continue and enhance customer service, business success continues. Service as a core value is self-sustaining; this is its power.

Making Service the Core Value

A core value implies commitment. Creating a core value in an organization is a long-term endeavor. There are four essential steps in making service a core value: 1) Leadership by example, 2) comprehensive service to all stakeholders, 3) truthful service, and 4) the reconciliation of power with service.

1. Leadership by example. It is the level of commitment that will distinguish a company from others in serving its stakeholders. Inspiring and creating commitment is the task of leadership. As we move to a business environment, where knowledge and information are the driving forces, there is increased interaction among all levels of employees. Leadership has increased visibility. In this environment, leadership actions must reinforce what is valued. The model of leadership that is most effective in inspiring commitment is leadership by example. "Example," said Albert Schweitzer, "is not the main thing in influencing others. It is the only thing."

2. Comprehensive service. If service is to be the core value, there must be a commitment to serve all major stakeholders—customers, employees, and shareholders. When Jack Welch, CEO of General Electric, states that the measurements he is focused on relate to customer, shareholder and employee satisfaction, he is recognizing that all the major stakeholders have to be served. Decline in service to any one group will inevitably lead to a decline in service to other stakeholders. Dissatisfied employees will deliver poor customer service, leading to a decline in financial performance and reduced returns to shareholders. Corporations are beginning to recognize that stakeholder interests are inter-twined and that serving one stakeholder requires serving all stakeholders.

All businesses operate in a societal context and have to respond to societal concerns expressed in laws, regulations, and policies. Recently the senior management of Pacific Gas and Electric, the largest investor-owned utility, formally acknowledged the interdependence of shareholders' financial objectives, customer service requirements, employee safety, and society's concern for public safety. In a pioneering activity, it has implemented a process with its unions for developing an ongoing labor-management partnership to maintain and operate the gas and electric systems to ensure the delivery of safe, reliable, responsive service to PG&E customers. "The concept of partnership implies service to each other and together serving all other stakeholder interests.

3. *Service must be truthful.* Service has to be performed within moral constraints. Goals, objectives and the means to achieve them must not violate moral principles. Executives who direct people by statements like "I don't care how you do it, just get me the results" do not contribute to truthful service. In businesses ranging from agriculture to financial services, intense focus on profit goals has caused individuals to commit illegal and unethical acts. These acts have resulted in disservice to all stakeholders through decreased morale, damaged reputations, and depressed stock prices.

The essential service a corporation provides for its employees is employment. In today's rapidly changing technological and competitive environment, businesses that have service as a core value have to think of new ways to meet their service commitment to their employees. Employees need to be told the truth about the future of the business; it is the only way they can respond to the realities of the changing environment, both in terms of preparing themselves to remain valuable contributors and in responding to immediate challenges. Andy Grove, chairman of Intel, has recognized that the corporation has an obligation to be truthful and inform employees about senior management's view about the future. Based on this future, he has expressed his view that the corporation should serve its employees by providing education and training opportunities so that employees can prepare for the future and thus increase their chances for continued employment.

In dealing with customers, truthful service implies delivering the promised quality in products and ensuring accuracy in advertising and packaging. There is increased evidence that dealing truthfully with customers results in higher customer satisfaction, creating better business results and increased shareholder satisfaction—reinforcing the concept that good service is comprehensive.

4. *Reconciling power with service.* The major difficulty in making service a core value is the corrupting influence of power. Through service, or at least the promise of service, organizations and individuals get elevated to positions of leadership. Organizations gain market leadership; individuals gain position and executive authority. Having achieved this position of leadership, organizations and more often individuals can forget that they should use their position for service. Power can cause arrogance and remove the desire for service—this is a pervasive human weakness and is a significant obstacle in maintaining service as a core value.

Mahatma Ghandi proposed the concept of "trusteeship" to reconcile power with service. Although Gandhi's primary emphasis was in the political arena, the concept has general applicability. According to the concept of trusteeship, power is not something that belongs to an individual or an organization, but is given to it by others. Businesses get power from customers, employees, and society. Executives get their power from shareholders, employees, and the organization. Trusteeship says that those who have power, and everyone has some power, should think of it as being placed in trust with them by others. People with power should think of themselves as trustees acting for the benefit of those who gave them power. With the trusteeship model, it becomes the personal responsibility of every individual to use whatever power he or she has for service toward all stakeholders.

The core value for a business should be service. The level to which a business lives up to this core value will be the basis on which it will distinguish itself from its competitors. Service gives a sense of purpose to the organization, which inspires commitment at the individual level. At a fundamental level, all commitment is individual—and individual commitment is the foundation of organizational excellence.

Leadership by example must inspire this commitment. This leadership has to exist at all levels in the corporation. Service as a core value must be comprehensive, truthful, and reconciled with power. A core value provides a sense of purpose to core competency. It provides the motivation to develop competency and the commitment to maintain it and thus create a sustainable competitive advantage.

Chapter 25

Quality Service: More Than a Smile

By Ken Myers, Principal,
Breakthrough Group, and
Jim Buckman, President,
Minnesota Council for Quality

Now, more than ever, executives share a responsibility to actively shape quality service. We recommend the following 18-point "checklist" to guide you.

Six Foundation Stones

At least six foundation stones are basic to providing quality service to internal and external customers.

1. Know your customer. Actively identify customers and suppliers, inside and out. Clarify and negotiate roles and relationships. This process reestablishes communication, makes the territory clearer, clarifies expectations, and often leads to the discovery of opportunities for improvement.

2. Make service a seamless experience. Most customers, inside and out, seek a seamless experience. They don't want anything to fall through the cracks. They want what was expected, when and where they were led to expect it.

3. Give and receive communication. To achieve quality service, observe the rules: communicate, communicate, communicate. Keep employees, management, customers, and suppliers in the loop.

4. Shape the environment. Quality service must be fostered within a positive work culture and climate. Adequate training, time, and resources are required, along with a commitment to remove disturbing "pinches."

5. Seek continuous improvement. Technology, processes, competitive demands, and customers' expectations all change over time. They keep moving the quality service "bar" higher. Maintaining your "edge" requires continuous improvement.

6. Celebrate and reward service excellence. Employees are paid to get the job done. But we all appreciate a little recognition along the way. If you want improvement, acknowledge progress early and often. Catch employees in the act of providing quality service and reward them.

Six Aspects of the Service Setting

Have you ever felt out of place, even lost, in service surroundings? Have you ever grown tired of waiting in line or seeking help? When this happens, too little attention has been paid to the utility value or "user friendliness" of the service setting.

1. Orient your customers. Keep customers from getting disoriented. Provide relevant, well-located information and signage. Make the system, facilities, and processes legible from the user's perspective. Ensure informed and authorized employees are available to help and solve problems.

2. Cut waiting times. Waiting is frustrating, even anger-provoking. It deadens the experience of otherwise superior service. It's often effectively managed by a first-come, first-served queue. Information, distractions, "handlers," or other features may be used to build a neutral, even positive experience of waiting.

3. Enhance the physical environment. Does the environment match the image you desire? Do the decor, color, and props convey desired messages? Are physical separations adequate for the service context? Is the environment cuing the customer to feel and respond appropriately?

4. Enhance the social environment. Ensure that service providers' appearance, demeanor, knowledge, spirit, and approach are appropriate. Review how people are managed and moved. Examine routine employee tasks to ensure they facilitate service delivery. Do service providers meet or exceed service standards at the "moments of truth" (points of contact)? Do service providers add value to the service experience?

5. Make the service tangible. Customers appreciate quality service more when it is tangible. Quality service should include "felt contacts" or mini-encounters to give pause to the customer. Signs, verbal messages, and "handlers" heighten customer awareness, helping them to form a basis for having and reporting a quality experience.

6. Don't let the rules get in the way. Nothing so galls customers as rules that block their way. Review rules with an eye to simplifying and limiting them. Try to make them "user friendly" and empower those on the frontline to make appropriate judgments and adjustments.

Six Action Levers

Here are six ways to manage those moments of truth with your customers, inside and out, to leverage quality service.

1. Being on target. This means setting and meeting expectations, and doing what was promised, when and where it was promised.

2. Showing care and concern. This means being empathetic, attentive, ready, and willing to help, tuning in to the customer's situation, frame of mind, and needs.

3. Encouraging spontaneity. Empower service providers to think and respond quickly. Give folks close to the action some discretion to "jockey the system."

4. Solving problems. Customers give their fullest attention when they experience a problem. Responding positively, taking care of the situation quickly, turns a problem into a chance to please, which sticks in the customer's mind.

5. Following up with flair. Attentive follow-up captures customers' attention, is associated with caring professionalism, and is the stuff of legendary quality service.

6. Believing in recovery. Making things right quickly is a powerful factor in creating an enduring image of high quality service.

We invite you to use this checklist to help assess your service quality and to help make Total Service Quality a reality in your organization.

Chapter 26

Four Keys to Service Performance

By Stan Brown, President,
Coopers and Lybrand Consulting, Toronto, Canada

*I*n building a house, you first construct a firm foundation; you then form a basic outer shell; you next add the essential fixtures and ensure that all systems work together; and you then maintain the house. Our research and experience shows that companies that improve customer satisfaction practice four parallel steps.

Step 1. Align senior management in the commitment to excellence. The first step requires an alignment of attitudes. This has to actively involve senior management.

A meaningful budget must be allocated to enable the organization to achieve its customer satisfaction objectives. There must also be visible executive involvement in customer satisfaction initiatives as well as a reasonable timeline and measurable goals for improving customer satisfaction and its payoffs, so that staff throughout the organization have something tangible to work for and can see the benefits of their efforts.

Part of a management commitment to improving customer satisfaction also includes a focused reward program designed to recognize excellence-in-service within the organization. Successful organizations know the magic of incentives and performance-based reward systems for employees. Less successful organizations recognize the error of their ways. When asked to identify those factors that limit their potential to succeed, they resoundingly state insufficient budget, lack of management support, and inadequate rewards and recognition.

Step 2. Listen to the voice of the customer. Successful organizations survey their customers extensively and regularly to determine their needs and the extent to which the company is meeting or exceeding them. Successful companies are more likely to survey customers on a variety of areas, including the effectiveness of complaint handling, customer satisfaction, conformance to standards, customer needs, and new product ideas.

But successful companies don't stop there. Not only do they measure their actual performance against the standards they have set, they research and compare themselves against their competition to see how they measure up. They know that a commitment to customer satisfaction must be backed up by a complete understanding of the customer, the competition and the marketplace, and an ability to identify and respond to areas where change is needed.

Step 3. Focus on customer-related processes. In addition to constantly surveying customer needs, companies that improve their customers' satisfaction levels are more likely to take a hard look at their customer-related processes and reengineer them. These processes include customer order fulfillment, billing, complaint systems, account management, sales force management, and other processes that deal directly with customers. Companies that focus on these systems see positive effects on both revenue and customer satisfaction; less successful companies tend to focus on systems that drive cost improvements and reduce labor strategies that bring only temporary advantage in the marketplace.

Successful companies also track customer complaints. These companies operate under the philosophy that "what gets measured gets done," and they actively encourage customer feedback. Management is made aware of customer complaints received in all departments and the corrective action being taken. This tracking information is shared with the entire organization.

Knowing where to begin a process improvement initiative requires an understanding of the company's options. This is where differences in company philosophy become strongly apparent. Companies that are achieving improved customer satisfaction know that a good rating from customers must be measured against ratings received by the competition. If, for example, Company A is seen as an "excellent" service provider, then Company B's "good" rating obviously isn't good enough. Company B must understand why Company A is seen as excellent and look at a variety of ways to make improvements, researching direct competitors as well as other industry segments. That's where process benchmarking comes in—and where less successful companies often drop the ball.

Process benchmarking is the art of finding out how others do something better, with the ultimate goal of imitating—or perhaps improving upon—their techniques. It is a continuous process already being practiced by Kodak, Milliken, Motorola and Xerox, and is an essential part of an approach to improving customer satisfaction.

Step 4. Support a culture of continuous improvement. Successful companies state the importance of understanding that improving customer satisfaction is an ongoing process, one that must be constantly nurtured with attention to the "human" side of the equation. It has to become part of the day-to-day operation of the organization, which means creating an internal service culture throughout the company.

Create a Service Culture

Use five main strategies to create a service culture.

1. Communicate with employees to determine their needs and level of job satisfaction. Successful companies follow the Golden Rule of Service: "Do unto your internal customers—your employees—as you would have them do unto your external customers." Satisfied employees create satisfied customers. And satisfied customers create momentum. They help the company innovate, by offering ideas on how it can improve.

2. Empower senior management with the responsibility for developing and maintaining the service culture. The commitment to improve customer satisfaction has to begin at the highest levels to ensure success. Executives must have both the authority and the responsibility for developing and maintaining customer satisfaction initiatives.

3. Establish service standards through the input of both customers and employees. Successful companies go one step beyond gathering customer and employee survey information. They produce a "Customer Bill of Rights" to inform customers of the quality of service they can expect to receive, to tell employees about the service they are expected to deliver, and to let employees know the standards management will abide by in delivering quality service to its staff.

Your Customer Bill of Rights should include some basic components: a vision statement for the future of the business; a mission statement; a core values statement; and a description of standards against which it dares to be measured and receive customer feedback.

4. Ensure that those standards are practiced by employees and promoted to customers. A Customer Bill of Rights should be posted throughout the organization. Customers must be made aware of it, and it should be incorporated into all employee training programs.

5. Encourage the service culture through training and reward programs to establish and recognize excellence-in-service. Provide motivation, positive feedback, and performance-based rewards and link a portion of employee compensation to the performance of the business. Also, recognize employee contributions and share authority by involving employees in the company's strategic plan. Customer satisfaction starts with the analysis of both internal and external needs and practices. Externally, successful organizations understand that innovation comes from what works for others. Accordingly, these companies constantly review the best practices of others and adopt those that suit their needs. Internally, successful companies know that although ideas may come from outside, change must start inside. Establishing an internal service culture must combine a commitment from management with the input of employees and customers. Although the initial investment is sizeable, developing a service culture ultimately results in revenue enhancement (increased sales) and improved profitability (decreased internal costs) without necessitating cutbacks.

Chapter 27

Innovation Imperatives

**By Charles Garfield,
CEO of the Charles Garfield Group**

Only by courting customers with product and service innovations can companies hope to win competitive advantage.

Innovation can spring up in the most controlled environments, just as flowers can force their way through the cracks in a sidewalk. But for innovation to thrive, for it to be continuous, the climate must encourage and nurture it.

Alvin Toffler believes that all companies are now faced with the "innovation imperative." He declares: "No existing market share is safe today, no product life indefinite. In everything from insurance policies to medical care to travel packages, competition tears away niches and whole chunks of established business with the weapon of innovation. Companies shrivel and die unless they can create an endless stream of new products."

Innovation—the product of knowledge (of customers' needs, market trends, competitors' offerings, distributors' concerns, changing technologies) and empowerment, autonomy combined with responsibility—is most likely to flourish in a climate where people are encouraged to learn, where open communication is the norm, where employees have easy and complete access to information, and where all employees are empowered.

Successful Innovation

PC Connection has created such a climate. In 1982, Patricia Gallup and David Hall invested $8,000 of their own money to launch a mail-order business that offers a broad range of software and accessories for IBM and Macintosh personal computers. Based in Marlow, New Hampshire, PC Connection boasted sales of $233,000 in its first year. By 1990, its annual revenues had grown to more than $100 million, and its staff had swelled to 250 employees. *PC World* magazine named PC Connection "Best Mail-Order Company" four times.

The odds against winning in the crowded, cutthroat mail-order industry are overwhelming. But PC Connection has thrived, thanks to an innovative approach. Patricia Gallup explains:

> When my partner, David Hall, and I started the company, we asked, "How do we want to be treated when we buy mail-order?" Our goal is to seek better ways of providing products and information to our customers. We talk to and listen to all of our contacts in the industry. We ask, "What's going to make us stand out?" We also do our homework, and it leads to creative ideas and new services.
>
> In the computer industry, you need to always be thinking about what the customer may want in the future. We realize many people are going to want products and information at their fingertips, and they are going to want it fast. Our responsibility is to make sure that people are as productive as possible with their computer equipment.
>
> We started offering toll-free technical support. Then we came up with the idea of including videotape instructions. We started our own video production studio. We now develop programs that help people with their purchasing decisions, as well as encourage better use of their equipment.
>
> We put ourselves in the shoes of both customer and vendor. We've created an environment of innovation by giving our management team the freedom to explore, experiment, and discover how to best accomplish the goals they set.

Patricia is understandably upbeat, but her suppliers are equally enthusiastic. Elliott Levine, vice president of Merisel, says "PC Connection almost single-handedly brought mail order out of the Dark Ages."

The stunning success of PC Connection can be explained largely by its ability to produce continuous innovations—ignoring the conventional wisdom that low price is the only "innovation" that attracts customers to mail order—and by the company's commitment to putting customers first. In many cases, PCC is not the lowest price competitor.

To generate continuous innovation says Patricia Gallup, "Learn to listen to your customers. Find out what they want, and don't assume anything. Give them what they expect—and more."

Enter into Partnerships

When employees are given free access to information, when they are allowed and encouraged to enter into partnerships and learn with others inside and outside the organization, innovative ideas multiply. A company's most important innovations often spring from such partnerships.

• *With customers.* PC Connection generates many innovations by partnering with customers, listening to them, encouraging feedback, and finding new ways of satisfying them. Positive response from customers prompted PCC to strive for faster delivery and to start an overnight service. It developed telephone support and instruction videos in response to customer needs. Elliott Levine of Merisel comments: "Rather than buying market share with their dollars, they focus their attention on what they can do to add value to sell their products." By listening closely to customers, by encouraging their feedback and suggestions, PC Connection is ensured of a continual stream of ideas, which it translates into service innovations.

• *With suppliers.* By considering the needs of its suppliers, PC Connection generates win-win innovations. One, for example, is PCC's policy of paying many of its suppliers on a "one day net" basis—unheard of in the mail-order industry (and rare in any industry). By partnering with its vendors, PCC benefits as well. Patricia Gallup explains: "We try to give our suppliers more than they expect. Because we are so prompt in our payments to them, we are always first in their minds, and that's a good place to be."

• *With employees.* Charles Hampden-Turner points out: "There is no escaping the underlying sense that the product or service can be no better, no more sensitive, subtle, aesthetic, congruent, or intelligent than are the relationships and the communication among those who create the product." Unless employees feel a sense of partnership with one another and with the organization, a high level of service, quality, and innovation can't be sustained over time.

• *With community.* The growth of the company must be reconciled with responsibility to the community. Innovation has sprung from PCC's partnership with the community, as reflected in its dedication to preserving the integrity of the historic old town. PCC set up headquarters early in an old mill, which it restored. The new corporate headquarters blend in with the town's architecture. Also, PCC purchased and restored the old Christmas Trees Inn for use as a corporate training center.

Innovative companies like PCC are constantly learning—from customers, competitors, employees, suppliers, distributors, and others. The innovative organization is a learning organization, a giant laboratory of learning where the gathering of information and the acquisition of knowledge are integral parts of every job. Learning is a central task for all employees. To keep its finger on the pulse of its industry, PC Connection is in constant contact with customers, suppliers, and other outsiders, monitoring hundreds of mail-order catalogs, looking for innovations, trying to identify emerging market trends, customer needs, and the activities of its competitors.

Patricia Gallup notes: "Innovation is just what we like to do. Our interest is in being creative and in making life more pleasant for the person whose path crosses ours. If you like what you are doing, success comes naturally because you are dedicated to keeping up with what's going on in your industry. You do your homework. You research the trends and note how people's needs and expectations are changing. You think about the impact these changes could have on your business, or the influence your business could have on people's changing needs and expectations."

An innovative organization ensures its opportunity for success by being well suited to the environment in which it operates, and by partnering with internal and external stakeholders to achieve maximum speed, flexibility, and responsiveness. An innovative company is far more likely to thrive in a world of constant change and intense competition.

Chapter 28

The Service Edge

By Ron Zemke,
President, Performance Research Associates, Inc.

*T*o keep your competitive edge, take the following eight steps to quality, knock-your-socks-off service.

1. *Find and retain quality people.* If you don't start with quality people, you can't end up with satisfied, loyal customers. But this is a two-act play: once found and brought on board, quality people must be kept on board. That means orienting them carefully, training them fully in the knowledge and skills necessary for success, giving them challenging assignments, and keeping them interested in the work. It also means empowering them to work for the customer, rewarding and recognizing their accomplishments—sometimes individually, sometimes as a group. In particular, it means celebrating the accomplishments of those who go "one step beyond" for their customers.

2. *Know your customer intimately.* Astute service managers recognize that the judgment of quality service begins and ends with customers. Only customers can say what high quality service really is; only good management practices can tap that knowledge. And, since customers' needs are constantly changing and their expectations are forever rising, remaining focused on the customer experience is critical. Only a persistent, ongoing dialogue with customers can keep a company on top. Knowing your customers intimately means more than having a passing acquaintance with the market research of your industry or company. It means understanding and responding—often in unique and creative ways—to the evolving needs and constantly shifting expectations of your customers. Customers come in so many varieties and shades of need and expectation, we need to be careful of the "one size fits all" assumption. Sometimes a single customer is so special, or so different, or so unique, or so important, that he or she rates his or her own rules, policies, and procedures. Managers are at a disadvantage with regard to gaining the customer's view of service. The longer people manage a service delivery system, the more they take it for granted and stop seeing it with cold objectivity and without bias.

3. Focus on purpose. Focusing on purpose means establishing a clear vision of what superior service is, communicating that vision to employees at every level, and ensuring that your vision of service quality is personally and positively important to everyone. When managers have a clear, no-nonsense statement of service distinction, employees can align their efforts. Concrete standards of service quality make the vision real and palpable; regular and extensive measurement makes it meaningful. The best organizations clearly articulate the vision, communicate the vision to all, set standards, measure regularly, and make results count.

4. Create systems that make you easy to do business with. The service delivery system is all of the apparatus, physical and procedural, that service people must have to meet customers' needs and deliver effectively the service promised in the service strategy statement. Your service delivery system is the physical embodiment of your service vision. What the service strategy statement promises, your system delivers. A service delivery system is, above all else, the rules you write for daily work. A good service delivery system is friendly to customers and employees and monitors satisfaction levels to enable self-correction. In a bad system, it is an easy—and grave—mistake to blame the frustrations caused by poor system design on poor people performance or rotten customers.

5. Train and support. Training turns potential into performance. Even an employee who has worked in another area needs to be trained in your ways of doing things. And someone hired from the outside—regardless of experience—needs to learn your approach to the job and to customers. Support is being there for new employees who are having problems learning and applying your way of doing things as well as being a resource for seasoned employees who are dealing with sticky issues and tough calls. Support is also backing up employees who have had to make a tough call and standing behind employees who have erred.

6. Involve and empower everyone. The best consultants you could possibly have are already on the payroll—your employees. They are ready, willing, and able to lend a hand and make improvements. You have only to involve them—in a sincere and meaningful way—in the business of your business, in creating and delivering high quality service to customers. Empowerment is delegation, or the giving over of power and responsibility to a subordinate. It enables an employee to perform better; it enhances the skills and scope of an employee;

and it helps an employee feel an increased sense of control over his or her work, decisions, and environment. Empowerment does not mean granting unlimited license, but rather, responsible freedom. The key to effective empowerment is understanding that it is not a gift bestowed by the manager; empowerment means removing the barriers which prevent service people from acting with power. People care when they share and contribute. Without employee involvement, there is no employee commitment. Service quality is a team sport. Teamwork ensures that the customer's passage from employee to employee, unit to unit, is efficient and effective.

7. Recognize, reward, and celebrate distinctive performance. Recognize and reward service accomplishments, sometimes individually, sometimes as a group. In particular, celebrate the successes of employees who go "one step beyond" for their customers. A celebration is a pause in the day to acknowledge success. Celebrations help to underline and emphasize an organization's mission and its values. They help bolster self-esteem by focusing on fun, purpose, and the "work family." When giving public recognition, make clear what the person or group did to merit the honor.

8. Set the tone and lead the way. Will Rogers said that "people learn more from observation than from conversation." He was right. Setting a personal example of doing things right, taking the time to listen to customers and employees without impatience, and focusing your energy on the things that say service quality to your customers—inside and out—is a critical part of your role. Just as customers' expectations are constantly rising and their needs changing, so too are your frontline service people in need of an occasional jump start and renewal. Effective service managers try new approaches to keep people focused on providing quality service.

Globally, we live and work in a service-centered, service-sensitive economy. In North America, for example, 80 percent of the jobs and 60 percent of the GNP come from the performance of services, rather than the production of products. More importantly, as manufactured products become more alike, it is increasingly the quality and variety of the service that is the critical difference between success and failure in the marketplace. Organizations that deliver high quality service see a greater increase in market share and have a higher return on sales.

If service quality is the competitive edge for business, why do we do a mediocre job of managing and delivering service? Because we try to manage the design, development, production, and delivery of services the same way we manage the production of commodities.

Four Traits of Service Winners

Organizations that successfully deliver quality service are distinguished by four characteristics:

• They understand their customer's wants and needs, and know that customer satisfaction is created "a moment of truth at a time."

• They have a well-developed and broadly communicated sense of what they want to accomplish with the customer, an articulated service strategy;

• They design their delivery systems with customer accessibility in mind; and

• They recognize the importance of having well-trained employees who understand the needs and wants of the customer, and who are aligned with the service strategy for meeting those needs.

Today's corporate hero will be the executive who understands the design, development, and delivery of high quality service, and who endeavors to meet the needs of both external and internal customers. Successful organizations will be known for their steadfast commitment to service quality, and their ability to deliver it without fail.

Customers today will simply not stand for bad service, poor quality, shoddy work, or lousy treatment. Today's consumers—wholesale, retail, commercial, or trade—are willing to pay a premium to have their needs met in a timely and efficient manner, and with a modicum of dignity, reliability, responsiveness, and respect.

Laments about rude, unhelpful salespeople who neither know their products nor care about their customers are all too common.

Organizations that deliver first-rate, knock-your-socks-off service to customers and clients are managed differently. They focus on understanding customers' wants, needs, and expectations; they have a well-conceived vision or plan for delivering top quality service; they have customer-oriented systems for delivering service; and they have customer-oriented frontline employees.

Outstanding service organizations also form service partnerships to build and maintain long-term, mutually beneficial customer relationships and alliances.

A key to an effective service partnership is your measure of you. At the very core of any relationship is two people struggling to meet individual and joint needs while maintaining some stability of the relationship. The relationship is most "at risk" at three points: 1) at the start when needs and expectations are being clarified, negotiated, and ultimately aligned; 2) when a blunder has occurred, and one or both parties is left feeling disappointed; and 3) when the relationship is in a state of change. Think of other partnerships in your life. During the forming (alignment), storming (blunders), and norming (change) stages, you experience the greatest anxiety. So too in a partnership.

Understanding what makes partnerships succeed and fail equips you to make them positive, long-term successes.

Chapter 29

Total Quality Service

By Karl Albrecht,
Chairman, Karl Albrecht & Associates

*T*he Total Quality Service (TQS) process provides methodology for assessing, defining, and improving service quality. Underlying the concepts of the TQS process are certain conclusions about what works and what doesn't:

• Outstanding service quality, as perceived by the customer, can give any organization a competitive edge in its marketplace.

• Establishing a superior level of service quality is challenging.

• Service excellence begins with management excellence. Frontline service employees can't deliver any better service than they are enabled to deliver through the support and encouragement given them.

• The only hope of achieving market differentiation and competitive advantage based on service quality is through a constant, concerted effort to make the entire organization customer driven, service oriented, and profit minded.

• To advance from a "so-so" level of service to a truly differentiated level of service that has competitive value, you must undertake a total effort that affects the daily working life of everyone, including those employees who work unseen by the customer. Top management must make a significant investment of resources to carry out a "wall-to-wall" service improvement effort that has any chance of succeeding in the long run.

• Implementing a service quality program presents some very tough challenges to leaders. Service initiatives have failed because many chief executives are leery of any major undertaking for fear of going down the wrong road, in terms of methodology, or of making a huge investment without seeing a satisfactory payoff.

• Middle management effectiveness is becoming more pressing these days, especially in larger service organizations. Many executives and frontline people feel exasperated at what they perceive as inertia, sluggishness, and bureaucratic attitudes on the part of managers. This issue must be dealt with if any service initiative is to succeed. We risk making managers into victims and scapegoats, rather than helping them adopt roles that can make them leaders rather than bureaucrats.

• According to J. W. Marriott, Sr., "success is never final." When the moments of truth go unmanaged, the quality of the service regresses to mediocrity. Any methodology for achieving service excellence should have within it the means for sustaining and even enhancing the quality of the service product over the long term. A major financial investment in service quality is questionable in its payoff if the results of the effort quickly regress to the previous level.

For all of these reasons, there is a strong need and desire among executives to have a clear, logical, and compelling methodology for carrying out a service quality program. This is what the Total Quality Service process is designed to do. Service-quality programs can fail for many different reasons, but most of the reasons relate to just a few factors: lack of top management impetus, "fluffy" approaches that don't affect anything, bureaucratic approaches that don't generate energy, sheer inertia, employee cynicism, and management inertia.

Implementation Options

I have identified three service quality implementation methodologies:

1. Cosmetic Approaches. Putting up posters for the customers to see, with messages like "The customer is king," "We're here for you," and "You count with us," typically have little effect on the customer's perception of service quality, and may serve to accentuate the difference between the promise and the reality. They may look nice, but they do nothing to correct the underlying mediocrity of the service product itself. Other cosmetic approaches include simply claiming to give excellent service in advertising and promotional media and hoping the customer will believe the claim rather than his or her own experiences. "Smile training" and "charm school" courses are another form of cosmetic application that appeals to some executives. The advantage of cosmetic approaches is that they raise energy and sometimes improve service quality, at relatively low cost. The disadvantage is that they seldom produce long-lasting results.

2. Standards-based approaches. A more sophisticated approach to service quality is the use of predefined service standards as management tools. This approach involves the analysis of service jobs, formulation of objectively measurable standards of performance, and management action to ensure that people meet the standards. The advantage of standards-based approaches is in the simplicity of their methodology. Each provides a clean, logical framework for implementing quality improvement processes in areas where objective standards are possible. The disadvantage of these approaches is that they have a manufacturing mindset at their foundation. Because a service product is profoundly different from a manufactured product, users of these methods find it difficult to take into account the psychological and cultural factors that may be crucial to service quality.

3. *Culture-based approaches.* In the search for a service quality methodology, I have concluded that cosmetic approaches are clearly not cost-effective, and that standards-based approaches are more suited to manufacturing than to service areas. I believe that culture-based approaches will ultimately emerge

The TQS Process

What is needed is not a standard "formula" for a service program, but rather a methodology system. Not a fixed recipe or a one-size-fits-all process, but a logical system of methods and tools that can be brought to bear in a unique way for the unique needs of a particular service organization. This is what the Total Quality Service process provides.

TQS is a family of interrelated methodologies for assessing, defining, and improving service quality. There are five key "methodology menus" involved in the TQS process. This model shows how these methodology choices fit together.

The sequence in which these methods are applied will depend on the situation, the market, the competitive environment, and the leadership style and attitudes.

1. *Assessment, measurement, and feedback.* This may be an appropriate place to start in some situations. Some of the better-known methods in this area are:
- Service Audits
- Dialogues with employees
- Organizational climate surveys
- Executive, leadership, and employee assessments
- Service standards development
- Service quality measurement systems
- Service quality feedback systems
- Staff recognition programs

2. *Market and customer research.* Two kinds of research are involved in the TQS process: market research and customer perception research. Market research, in this context, is the investigation of the structure and dynamics of the marketplace the organization proposes to serve. This includes segmentation analysis, demographics, niche analysis, and analysis of competitive forces. Customer perception research attempts to understand the thoughts and feelings of the customer toward the service product and the

service provider, in hopes of discerning one or more critical factors in the customer's perception of the product. This research can give invaluable information about how the customer sees the service product as presented, and what he or she is trying to buy. Methods used in market and customer research include:

- Demographic analysis
- Customer focus group research
- Customer questionnaire research
- Market segmentation analysis
- Market niche analysis
- Product attribute analysis
- Competitive analysis
- Company image analysis
- Report card development

3. Strategy formulation. At times you may need to review various aspects of the competitive strategy, or to rethink the mission, strategy, and basic direction. You can't do the things necessary to build service quality until you have a clear definition of what the service product is, to whom it will be sold and delivered, and what level of quality will be required to compete effectively. Methods of strategy formulation include:

- Executive strategy retreats
- Environmental scan
- Market matrix analysis
- Organizational scan
- "SWOT" analysis
- Scenario planning
- Strategic option analysis
- Strategy documents (mission, competitive strategy, core values, etc.)

4. Education, training, and communication. These methods come into play in helping everyone understand the service philosophy, service strategy, service product, and service quality standards. Some methods are organization-wide, serving to build awareness and commitment. Others are more targeted to specific aspects of service quality. Others help employees to acquire specific skills and knowledge they need to handle service jobs well. Methods include:

- Executive education
- Management training
- Management reading plan
- "Walk around" management
- Dialogues with employees
- Leadership training
- Specialized staff training
- Performance coaching

• New-employee orientation
• Organization-wide communication events
• Service awareness media

5. *Process improvement.* A key part of any wall-to-wall service quality program is a means for grass-roots efforts to improve the various processes, systems, methods, tools, policies, and procedures involved in the delivery of service. These process improvements can originate with management analysis, or from the initiative of frontline people who want to improve their work process. Typically a high-level task force can play an important role in guiding those efforts. Methods of process improvement are:

• Task force development and training
• Middle management leadership workshops
• Service team development
• Quality service, action team development
• Redesigning and realigning operational systems
• Redesigning and realigning organizational systems
• Service standards development
• Management standards development

Applying the TQS Process

The five major components of the TQS process work together to build service quality. There is not one starting point for all programs. Where you start depends on where you are. The appropriate starting point, sequence of activities, and choice of methods all depend heavily on the organization's current state and the orientation of the executives who lead it. This is one reason why many service programs fizzle: the choice of methodologies is not appropriate to the situation.

The TQS process recognizes the need to customize the methodology to the organization's reality. The key to success in applying TQS is in the choice of program strategy, the unique way of putting together the elements of methodology, resources, timing, and sequencing of actions to create a successful program.

Arriving at a successful strategy requires a great deal of expertise and experience with service quality programs and a skillful analysis of present status and opportunities. Too much rides on a venture of this magnitude to risk launching it with a poorly-conceived strategy.

Careful thinking and good judgement in the early stages can ensure the success of a service initiative, and the TQS process can provide the necessary methods.

Chapter 30

Delight Customers

By Kirtland C. Peterson,
Executive Vice President, Staub-Peterson, Inc.

*C*reating customer-focused cultures isn't easy, but it's the task of today's leaders to ensure that it gets done. As W. Edwards Deming said: "It is not enough to satisfy the customer. You've got to move beyond customer satisfaction to customer delight."

Quality no longer guarantees success. Technological advances are emulated, or improved upon, so quickly by competitors that they guarantee nothing. In harsh markets, many corporations will perish. But those that leverage superlative customer service stand a chance of not only surviving, but thriving. The company that treats its customers well will gain the lion's share of the market—by default. And those companies that delight their customers may create an advantage difficult to challenge.

Service Imperatives

Here are five reasons why delighting customers is so important.

1. Customer expectations are higher than ever before. Customers want quality products, responsive service, value for money, timely delivery, user-friendly features, money-back guarantees, and customization. What is frightening is that you compete on service not only against those in your industry, but against anyone offering good service. If I am treated well at Nordstrom or L.L. Bean, I will expect the same from your business.

2. We are all in service. Horst Schulze, President and COO of Ritz-Carlton, says that many companies have processes for developing quality products but have none for improving service. And yet we are all in service. It is the human contact that is critical. When I buy a product, I buy it from a person, not a machine. And when I have problems with that product, I want a timely response from a person. As the customer, I don't want to hear you say, "That's not my job." If I have a problem with a product or service of yours, I want you to solve it.

3. Competition is fierce. Customer service may be your only edge. In just about every industry, competitive pressures are on the rise. Customer service can give you an edge.

4. Superlative service means repeat business. If you treat me well, I'll come back. If you treat me poorly, I'll look elsewhere. When I asked if I could exchange a CD at CD Superstore, I was told, "No problem. What would you like to exchange it for?" They've got my business from now on.

5. Quality service is profitable. Research shows it costs five times more to prospect a customer than to maintain a current one. Some put the differential at 10 to 15 times more. Yet in many companies, the focus is on new clients, often at the expense of current ones.

One study revealed that 26 out of 27 customers fail to report bad experiences. If only one in 27 of your customers is telling you what's wrong, your ability to make quality improvements is limited.

Action Items

Since nine of every 10 customers who complain won't come back and since someone who has been "burned" will tell, on average, 10 to 20 other folks, you need to take action.

• *Focus on delighting the customers you already have.* Many businesses are built by word of mouth. Make sure your employees know that replacing lost customers is a costly business.

• *Actively seek out dissatisfied customers.* Ensure that your customer surveys ask questions that reveal dissatisfaction. And get on the phone and ferret out problems.

• *Take service training seriously.* Off-the-shelf programs do little to impact your culture or your bottomline. But focused customer service training for all employees can have a major impact on your success.

• *Select service people carefully.* Make sure that those who deal with your customers are the right folks with the right training. Many people who deal with customers every day are not well suited for customer contact. The Ritz-Carlton interviews 10 prospects for every job opening in a new hotel, and each interviewee goes through at least three interviews to ensure each person fits the job.

• *Treat your people as your highest asset.* Disempowered employees can't provide quality service. The correlation between employee satisfaction and customer satisfaction is nearly one-to-one. People deal with people. Only satisfied employees treat customers with dignity and respect consistently. Take steps to empower your employees to satisfy customers. An immediate, cheerfully offered solution will get me coming back.

• *Ensure that management is committed to quality service.* Managers cause service difficulties if they are not committed to quality service and fail to ensure training for employees. A "follow the rules" not "satisfy the customer" dictum leads to a customer-insensitive system. Failure to reward excellent service means that less value-added behaviors are being reinforced.

• *Establish a service-oriented culture.* Your culture is that reality your customers experience whenever they do business with you. Establishing a customer-friendly culture is a massive challenge, but one worthy of your attention.

Changing Paradigms

Developing service-oriented cultures dedicated to delighting the customer amounts to a paradigm shift.

• *Financial performance.* We need a shift from a "productivity of capital and labor" perspective to one that sees the quality of service driving profit.

• *The nature of work.* We must shift from meeting specific "job standards" and "performing tasks" to "managing moments of truth" and learning how customers experience your organization.

• *Metrics.* Output measurements are valuable, but evidence of customer satisfaction is more important. Ensure you are measuring the right thing and getting the data that helps you improve.

• *The role of the employee.* We need empowered employees willing to work with customers. And since dealing with customers is never easy, employees need management support and assistance.

• *The new organization.* The old focus on structure, process, and legislative control must give way to a new organization dedicated to creating a service culture.

• *The role of senior management.* Senior management must take delighting the customer seriously, and personally.

Chapter 31

Customer Dialogue

By Kevin Daley, CEO of Communispond and author of *Socratic Selling*.

*A*ny company that is serious about leveraging customer service as a competitive strategy would do well to start building satisfaction with the very first contact. Creating happy customers is not a matter of promising more, giving up more, or wowing the prospect with fancy displays and a barrage of statistics.

One approach to customer satisfaction taps the wisdom of Socrates, the ancient Greek philosopher who drew out his students' intelligence and problem-solving abilities through a series of questions. The Socratic method can be applied with equal effectiveness by anyone who has a product, service, or idea to sell. As tried and true as the method is, it flies in the face of what most people believe and behave. The Socratic method demands that you talk less and listen more, that you show deep respect for the customer's knowledge about his or her needs and problems. It requires a sincere belief that every customer is unique, and a commitment to understand the particulars of each situation.

A Socratic sales call is not a pressurized pitch; nor is a Socratic service encounter a masterful manipulation. It is real dialogue. At every stage—from the opener, through dealing with objections, to negotiating terms—you and the customer are building the candor and trust you need for a satisfying relationship.

Socratic service and sales work because they are in tune with today's customer. The buyer of computer software or training program or benefits package or printing service is first of all a well-trained person, with access to mountains of information about what's on the market, experience in how his or her company has handled the needs in the past, and decision-making authority.

The buyer of today is more accountable than his predecessors. Improved management practices have made it hard to hide mistakes, and buyers are acutely aware that bad decisions put their careers in jeopardy. This customer is highly motivated to make good buying decisions; and the Socratic approach provides him and her a thorough, systematic way of arriving at sound, informed decisions.

Think of a sales call as entry into another world, the buyer's world. Like a guest in another person's home, you need to be very attentive to what is going on and what is being said. This is the customer's turf, and it's up to the outsider to pick up on the rules and customs of the place. Respect for the customer begins with this stepped-up awareness of the customer's world, which is far removed from the more common practice of going in with your mind filled with what you are planning to say.

Most people want to cut to the presentation. They've gone to some effort to arrange the meeting; they're aware that they're competing with other sellers, and they're comfortable putting on their dog-and-pony show. Others want to talk about their company and what it has to offer. Handing over the glossy brochures diffuses the initial tension and gives the rep the feeling that he or she is getting down to business. Still others like to jump in with a few pointed questions that tie the customer's world to the seller's product. Again, the salesperson or service agent is controlling the way the customer is involved in the discussion.

These approaches are offensive to customers, who naturally think that this meeting is about them and their needs. They want to do the initial talking, because no matter how much the salespeople think they know about the customer's world, the customer knows more. Even regular customers have plenty to say, because their world changes every day.

Opening a Dialogue

To open a Socratic dialogue, say something like this: "Ms. Smythe, I'm ready to talk about our leasing program. However, if you could give me your perspective, we can focus the meeting on what interests you."

This approach, far from being casual, is carefully structured to immediately satisfy customers on three counts: 1) you are prepared for the meeting; 2) you are inviting customers to talk about anything they feel is pertinent to the subject; and 3) you are committed to making the meeting time productive for them. One salesperson I know met with 10 people from a major computer manufacturing company. After she gave her Socratic opener, the customers started talking, and she started making notes.

When she glanced at her watch, she saw that 40 minutes had passed. The customers told her not to worry about the time, that it was important that she understand the situation. The meeting lasted

90 minutes and led to a sale and a lasting business relationship. This experience is commonplace with people who use the Socratic approach. When you are talking, your customers eye their wristwatches anxiously. When the customers talk, time becomes very elastic. Explaining their circumstances, pressures, and needs is so important and satisfying to buyers, that they aren't even aware of the passing of time.

The Socratic opener leads customers to the first in a series of logical conclusions: that the meeting has been about the customer, that the priorities are in order. Your customer's perspective is on the past: what went wrong, what went right, what worked then that doesn't work now. You are focused on the future: what you can promise, how the customer will benefit, what a great solution you have in store. But you lose trust and sales when you force customers into the future too quickly.

Socratic probes help customers think through their needs and give you information you need. Draw probes and access probes are easily answered questions: *Tell me more about how you relate to the R&D function. Give me an example of the problems you're having with deliveries. What else should I know about the causes of turnover? How do you handle vehicle breakdowns? How does sales training fit into the picture?*

In this process, the customer does 80 percent of the talking. You have to experience this to believe that the process of bringing ideas to light is not wasted time. The customer has now reached two more logical conclusions: *you are looking in the right place for what you need to understand, and you make good on your promise of using the meeting time productively.*

Price advantages, product improvements, and almost every competitive edge you have to offer can be lost in a twinkling. Really listening to the customer is the one competitive advantage that has lasting value, and one that will immediately set you apart from most of your competitors. Just as the most popular person at a party is the one who draws other people out by encouraging them to talk about themselves, the most welcome and valued salesperson or service rep is the one who does more listening than talking. The desire to be heard and understood is universal; and a person who gives a buyer this satisfaction has laid the groundwork for a solid business relationship.

Listening is at the heart of the Socratic method. If you go in thinking you have the answers because you have worked with similar customers, if you just listen for cues that allow you to jump in with your pitch, you aren't listening. Only by fully attending to everything the buyer says, playing back what you have heard, and asking the buyer to elaborate on his statements will you gain the buyer's confidence and the information you need to make a proposal that fits the need. Listening enables you to draw out both facts and the feelings that drive the sale. When you hear, "I've got a lot riding on this," you know that you have gotten past the foyer in the customer's world. You are in the family now, where formalities are dropped and people feel free to say what's really on their minds. You can ask for elaboration on exactly what is on the line in this buying decision. When you hear, "We've got to cut marketing costs," you can ask the buyer to clarify exactly what is meant by that. Socratically trained sales and service people don't mistake customers' short-hand statement for the full story.

The most powerful tool you have in discovering needs, answering objections, negotiating terms, and closing sales is the simple phrase, "Tell me more." When your customer interaction is a dialogue instead of a pitch, customer satisfaction is off to a flying start.

Chapter 32

Reciprocal Relationships

by Stephen R. Covey,
Co-Chairman of FranklinCovey Co.

What's in it for me? That's the only question some customers and suppliers will ask unless the leaders of organizations cultivate reciprocal service relationships with all of their stakeholders.

In some organizations, service is a one-way street. Just listen to front-line service providers: "You give and give, and they take and take without any thanks. There is not much customer loyalty anymore. If there's a better price, product, or program on the market, customers will shop and switch. Even when we do our best to build strong customer relationships, many customers will go where the price is lower. When we make our customers the beneficiaries of a wonderful service program, they take advantage of it and run."

Seven Steps Beyond Hit and Run

How can executives ensure that customer service is a value-added benefit that brings returns to the bottom line? So much depends on the nature of the customer-supplier relationship. If that relationship is based upon a deep mutual understanding, then bonding starts to happen, and the relationship becomes reciprocal and mutually beneficial.

Here are seven ways to build bonding, win-win relationships.

1. Look first to yourself. To improve your relationships, don't look to others to change and don't look to easy shortcuts. Look to yourself. Be honest with yourself first—the roots of your problems are spiritual, and so are the root solutions. Build your character and your relationships on the bedrock of principles.

Our relationships with ourselves affect and are influenced by our relationships with others. Our ability to get along well with others flows naturally from how well we get along with ourselves, from our own internal peace and harmony. To get closer to business partners or customers, for example, we may need to make some changes in our own attitudes and behaviors. When I like and respect myself more, I find it easer to like others more. I give more freely of myself. I'm less defensive and guarded, more open and respectful of the feelings of others.

Too often we take either the route of living for appearances, or the route of freezing our views, opinions, and conclusions about others. Understanding requires openness and empathy, but these efforts carry a risk insecure people can barely afford—the risk of changing judgments. Force, coercion, and compulsion will never establish an ideal working and living environment. This only comes through transformation of the soul—a life brought into harmony with timeless principles. By observing laws and principles and by committing to noble purposes, we gradually develop deep unity and integrity. Harmony and security replace estrangement and insecurity. Our security comes from within, not from what others think of us, from our social station, or material possessions.

The test of the quality of any relationship is found in the little things of every day, the little courtesies, acts of kindness, the give and take in moments of truth. We show our true character in the small things, when we are not on guard. In the seemingly insignificant matters and the simplest habits, we see a range of behaviors—everything from the egotism which pays no regard to the feelings of others and denies nothing to self, to selfless, considerate, and compassionate service.

Unless our relationships are rooted in character, they only tranquilize and anesthetize. They will likely buckle when the storms move in. People may then lose their tempers, condemn, criticize, take out hostilities on others, withdraw in indifference, or even turn on themselves.

We all need love, understanding, and acceptance; but fearing we may not receive such warmth, we learn to play roles and defend ourselves against being hurt, to guard our communication, to pretend and stand behind facades, to elevate ourselves artificially above others by judging and labeling them. Because of this behavior pattern, we do not receive the love we need, even though others may try to give it to us. Self-alienation is the root cause of relationship breakdowns.

Our cultural models may teach us to exploit and manipulate relationships, to defend our pride, and to hurt before being hurt, to suspect and doubt, to pretend and to take shortcuts, to gratify our appetites and selfish desires and interests—even at the expense of other stakeholders. But as we rise above the negative cultural norms and follow higher moral laws, we are increasingly free from this cultural conditioning.

2. Create customer intimacy by practicing Habits 4, 5, and 6. The key to creating this bonding between customers and suppliers is practicing Habits 4, 5, and 6 in our interactions. Habit 4 is to go for win-win or no deal: to create a mutually beneficial interdependency. Habit 5 is to show empathy: to seek first to under-stand, and then to be understood. Habit 6 is to seek synergy: to involve stakeholders in problems to create third-alternative solutions. When you create that bonding, the customer comes to say, "You may know our needs better than we do. We only know what our current wants are. We are blinded, in a sense, by our own forest. You have a larger view. We will let you deal with our real needs and our anticipation, and we will also tell you things you don't know about us—even things you don't know about yourself."

As dialogue develops, more insight comes into the relationship. Once you bond with a person or company you don't just ask, "What's in it for me?" The more you bond, the more you care. You go the second mile for each other. People who are closely bonded in a reciprocal relationship can't be selfish. Bonding and selfishness are mutually exclusive.

3. Sacrifice in service to others. I've learned that unless there is a spirit of sacrifice in the practice of Habits 4, 5, and 6, the bonding between supplier and customer never happens. I've got to sacrifice my ego and willingly say, "I will be open and listen to you and see what we can create together for our mutual benefit." That involves some personal sacrifice.

To sacrifice means to make sacred. You can't bond with an entity (a company)—you can only bond with the people who work in the company. And that bonding occurs when a sacrifice makes sacred what otherwise might be disregarded. As we treat one another with more love, kindness, courtesy, humility, patience and forgiveness, we encourage the same in return. For example, a vice president once traveled on assignment to Egypt with the president of the organization. After a particularly weary and dusty day together, he awakened the next morning to find the president quietly shining his shoes, a task the president had hoped to complete unseen.

Such quiet service in the daily and ordinary things bonds souls and awakens the spirit of reciprocity in relationships. Can you imagine that vice president refusing to do anything the president asked of him on that assignment? A successful manager is one who has loved, sacrificed, served, cared for, taught, and ministered well to the needs of people. It partakes of the same spirit as Gandhi or Mandela or Sadat or Christ. It is the spirit of sacrifice that bonds people like nothing else. If I subordinate my ego to attend to your needs, then you begin to say, "I'll subordinate my ego to attend to Stephen's needs." And then we will ask, "What can we do to serve each other?"

To me this spirit of sacrifice is the very essence of the bonding in marriage and family relationships. For example, when I arrived home one night, I learned that my daughter Jenny was under tremendous pressure with all her papers and final tests, and on top of all that she was putting on a party. My wife, Sandra, stayed up until 2 a.m. to help Jenny. That's why our children are so close to Sandra. She gives most of her evenings to them. She will sacrifice her sleep, staying up for them and then dragging herself out of bed in the morning to serve them and attend to their needs. The kids know they can trust her.

4. *Share knowledge and information.* People have to be willing to share information and share their problems and challenges with each other. They must try to understand each other and look for ways to help each other. They must engage in dialogue: "I can see you are having difficulty getting costs down in this area. Here's what we have learned."

It's mostly through two-way communication and seeking to understand each other that the supplier-customer relationship gets nurtured at a deep level. I once asked a group of CEOs, "How many of you are doing 360-degree performance feedback or assessment?" Most of them were, and that was very unusual. They are outstanding leaders. For most of them there is no disconnect between shareholder relations and stock value, between employee relations and bottom-line returns. They're all integrated together. They know it's an ecosystem. Today's world is making supplier-customer interdependency more apparent.

5. *Include all stakeholder relationships.* If you only focus on one stakeholder to the exclusion of others, you may move away from total stakeholder satisfaction to total customer satisfaction at the expense of employees. Effective managers wouldn't think of taking advantage of their employees because they are their suppliers. All of us are suppliers and customers. I'm a supplier to my customers, and I'm a customer to my suppliers. I meet your needs as you meet my needs.

Business is all about relationships. Sure, there's a technical side to business, but I think it is better to deal with needs of people—all stakeholders. There are no small people. I sometimes encounter a company that has tremendous relationships with customers, but then they treat suppliers poorly. It's as if they departmentalize things. Or they ignore one vital community. They kill the goose that is laying the golden egg. They pollute the environment, penalize the next generation, or ignore the dealer organization.

That's what I admire about the Saturn Corporation. It's not just a different product—it's a different way of doing business. The way they treat their dealers is unprecedented in the automobile industry. Too often the manufacturer and dealer make no effort to understand one another. Saturn is different. They are not perfect, but they have a unique relationship with their customers and dealers. They invite them to come to Springfield, TN, to see the plant, and thousands of Saturn owners respond. Saturn is one of the best corporate models of win-win thinking. They are in partnership with a union that historically had an antagonistic relationship with management. At Saturn, management can't win if labor loses; they prosper together. They started and built the company with that end in mind. Before they had a building or a product, they made a movie about a day in the life of a Saturn employee—and their work day now follows that vision. It's an environment where they can build people as well as cars.

6. Care about those on the front lines. The front-line service providers— people who tend to get beat up and abused and used— are the keys to success in any service organization. What do you do to cultivate that relationship so they provide exceptional service? The same principle of reciprocity applies. You realize those people are in the crossfire between the demands of the customers and the operational policies of management. They are really in no-man's land, and they need to be understood and appreciated. I've seen stewardesses on airplanes, for example, shed tears and share sad stories as they get treated poorly. Over time, some grow calloused by the sheer numbers of people they are processing.

In his book *My American Journey,* General Colin Powell writes disparagingly about a particular general's leadership style. "He was a tough overseer. The job got done, but by coercion, not motivation. Staff conferences turned into harangues. Inspections became inquisitions. The endless negative pressure exhausted the unit commanders and staff." In sharp contrast, the leadership style of General Bernie Loeffke, a colleague and mentor of Colin Powell, created an esprit de corps that invigorated the troops. In Vietnam, Loeffke rewarded the top performers in his unit by allowing one man each night to sleep in his tent as he took his place on the front lines. Who would not fight for such a leader?

7. Choose mercy over measure for measure. In his plays *Measure for Measure* and *The Merchant of Venice,* Shakespeare explores the moral dilemmas of exacting "a pound of flesh." Near the end of *Merchant,* the fair Portia poetically expresses the virtue of mercy: *"The quality of mercy is not strained. It droppeth as the gentle rain from heaven upon the place beneath. It is twice blest: It blesseth him that gives and him that takes. Tis mightiest in the mightiest. It becomes the throned monarch better than his crown. His scepter shows the force of temporal power, the attribute to awe and majesty wherein doth sit the dread and fear of kings. But mercy is above the sceptered sway. It is an attribute to God himself, and earthly power doth then show likest God's when mercy seasons justice. In the course of justice, none of us should see salvation. We do pray for mercy, and that same prayer doth teach us all to render the deeds of mercy."*

Customers to the Rescue

In some cases where there is this reciprocal relationship, customers have rallied to support, even save, a company in need. In the case of Pan Am airlines, several lifelong customers felt deep loyalty to Pan Am and wanted to help the company out of financial trouble. Some tried to help, while others merely took advantage of last-minute offers to fly at deep discounts. Company leaders never really organized and rallied customer support, perhaps underestimating the value of the equity built up over the years in the emotional bank accounts of people.

Historically, just when you are about to go belly-up, you become very open and honest with all stakeholders—and often they jump in to salvage you. Sadly, when the company recovers, some leaders forget the people and the principle that saved them.

Reciprocal relationships return on investment. Sacrifice pays. You always reap as you sow in the long run. It's a universal law. Sacrifice so affects the spirit of other people that it will usually come back to you tenfold. Again, there are only two relationships in business: customer and supplier. All of us play both roles all the time on both an internal and external basis. If our relationships are firmly based on principles or natural laws, they produce their own fruit. Charity never fails; it's an energy that will always return benefits.

You may cheat your customers for a while, but Nature is never deceived. She credits and debits according to merit. The law of retribution is just as constant as the law of compensation. You can't violate a moral principle without suffering the consequence. We all have the balance of our daily operations paid over to us at the end of every minute of our lives.

Chapter 33

Welcome Complaints

Janelle M. Barlow,
President of TMI

When customers feel dissatisfied with products and services, they have two options: they can say something, or they can walk away. If they walk away, they give us virtually no opportunity to fix their dissatisfaction. Complaining customers are still talking with us, giving us a chance to return them to a state of satisfaction so they will be more likely to buy from us again. So as much as we might not like to receive negative feedback, customers who complain give us a gift.

If we see complaints as gifts, we can more readily use the information the complaints generate to grow our own businesses. Customer complaints are one of the most available and yet under utilized sources of consumer and market information; as such, they can become the foundation for quality and service recovery programs. This is no small gift! We must welcome these complaining customers and make them want to come to us with their feedback. Complaining customers tell us what their problems are so we can help them, and so that they will be encouraged to come back, use our services, and buy our products.

Unmet Expectations

A complaint is a statement about an unmet expectation. It's also a chance to satisfy a dissatisfied customer by fixing a service or product breakdown. In this way, a complaint is a gift customers give to a business. The company will benefit from opening this package carefully and seeing what is inside.

Most service representatives hear the surface complaint, not the deeper message, and the end results are mismanaged complaints and loss of customers. When organizations listen to customers with open minds and more flexible points of view, they can experience complaints as gifts. Unfortunately, most people do not like to hear complaints, and we put up enormous psychological blocks to hearing them. Even more fundamentally, most customers simply do not grace us with their complaints. They just take their business elsewhere.

On the surface, it seems apparent why complaints have a bad reputation. Someone is saying that he or she does not like what took place. Who likes to hear that? Complaints are a negative attribution or blaming behavior. When something positive happens, we tend to attribute it to ourselves. But when a failure occurs, most of us blame other individuals or systems. For customers, this means that employees, specifically those most accessible, are to blame when there is a product or service failure. Employees do the same thing. When they hear complaints, they tend to blame customers or company policy.

Unfortunately, the strategy of blaming policies does not work for customers because it does nothing to resolve the customers' problems. Nor does it stop customers from blaming the employees. Most customers find it difficult to separate employee behavior from company policies. For example, if a service provider says, "I know this sounds ridiculous, but I need . . . " customers will think, "If it's ridiculous, then why are you enforcing it?" Complaining customers tend to blame the service provider when things go wrong, regardless of the cause or circumstances.

To consider complaints as gifts, we first have to accept the notion that customers always have a right to complain even when we think their complaints are stupid, unreasonable, or cause inconveniences. To treat complaints as gifts, we need to separate the message of the complaint from the emotion of being blamed, which in turn, means understanding the dynamics of disappointed people and rethinking how complaints can help us to achieve our business goals.

The Gift Formula

We must become so comfortable with the idea that a complaint is a gift that when someone complains to us we will welcome it as something of value. We will not have to think our way through this; our natural response will be as if we have received a gift. How can we do this? First, the company must talk the language of complaint giving as gifts. The idea needs to be reinforced at every meeting, on wall posters, and in all conversations and training sessions on customer service. Second, the company's policies, compensation systems, mission, vision, values, and managerial behavior must be aligned to support the gift-friendly philosophy. Finally, we must learn some fundamental techniques for handling complaints.

Here is an eight-step process for handling customer complaints as gifts:

1. Say "Thank you."
2. Explain why you appreciate the complaint.
3. Apologize for the mistake.
4. Promise to do something about the problem immediately.
5. Ask for necessary information.
6. Correct the mistake promptly.
7. Check customer satisfaction.
8. Prevent future mistakes.

Make the complaint widely known so the problem can be prevented in the future. Fix the system without rushing to blame staff. Punish your process, not your people. Staff members will be more likely to pass along complaints to management if they know this is the company's approach to complaints.

Most executives react to complaints as they occur, rather than use them as a free source of information to improve quality. Complaints are not fully used if they sit in a complaint-handling center; they must be used as a feedback mechanism to help the company improve itself.

Chapter 34

Achieving Quality Through Customer Service

By Kathy Welch,
Director of Customer Service,
The Coleman Company

*A*merica has become a nation obsessed with quality customer service, because it is so profitable. It costs a company five times more to attract a new customer than to keep a current one. If this is true, why are there still so many companies providing nothing more than lip service to customers?

The high cost of attracting new customers underscores the need to keep existing customers through effective service. This can only be done through commitment, people, and technology. Something as simple as answering the phone, "How may I help you?" after giving the name of your firm, can increase the caller's positive attitude.

If company executives expect employees to deliver quality customer service, they need to express a philosophy of service and reinforce it through a culture of service at all levels. Without this commitment from upper management, employees won't be motivated to provide customers with the best possible service consistently.

Ten Service Commandments

Our customer service professionals recommend the following 10 methods for improving customer service:

1. Don't treat customers as an inconvenience. Work with them to fulfill needs and solve problems.

2. Don't treat customers as if problems are their fault. Anticipate problems so you can stay on schedule.

3. Never ignore customers. Return every call within 24 hours.

4. Work with your customers. Even slow-paying customers are entitled to your attention. Work together on any problem and find a mutual solution.

5. Follow up. Ask your customers if they are satisfied. It shows them you care and provides valuable feedback.

6. Know your products and services. After all, every employee is, in effect, a sales rep for the company.

7. If mistakes are made, smooth out the situation as soon as possible. Apologize, show empathy, and atone by offering to waive or reduce charges where applicable.

8. Understand the needs, wants, and expectations of your customers. It will help both of you achieve your common goals.

9. Create a service strategy. Involve everyone on your team and ask for their suggestions and ideas.

10. Remember to treat your customers in the same way you wish to be treated.

Education and training are critical to the success of your customer service. How many times have you found yourself in a situation where your employees feel as if they aren't part of the team, or customer service representatives can't answer a question about a product or service because they weren't trained properly?

Commit the resources needed to train employees and work with them so they are fully aware of the company's history, policies, and products. Train employees to use the technology available today. An informed employee is most often a satisfied one, and a satisfied employee is often the key to a satisfied customer.

Keeping good people is a challenge, of course. But it can be done if the company provides people with positive reinforcement, personal and professional growth opportunities, and a comfortable working environment.

Make every member of your staff feel important. Treat your people with respect and reward them for excellent service performance. Instill the quality image in their minds. If they feel good about themselves and believe in the company and its products, their positive feelings will come through in every contact and transaction with customers. When your people believe they can make a difference and that they can somehow affect the success of the company, they will go the extra mile for your customers—and those miles result in return business.

In the next century, technical advances, continued emphasis on quality, and increased international demands will challenge customer service professionals. As these demands increase, service will become an ever-increasing factor in the consumer's decision to buy. Therefore, out-servicing your competition should be your primary goal.

SECTION 4:

Case Studies

Chapter 35

Employees as Ambassadors

**By Edwin L. Artzt,
Chairman and CEO,
Proctor & Gamble**

*O*ur employees are ambassadors to our customers and the stewards of our products, brands, and our image. Traditionally, Proctor & Gamble has separated its corporate name and activities from its brands, but our traditional approach is changing. Proctor & Gamble is fast becoming one of our most important brands. The integrity of the company and its policies and practices concerning the environment, nutrition, safety, and social consciousness all have an important bearing on how the consumer feels about our brands. It is still our policy that our brands must stand on their own. But today our image and reputation visibly stand behind them as well. Our employees have always represented both our brands and our company very well.

We see ourselves, first and foremost, as a quality company. Quality is the essence of Proctor & Gamble's positioning as a business. We started out selling soap and candles of high quality at good value, and that commitment to quality has carried through to this day—in the brands we sell, the people we hire, and the plants we operate. We're also a company of great integrity—we're an ethical and socially responsible company. The values of our people and our determination to try to do the right thing have always guided the way we do business. And we're a company of winners. We strive to be number one in the market and to gain competitive advantage in all we do. That's our culture. We're product driven, financially oriented, innovative, fast on our feet, and truly global. We're a great place to work and a great company to do business with from the standpoint of both customers and suppliers.

Put all of that together, and it's the ultimate corporate product. We need to protect it and market it with the same care and skill that we bring to all of our brands. Our employees personify this image. And so when we talk about our company, we are really talking about P&G people.

I don't think it's passé for employees to be proud of the companies they work for. One characteristic of P&G is the pride our employees take in both the company and the role it plays in the community. Our employees get enormous satisfaction out of the fact that they work for P&G and that the company is so highly regarded in the community. Their pride in Proctor & Gamble is a real asset for us. It makes them feel good about their work, and it also helps us recruit and retain the best people worldwide.

That pride ensures cultural continuity. Two simple things preserve the culture of a company. One is a set of principles that survive change. And the other is management that's been through it all and has a historical perspective of what has made the company successful. If we preserve those two things, then 100 years from now, Proctor & Gamble will still be Proctor & Gamble. We may be in different businesses, and we may be doing many things we wouldn't recognize today. But we would recognize old William Cooper Proctor's simple principles of trying to do the right thing; conveying respect and concern for our people; conducting business in a fair and honest way; and besting our competitors every chance we get, in fair competition.

We look for people with high levels of energy, intellect, leadership, and character. That brings together a lot of very different people. It's amazing how different our people are as individuals and yet how well we work together. We tend to be hard-driving and results-oriented.

Because we operate in many countries, we have to work at maintaining our standards, our values, and our culture. We find that our values and culture travel very well. We sell our products in over 140 countries, and we have major operations in more than 50. We transmit our standards and values through our principles, our training, and our people. Our managers in those countries have grown up in Proctor & Gamble, and most have experience in more than one country.

We want our managers to have a parental relationship with our brands. We want them to be aware of the heritage of the brand. Their job is to take the brand asset entrusted to them—to keep it healthy and to make sure that its value is greater when they turn it over to a successor. We don't believe in marketing life cycles. We want our brands to be eternal. Anyone who starts thinking about life cycles is in the process of creating a self-fulfilling prophecy. We don't want to sacrifice our brands to short-term strategic expediency.

Just as we won't allow our brands to go out of style, we have a set of basic principles that won't go out of style. Those are the things that bind P&G people together with a sense of loyalty and commitment that they transmit to the outside world.

Chapter 36

Redefining the Role of Customer Service

**By Don Flamm,
Vice President and General Manager,
Honeywell, Home Control Division, Inc.**

*E*verywhere today, people are talking about the changing role of customer service as a competitive reality. Customers have become far more demanding about the services they receive and are more likely to focus on service quality when making a buying decision. While product quality remains important, customers demand and expect higher levels of service. Businesses can no longer afford to view product quality and service quality as an "either-or" proposition. They have become one and the same in the eyes of the customer.

Our guiding vision is centered around "satisfying the customer" in a superior fashion. This means every employee understands how his or her contributions impact our customers. It also means our Customer Satisfaction people provide superior frontline service to our customers. We firmly believe that to compete effectively, customer satisfaction and service must be viewed and supported as a major strategic weapon. Our success and ultimate survival depend on it.

Three Support Strategies

To demonstrate our recognition of the strategic importance of customer service, we have adopted three support strategies.

1. Measure satisfaction from your customers' perspective. To have satisfied customers, you have to put yourself in the customers' shoes and understand requirements from their perspectives. To do this, you must redefine and develop customer service systems that allow you to rapidly understand, measure, meet, and exceed the individual service needs of each customer. We do five things to determine customer requirements, performance, and future needs from the customers' perspective: 1) customer interviews (conducted by outside consultants); 2) executive visits to customers; 3) customer service representatives' visits to customers; 4) customer-vendor performance evaluation rankings; and 5) cross-functional corrective action teams.

2. Ensure structure supports speed and responsiveness. Speed is perhaps the single most crucial element in satisfying customers. Speed is a function of time—how fast something is done, such as answering phones, shipping products, correcting errors, developing, producing, and delivering new products and services.

Customers are constantly challenging us to reduce new product development cycles, to reduce delivery lead times, to improve response time on inquiries, to provide faster access to information, and to offer special customized services to meet their different needs.

We distinguish between our perception of speed and the customer's perception of speed. While a company may be meeting its targets and indices for speed, these targets are typically set and defined according to industry standards for all customers regardless of the circumstances. But the customers' perception of speed focuses on the company's capability to respond to a particular need at a given point in time. A customer's need varies with its different circumstances. Thus, speed should be measured by the company's responsiveness to a customer's circumstances at a given point in time. Measurements of "real" speed and responsiveness to customers' "particular" circumstances go beyond standard, company-focused measurements to specialized, customer-focused measurements.

To support this strategy, we first had to create a new structure that supported improvements in speed and responsiveness and reduced delays in our distribution chain by creating unified accountability for delivering products and information to the customer. Under the old structure, we had an "internal out" allowing us to say: "It's not my fault—the order was entered wrong by Customer Service"; or, "The Shipping Department picked, packed, and shipped the wrong item"; or, "It got damaged or lost in transit, check with Transportation"; and so forth and so on. No one person or area owned the responsibility.

To unify this accountability, we created the Department of Customer Satisfaction and placed all functional areas of distribution under one unit, led by a director of customer satisfaction. The director and her staff not only have direct responsibility for swift corrective action when problems occur, but they are empowered to do what is necessary to determine the root cause of problems and to ensure appropriate changes occur to prevent a reoccurrence.

This department is recognized as "equal partners" in the business and is actively involved at all levels of decision making. Customer service managers and representatives participate in the development of marketing programs, business unit strategic reviews, and on cross-functional, corrective-action teams. The customer satisfaction function is the focal point for external customers. Internally, it monitors and challenges all groups to ensure their activities are in concert with our goal of being first in customer satisfaction.

By redefining and changing the role of customer service, we increase the possibility of establishing a speed-response time advantage as a means to create competitive advantage. We want to leave customers happy, exhilarated, surprised, and pleased—not just satisfied. We don't just want satisfied customers—we want ecstatic, happy customers. To us, "satisfaction" represents a minimum level of acceptability, while "exhilaration" represents the maximum level.

Happiness builds relationships, and relationships create business opportunities. For instance, a company at the beginning of the quality process focuses on meeting customer requirements. As the company progresses, it reaches out to exceed them. If it is really good, it begins to anticipate requirements. When the point of creating the requirements is reached, then the competitive advantage is acheived.

3. Identify opportunities that differentiate you from your competition in the eyes of your customers. For example, Honeywell Home and Building Control is the first company in the industry to offer customers remote on-line access into our computer system for order status information and electronic messaging between customer, field sales, and customer service representatives. With this system, we provide real-time information, allowing our customers to save time and allowing us to minimize errors and to respond quickly to requests for information.

Do we have a sustainable competitive advantage? Only time will tell. But we do have a window of opportunity to tie customers closer to us by differentiating ourselves from the competition.

We identified this as an area where we could differentiate and distance ourselves from the rest of our competitors. These services were not requests from our customers that others were providing; instead, these were ideas we identified, developed, and took to our customers—and they recognized them as value-added services that increased either their productivity or their sales, resulting in improved profits to their bottom line. We are not settling for meeting requirements; we are creating the requirements of tomorrow. We can no longer take the conventional viewpoint that customer service adds cost, not profits. Commitment to a sound Service Quality Strategy can add up to four margin points to your profit line.

Our challenge is to continually examine existing customer service processes and set priorities that improve service and lower cost. Happily, none of these strategies add cost. To the contrary, when a job is done well, customer satisfaction and service increases the bottom line and becomes a profit-making component of the company.

Chapter 37

Unleashing Power

By John E. Martin,
Chairman and CEO,
Taco Bell

Discovering the power of our people has been the single-most important aspect of Taco Bell's success and growth.

Today's marketplace is marked by constant change and turmoil. Here in the U.S. we've seen paradigm shifts in consumer expectations. Consumers have gotten tough-minded. They're paying down their debts, cutting back on expenses, limiting their expectations, and demanding that institutions and their leaders do the same.

Taco Bell has certainly changed a lot in response to our customers since Glen Bell opened his first taco stand back in 1962. In recent years, we've found that embracing change can be a catalyst for growth. Listening to our customers, and continually innovating to meet their needs, is enabling us to thrive instead of simply survive.

Just about everyone is faced with a mandate of reducing costs while improving service. Businesses today don't necessarily need more people to become more service oriented. All they need is a workplace full of people who are empowered, self-sufficient, and highly motivated.

Where can you find a work force like this? The answer is that you don't find it—you build it by providing your people with the tools, training, environment, and freedom they need to take charge. You build it by trusting in the premise that people have a strong desire to succeed. Why don't more companies do this? Fear. I know firsthand what this fear feels like. At Taco Bell, we spent years doing everything possible to keep our workers "under control," which resulted in high turnover, low morale, and slow growth. Fortunately, we recognized that our company would only go as far as our people would take us.

A Journey of Change

Taco Bell will never become complacent. We believe that "if you wait until something's broken to fix it, there may not be anything left to fix."

We learned that lesson many years ago. In the early 1980s, Taco Bell was badly broken. Before the current management team came on board, the company had experienced several consecutive quarters of negative sales growth—and for good reason. Our stores were dark, our menus were limited, and our advertising was flat. The running industry joke was that Taco Bell was such a well-kept secret that people east of the Mississippi thought we were a Mexican phone company.

So, during the next few years, we began a change, with the most important initiative being the way we listened to and responded to our customers. We asked them what they wanted for their money, instead of continuing to give them what we thought they needed. We listened, and they told us that they were getting less for more. What they were asking for was value.

We realized that products, systems, and prices that may have served us well in the past wouldn't satisfy our customers in the future. Following extensive market research, we implemented the first phase of our value program and turned our business upsidedown to give our customers better quality, better service and greater convenience—and all at a significantly lower price.

We began to remove many tedious food preparation tasks. Our customers told us they were primarily interested in getting a quality product and fast service at a low, everyday price; so, how we got the food from the kitchen to people's stomachs became less of a concern.

With the help of new technology, we moved much of the slicing, dicing, and cooking that took place in the back of our restaurants away to consolidated sites—which allowed our people to focus instead on final product assembly and service.

These initiatives helped ensure food quality, order accuracy, speed of service, enhanced safety, and improved quality of life for our people. Through our reengineering efforts, we returned prices to levels they hadn't been at in a decade, and we committed ourselves to keeping them there, even though industry critics predicted that value pricing eventually would mean our demise. History has proven otherwise. Our customers told us that we were on the right track, and they voted favorably with their wallets.

By embracing value, Taco Bell was able to leapfrog from being a regional, Mexican-food restaurant chain to a fast-food industry pacesetter. Our success with value opened the doors to even greater expansion. We began to envision a world that would take us beyond our traditional restaurants. We discovered that customers no longer saw Taco Bell simply as a restaurant chain—but as a respected brand. Our goal is to have over 200,000 points of access by the year 2000. We want to have Taco Bell food available wherever hungry people gather, and have opened nontraditional operations in places such as schools, colleges, airports, malls, theatres, convenience stores—even subway stations in Moscow.

As our fast food customers pass through their life stages, and their eating habits and expectations change, we want to travel with them by building upon the lifetime value of those consumers.

We felt these were exciting breakthrough ideas that would reshape the industry. But it didn't take long for a megadose of reality to sink in. The reality was that our management processes were all too linear, too labor intensive, too costly and too time-consuming. So we embarked on a new voyage of change—a reengineering voyage that has enabled us to become far more innovative, entrepreneurial, and responsive to our customers.

The Power of Teaming

The key to our success is the empowerment we have given to our people. We operate under an empowerment philosophy that is rare, not only in the food service industry, but in retail as a whole. The philosophy is based on the premise that to change what people believe they can do, you must first change their experience.

At Taco Bell, we felt that our people could do far more than our industry gave them credit for. If we were serious about reaching our goals, we could either build a work force of unmanageable proportions, or we could create an environment that encouraged self-sufficiency and empowerment. We chose the latter.

We committed ourselves to leveraging the talent of our people, and the more responsibility we gave them, the more they wanted. At every level, our people exceeded our expectations. They were turned on by the opportunities we presented and inspired by the challenges.

For example, the position we call Market Manager was once an extension of the restaurant manager. Today, just five years later, that same person manages a multimillion-dollar portfolio that comprises up to 50 points of access.

Empowering our Market Managers brought about a new mindset. They needed to become coaches and counselors to manage a diverse and growing business; they needed to empower others to take personal ownership in creating customer satisfaction.

The best example of how we're changing the experiences of our people is through teaming. We've extended the notion of ownership and responsibility to the people who interact with the 50 million customers we serve each week. Our crew people handle nearly all activities required to run a restaurant from the time it opens to the time it closes.

For many young people entering the work force, Taco Bell represents their first work experience. Through a teaming environment, they learn to accept responsibility and to establish a work ethic. We're lighting a spark among young people—one that is paying off with dramatically reduced turnover, greater morale, better profits, and more satisfied customers.

As part of our reengineering efforts, we are striving to break down the functional silos that limit what our people have been told they can do. Today we are seeing more initiatives coming from the field. By empowering our people, we have sent the message that everything within our business is fair game. If you recognize a marketing opportunity, you may find yourself working on a special-projects team.

We are creating a rich pool of highly-confident, self-sufficient, empowered individuals. In our work force, the power of diverse thoughts is creating tremendous results. I urge you to instill an entrepreneurial spirit within your organization. And when you do, you'll discover a tremendous new world of performance, prosperity, and personal reward.

Chapter 38

World-Class Service

**By Robert O'Neal,
Senior Manager,
AT&T Universal Card Services**

*W*hen you're delighting associates, it's not that great a leap to delighting customers. Delivering world-class service is like any business activity that produces a competitive edge. It comes from what passes for genius—1 percent inspiration, 99 percent perspiration.

All of us at AT&T Universal Card Services (UCS) share the same job title, "associate." We also share a belief in two customer service equations: 1) associate delight equals customer delight; and 2) world-class customer service equals customer and associate delight plus continuous improvement.

These equations are the result of paying close attention to our industry. AT&T faced an interesting challenge when it entered the credit card business in 1990. We had to distinguish ourselves from thousands of smart competitors. We'd learned, through benchmarking, that not many credit card companies were focused on customer service. The prevailing wisdom seemed to be that it was a customer's privilege to hold a credit card. It occurred to us that we could attract and hold customers by turning the situation on its head and making it our privilege to serve the customer.

We have learned that world-class customer service is a goal that can be won or lost in every contact with our customers. It's a worthy goal, and striving for it has served us well. Customers and industry observers have given us high marks for our customer service, and our focus on customer service was a major reason UCS won the Malcolm Baldrige National Quality Award in 1992.

The customer delight part of the equation translates directly into market share and growth. It's not easy because what delights customers today merely satisfies them tomorrow. When you're the industry leader, the competition studies your success and copies you so you can't rest on your laurels for long! That's where continuous improvement comes in.

To lead in this highly competitive industry, we must learn to solve the value equation for our customers and continuously delight them.

The credit card industry is fiercely competitive. Issuers are working hard to get different offers out to different customer segments. No longer is this a "one size fits all" business; yesterday's assumptions and approaches are obsolete.

Of course, this puts added pressure on all our associates: from marketers who must find better ways of knowing what delights our customers, to systems managers who must write better programs to support new initiatives, to customer service representatives who need to know everything about our product.

One tool we use to meet these challenges, and to strive for world-class customer service, is the development of our associates through education and training. It's a strategy that helped us become the second-largest issuer of bank credit cards in the United States and continues to propel us forward, growing both our business and our profitability.

Why a commitment to education and training? Because delighting customers requires knowledge and motivation on the part of associates. An associate dealing with an angry customer can have all the knowledge in the world; but if he is not motivated to turn the situation around, the customer will likely move her account to a competitor.

Our education and training programs contribute to associate delight by empowering them with the skills and knowledge they need to delight the customer, and to grow in their careers.

We've placed all our training and education programs under a single umbrella organization called Universal Card University. The "university" metaphor underscores our commitment to continuous development. It gives all associates a single point of reference for their training and education. It also gives UCS a single data pool so we can track, analyze, and measure the effectiveness of each program. And the university structure ensures that our programs stay linked with our business strategy and objectives.

Universal Card University is organized into "institutes." Customer Service has its own Customer Services Institute. In addition, we have the Professional Skills Institute, Quality Institute, Information Technology Institute, and Executive Institute.

Each institute is closely linked to its internal customers through a Dean's Council. This council sets broad university policy and approves the institute budgets. In this way, the customers of the university control the service they receive. Operation of the university is managed by curriculum managers of each institute who report to the senior manager of the university. This structure is designed to keep training and education focused on achieving the business goals.

Customized curriculums exist for almost every job at UCS. For instance, newly hired associates in the Customer Services area would begin development on their first day with the company. Like every new hire from CEO to entry level, they would attend our "Passport to Excellence" program—a two-day learning experience which introduces the unique UCS cultural environment, our corporate values, vision, and mission. Next, they will attend Customer Skills Training for up to six weeks, and another two weeks of on-the-job training. Our entire curriculum is custom designed, maintained, and delivered by our in-house staff of training professionals and credit card experts. The training integrates our corporate philosophy of delighting the customer with job skills and product knowledge.

Given the crucial and demanding nature of the Customer Service job, initial training is intensive. Depending on the associate's functional area, he'll take courses in telephone relationships, claims, credit relationships, or customer assistance (collections).

Continuous improvement is addressed by our requirement of 10 days of training per year beyond initial training. Additional training may or may not be directly job related. For example, a smoking cessation class can help fulfill the requirement; or an associate might want to take an "Introduction to Finance" course from the Professional Development Institute.

We've also developed a way for associates to actively learn about one of 23 different areas of our business. Called the "Associate for a Day" program, associates spend half a day in an unfamiliar department, watching their colleagues work and asking questions.

Universal Card University reaches outside to enrich its range of programs. We offer an enhanced tuition reimbursement program in partnership with local colleges and universities. Under its guidelines, UCS pays for any course as long as it comes from an accredited institution; this is done whether or not the course is directly related to the associate's job.

Nontraditional training environments include an on-site resource called the Associate Development Center. Reference materials, PCs, and software tutorials are included. These resources deliver training at the convenience of the associate, as do our computer-based multimedia training programs. Associates are encouraged to work with their supervisors to determine the training mix that is best suited for their professional and personal needs.

Other Customer Service Institute courses are designed to build and augment skills as associates grow on the job. They include instruction on quality, effective team membership, problem solving, and communications skills.

We integrate the company's principles and philosophy into our training efforts wherever possible to reinforce the culture and ensure consistent messages. For example, at the Customer Service Institute we emphasize three themes: all training instills the concept of personal empowerment; all training strongly conveys our corporate values; and exceed customer expectations with world-class service.

A good education and training program ensures that customer service associates have the skills and knowledge required to do their jobs. It also ensures continuous improvement and delights associates. Access to high-quality training and education that is flexible enough to serve associates' personal and professional needs sends them a clear message: their employer values and supports them. Delivering that message is worth every effort.

Chapter 39

Results Through Relationships

**By Bryan L. Kinnamon, General Manager,
Commercial Truck Tire Business,
The Goodyear Tire & Rubber Company**

*D*ramatic changes in customer and employee relations have generated big results for us as measured in new products and growth. By providing direction and encouragement, we have made major revisions in the thinking and processes that drive our manufacturing and marketing.

The new programs, plans, and directions are combined with new attitudes about customer service and customer relations. The objective behind the changes is to lay the foundation for a cultural transformation. To ensure that the ideas and their message of change permeate the entire corporation, we have extensive education programs.

We recognize that the company must embrace change if it is to prosper in the competitive commercial tire arena. Costs in the trucking industry are high. After fuel, the cost of tires is the next greatest operating expense. So we learn what customers expect from the tires they use in their business and what the tires could do to contribute to improvement at the bottom line. For example, before our most recent truck tire introduction, we learned what performance factors and product characteristics influenced customers' purchases. We surveyed companies and interviewed the people responsible for both tire maintenance and purchasing.

Although Goodyear products already meet many of their requirements, our engineers make certain that issues that are important to our customers are reflected in the creation of our newest products. We then put more than 20,000 tires into test service in major fleets around the country, and we ask fleet management for feedback.

Collectively, test fleets put more than one billion miles on our new 300 Series tires before the tires were introduced to the market. We wanted to be sure we gave our customers what they wanted. Listening to our customers paid off: the 300 Series was the most successful new tire in our history.

Unless we talk to and work with our customers, we can't know what they want. We may be manufacturing experts, but customers' requirements are the demands that drive our operations. The customer knows far better than we what their tires must do. Good business sense dictates that we must help our customers do the things that enhance their businesses.

Another change is the creation of an internal group called a Tactical Business Unit (TBU). Throughout the TBU, the energy, imagination, and creativity of each individual is tapped. Each team member seeks a better way to provide service to the customer at lower costs. The unit takes a team approach toward achieving more effective communication and problem-solving. Virtually all business challenges that could impact performance are scrutinized. Often, the TBU intercepts negative events or circumstances and reverses their momentum. The TBU also elevates positive events to higher levels, making more associates aware of opportunities and empowering them to take action. Within the TBU, management makes prudent use of the physical, human, and financial assets, and employs good communications and human relations with all associates.

A Shift in Thinking

Since 1990 we have charted a course that encourages deviation from the status quo. At stake is the Goodyear name as the industry leader. All elements of the corporation embrace the shift in thinking. Goodyear's basic culture has moved into a new era, developing directions and ideas that are foreign to anything experienced in our 94-year history.

At the heart of the change is a single tenet: the customer is first. The customer's needs are the reasons for our existence and the cornerstones on which our success is based.

The TBU routinely surveys customers to learn about tire performance and determine how we're doing. Previously, such surveys were extremely rare anywhere in the industry. Today, customer surveys are common, and our customer satisfaction levels have increased. Our teams spend time in the field surveying trucking operations, visiting locations, inspecting fleet equipment, interviewing tire managers, and working with financial-side customer associates and management to find answers that exceed customer requirements.

We recently introduced the Goodyear Tire Management System, a computer software program designed to help fleet managers reach sound business decisions about the tires they buy. The program is not skewed to favor Goodyear, but presents tire information and vehicle parameters objectively.

As we increase our ability to meet customer needs with products and services that exceed expectations, we earn the privilege of serving our customers again. We learn all we can about our customers' businesses, viewing their problems as our own problems. In this way, the customer becomes Goodyear's partner.

Such partnering and its very positive effects are clearly seen in our relationship with Navistar, makers of a highly effective fuel-efficient truck. To assure Navistar of maximum fuel efficient performance, Goodyear assigned truck tire engineers to work with the Navistar technical design team. The product of that partnering was a tire with capability to enhance the new truck's fuel savings.

Goodyear also takes customer projects to company test sites, including our Technical Center in Akron, Ohio, and our proving ground in San Angelo, Texas, where tires are subjected to murderous abuse and sophisticated analysis. Company resources in these test facilities are focused on the problems of our customer-partners. We have a long history of partnering with customers and building relationships of trust with them. Our motto speaks volumes: *Protect Our Good Name.*

Goodyear's name is our company's most powerful asset because the name has been built on trust. We try to show customers that we are worthy of their trust and that our products, service, and support are intended to benefit their bottom lines.

Chapter 40

Quality Service

By Robert W. Schrandt,
Vice President for Customer Service,
Toyota Motor Sales

*T*he Toyota Touch reminds us that our relationship is with the customer, not with the car, and that people are not things.

Despite recessions and a soft market, our share of industry has increased 3.6 percentage points in recent years. We currently have about 9 percent of the U.S. market.

We attribute this increase to the commitment we made nine years ago to make customer satisfaction an integral part of our business plan. Toyota, U.S.A. is in the service business. We service customers before, during, and after the sale. We have about 1,190 Toyota and 130 Lexus dealers, each independently owned and operated. Through these dealers, we sell over a million cars and trucks a year. Our challenge is to remember that our relationship is with the customer, not with the car. Dealing with people is more difficult than dealing with things. However, it's often tempting to deal with people as if they were things.

If we take care of the customer, the customer will take care of us. We have made total customer satisfaction the cornerstone of our business plan and part of everything we do. Satisfying customers' needs and expectations is our prime goal and the focus of our marketing strategy.

Our emphasis on people started in the mid-1980s. Back then, our dealers had great success under the Vehicle Restraint Agreement that limited the number of vehicles Japan could ship to the U.S. and thus created a seller's market, since vehicles were in high demand and easy to sell. Unfortunately, in this market, dealers had a take-it-or-leave-it attitude about putting the customer's needs first. Also, the industry experienced rapid increases in vehicle price, resulting in longer finance periods, higher insurance costs, and improved vehicle reliability.

These factors resulted in a market shift, from a seller's market to a buyer's market, and customer satisfaction became crucial. As the market shifted, we saw a need to build a solid business plan on a foundation of total customer satisfaction. We realized that we had to set ourselves apart from our competitors. Our challenge was to go beyond what others do—and beyond what others think anybody should do.

We started at the top management level. We knew that without a high level of commitment and leadership from top management, we would not succeed. Top management involvement ensures that operational departments understand the company's commitment. It also sends a very important message: Customer Satisfaction is critical to our success, and it must become an integral part of our daily activities, and the whole organization must be involved in making it happen.

Top management's first commitment was to change our corporate attitude toward customers. We needed to focus on the customer, not just the product. We needed to ensure that the quality of our service matched the quality of our products. Our president directed the top management team to draw up a blueprint for an "umbrella" business philosophy, to encompass all our activities impacting customer satisfaction. We had too many departments going in different directions, trying to address the same problem. The goal was to get everyone heading in one direction to produce consistency in concepts and applications. We called the business plan we developed The Toyota Touch. It represented a long-term philosophy for Toyota—Customer First. Through The Toyota Touch, we attempted to create an umbrella marketing system that established a special relationship between our customers, dealers, and Toyota. The Toyota Touch is commitment to excellence, concern for superior quality, and caring for people based on communication, cooperation, and consideration. These 3 C's are a way for people to interact with each other—human being to human being.

Our next challenge was to get everyone involved and assure that each person understands our new philosophy. To do this, we developed a Corporate Committee to give policy approval for all elements of the Toyota Touch; a Management Committee to formulate, review and integrate specific programs; and a Task Group to review and develop specific activities.

At this point, we found that not all of our middle management was fully committed to the spirit of the 3 C's. As we started program development and review, many barriers were erected and turf battles developed among departments. It took a lot of support and commitment from top management to get everyone moving together. Once we secured the support of management, our next action was to gather feedback from customers, find out exactly what they wanted, and then act upon it. We refer to this information as the "Voice of the Customer." To get this information, we formed a separate corporate level customer relations organization that reports directly to top management. Their charge is to coordinate all customer satisfaction activities and to establish systems to proactively communicate with the customer. For example, one proactive activity was to establish a Customer Assistance Center (CAC), using a nationwide, toll-free 800 phone number, and a customer satisfaction survey to measure the customer's perception of their sales and service experience and vehicle quality.

The CAC handles customer inquiries and assists customers with any problems or concerns they may have. The center is staffed by about 40 full-time representatives and operates from 6 a.m. to 6 p.m., Monday through Friday. Last year the center handled over 300,000 customer calls, establishing a direct line of communication between the customer and corporate headquarters, and between the customer and dealer.

Through this link, we find many customers who, though dissatisfied to some degree, might never have bothered to contact Toyota. Another advantage of the 800 number is when customers know we're only a phone call away, they feel the company really cares about their satisfaction. As a result, we can save valued customers who otherwise may have said "goodbye." Our dealers know this also, and are motivated to "do the job right the first time" and take care of the customer's needs. This results in the dealers having a more positive attitude about the customer, since they now have a better understanding of their concerns. If a call cannot be resolved by our CAC, it's assigned to the appropriate dealer as an "Action Dealer" contact. The contact information is sent directly to the customer's dealer via a direct computer link-up. At the same time, the information also goes to our field offices for their information and follow-up.

The dealer then has two working days to contact the customer and 15 days to resolve the problem. Our average resolution time is currently six days, down from 27 days before our 800 number system.

If the customer is still not satisfied after we've made every effort to resolve his or her concern, we inform the customer of our third-party arbitration program. We don't want to drop an issue if the customer still believes it's our responsibility. We promote customer satisfaction by offering an additional service of dispute resolution to them at no cost—providing customers with an impartial, nonaffiliated, third-party organization to equitably resolve their complaints. Our arbitration services are handled by the AAA. To initiate arbitration, customers just complete the form found in each vehicle and mail it directly to AAA, or they can call our 800 number and request the form.

Our next proactive effort was to survey customers to obtain information about their experience with the buying process, delivery experience, service experience, and product quality. The survey process helps to ensure that the sales and service people act as professionals and that the product actually meets the customer's expectations.

With systems in place to collect information from the customer, we then use the feedback to gauge our progress and performance. The reports that we send to the dealers are not factory essays on how we think our dealers treat customers, but are based on what the dealers' own customers think. The survey results are used as diagnostic tools to provide ongoing customer feedback to identify product or dealership strengths and weaknesses. This means the survey information can then be used to recognize outstanding dealer efforts or focus on areas of improvement.

These surveys are important because they put the dealers in touch with their customers, and let them know what customers want. We also use these surveys to get the customer's evaluation of vehicle quality. On a monthly basis, we send the product quality data directly to our manufacturing and engineering groups, both in the U.S. and Japan. These groups then analyze and use this data to make timely ongoing improvements in the product and manufacturing procedures.

To ensure that people maintain their focus on customer satisfaction, we establish annual performance objectives for each of our indexes. As I said, "What gets measured, gets done." Our goal was to motivate dealers and to help them focus on improving customer satisfaction at the grassroots level. To do this, we launched several programs which impacted all areas of the dealer's operation. One of the programs we developed is the Bottom 20 Dealer Program. This program is used to turn the heat up on poor-performing dealers. Once dealers are notified about a low standing, they are asked to send a personal reply outlining the specific actions to be taken on how and when they will improve their satisfaction rating. Another program is Dealer Consultation. This program targets high-volume dealers who have low customer satisfaction indexes.

Salesperson turnover is a major problem in our industry. A high degree of turnover indicates a lack of career commitment by the salespeople and a poor dealer attitude toward training. To address this problem, we established the Toyota PRIDE sales certification program: Professionalism, Respect, Integrity, Dedication, and Excellence. We follow up after the sell and service, and if any customer is not satisfied, we take action. Our research shows that if we follow up with the customer after their sales and service experience, their overall satisfaction as measured by our indexes is a full 20 points higher.

Our next activity was to get the attention and continued support of our dealers. To do this, we developed several recognition and incentive programs. We include customer satisfaction criteria in all of our major national dealer recognition awards, and in various incentive programs. We call our top dealer award "The Toyota Touch" President's Award. We challenged our dealers to provide their customers with the very best possible dealership experience.

We coordinate and energize customer satisfaction efforts in all operations through an executive level Customer Satisfaction Committee. This committee is probably the most important part of our business plan because it ties all our customer satisfaction efforts together and serves as the major conduit for communicating Voice of the Customer information to all areas of the company. We use this information to make company decisions and improve teamwork among the various departments. The committee is driven by input from customer relations, operational department involvement, monthly meetings, and top management involvement.

If we begin with 1,000 Toyota customers and satisfy them in their sales and service experiences, we can expect over 871 of them to return to the same dealer. If dissatisfied, only 22 will come back to buy another Toyota from the same dealer. These numbers help everyone in the organization understand the cost of dissatisfaction.

Customer satisfaction can't be just another program—it must be a part of your corporate culture and your daily activities. It must be based on a solid foundation, involve all areas of the organization, and provide a means for checking and monitoring activities. It's a process that takes time and perseverance.

Only when we track satisfaction over time can we see the results of our efforts. Our survey indices are at an all-time high, and we made significant sales gains, despite a very difficult market. These sales gains are mirrored by our customer satisfaction gains, indicating that our customer satisfaction activities are a major reason for our sales success.

Customer satisfaction is challenging and does not come cheaply or easily. It takes teamwork and commitment. Customer satisfaction promotes customer retention and generates positive word-of-mouth comments, essential for future success. Customer satisfaction means listening to the voice of the customer, determining areas that need improvement, and developing action plans that have the commitment of the whole company.

Chapter 41

The Customer Is Always Right

By Stew Leonard, Jr.,
President of Stew Leonard's Grocery Stores

*A*t 6:20 p.m. one evening, one of our customers answered her doorbell and found Stew Leonard's Produce Manager, Les Slater, on the doorstep with a complimentary two-pound package of fresh Perdue chicken breasts.

Less than one hour before, she had dropped the following note in the suggestion box at our Danbury store: "I'm upset. I made a special stop on my way home from work to buy chicken breasts for dinner, but you're sold out, and now I'll have to eat a TV dinner instead."

This outstanding example of customer service was the result of a fortunate confluence of events. My brother Tom Leonard who runs the Danbury store, reviews customers' complaints several times each day. He was reading the note just as the Perdue truck arrived—and as Les Slater was leaving for his home in Danbury. The rest, as they say, is history. But the idea behind the gesture, and its speedy implementation, reflect the philosophy that built our business.

The moment you arrive at the Stew Leonard's stores in Norwalk and Danbury, CT., your attention is riveted on six-foot-high, 6,000-pound boulders at the entrances. Carved in those stones and designed to be seen and reinforced every time a customer or an employee enters the stores, is the concept upon which our business is based:

Our Policy:
RULE 1. THE CUSTOMER IS ALWAYS RIGHT.
RULE 2. IF THE CUSTOMER IS EVER WRONG, REREAD RULE 1.

It bears a facsimile of my father's signature and our commitment to that philosophy is the basis for the decisions that have turned a small family dairy into one of the leading retail operations in the world.

The success of Stew Leonard's had its origins in the insights my father gained accompanying his father on his milk delivery route. The milkman was a trusted friend to his customers.

When construction of a new highway forced the family dairy to close, my father asked his customers what factors they considered important in the purchase of milk for their families. "Freshness and price," they told him. If there were significant savings to be had, they would be willing to give up home deliveries.

Stew Leonard's Dairy Store, which opened in 1969, was built around a milk processing plant where customers could actually see the milk being processed and then buy it as it rolled off the line. Because delivery costs were eliminated and container sizes standardized, our prices were 6 to 8 percent below retail. The store also carried a limited line of fresh foods.

Bucking Trends

From its inception, Stew Leonard's has defied conventional wisdom.

• Two-thirds of all family businesses in the United States fail every year, and yet, for 22 years, we have employed as many as 22 relatives and prospered.

• There are 93 food stores within a 15-mile radius of Stew Leonard's in Norwalk. Customers drive as much as 50 miles to shop here, and 99 percent of them are repeat shoppers.

• The average supermarket carries a product line of over 20,000 items. Stew Leonard's carries only 900 products, requiring customers often to shop twice. Yet we have the highest retail turnover rate in the world, yielding sales of $3,470 per square foot.

Today, in addition to my role as president, my sister Beth runs our bakery operation, my sister Jill is Director of Human Resources, and my brother Tom manages Stew Leonard's in Danbury.

We have been able to work together successfully because we were trained to do so. My father allowed no favoritism for family members, and from childhood on we have been involved in day-to-day operations. The feeling that they are part of a family extends to our employees, creating a sense of permanence and security.

The results have been phenomenal: 25 percent of our 1,200 employees have been members of the Stew Leonard team for over five years, and more than half of them have family members working here too.

Happy Employees, Happy Customers

Retailing is a "people" business. Our employees' attitudes and actions form the basis for the way customers view Stew Leonard's. As my father said: "Enthusiasm can't be taught, it must be caught."

What we look for in an employee is friendliness, concern for others, and a can-do attitude. We interview 15 to 25 applicants for each position to find an appropriate team member.

Our goal is to create a team spirit in every employee. With team spirit we can impart pride, and with pride we can instill a desire for excellence, which is the foundation of our success. Every employee attends a one-day training session before they have any contact with customers. Customer service cannot be a sometimes thing. It must be repeated over and over every day. In training, we use the acronym YES: Y = you = put yourself in the customer's place; E = encourage = encourage customers to talk about their problems with our products, services, or employees because the more we listen, the more we learn; and S = support = our employees can make decisions on the spot, knowing that they will be supported by management.

Our employees are involved in the development of ideas. The One Idea Club consists of employees who go out together to visit competitors or other interesting businesses looking for ideas. We also have a suggestion box for employees.

Members of the Stew Leonard's team are highly motivated because we promote from within. People who start at the bottom and work their way to the top are the backbone of our business. They make good managers because they know what it is like on the firing line.

Staff motivation requires four management qualities: 1) you must genuinely like people; 2) you must be a completely fair person; 3) you must be obsessed with perfection; and 4) you must find out what your employees' hot buttons are and press them.

Learning by Listening

In a highly competitive business, customer satisfaction is a critical concern. At Stew Leonard's we encourage our customers to give us their suggestions as well as their complaints and try to tailor our organization to meet their needs.

For example, customers tell us that they get bored with the tiring, repetitive nature of food shopping. Our response is to make a trip to Stew Leonard's a special event for the whole family. The festive atmosphere includes audio-animatronic characters, employees in animal costumes, and live barnyard animals.

We make extensive use of focus groups to help us target necessary changes and new ideas. Each month we invite 12 to 16 customers to a "Customer Action Breakfast" with six of our managers. Ideas generated at these sessions are generally implemented within 24 hours.

At one session a woman complained that our fish "wasn't fresh," and yet it was trucked in fresh every day. But because the fish was wrapped in plastic, she perceived it as "packaged" and not "fresh like when she used to buy it packed on ice." The very next day our fish department displayed its wares in a steel tub filled with ice, and its sales doubled!

Customers consistently express appreciation for the freshness of our produce and make suggestions for improving it. Following complaints about strawberries packed in the ubiquitous green plastic containers, we began to display them in bulk. Again, the product sold itself, and as customers filled their bags, the size of their purchase increased. Similarly, even though our store opens at 7 a.m., we do not offer corn for sale until 11 a.m., because to do so any earlier we would be forced to sell day-old corn.

Our policy is to buy in bulk, directly from the producer. By eliminating the middle-man, we can guarantee fresh products and control costs. Our prices are typically 6 to 8 percent below market.

Responding to customer requests for freshly prepared gourmet food, we hired Chef Georges Llorens, who presided at prestigious restaurants in Paris and New York, to head our in-store kitchen. His gourmet specialties are a resounding success.

Some of the ideas we implement are the result of complaints. Complaint boxes are prominently displayed in our stores and customers are encouraged to use them. The contents are read daily and by 11 a.m. the next day are distributed to department heads who analyze them, act where possible, and report at our weekly management meeting. Customers who complain are called "Friends of Stew Leonard's," because it is by learning what we do wrong that we can do better.

Chapter 42

Service Sells

**By Michael S. Dell,
Chief Executive Officer,
Dell Computer Corporation**

*O*ur company has grown fast because we are responsive in delivering custom products and support services to customers.

Our company started in 1983, when the PC business blossomed. I was in high school at the time and became interested in computers. I realized then that the industry's distribution and sales systems were poor. When I would go to a computer store, I would pay a 25 percent retail markup for a computer and be served by a person who knew little about computers.

I thought that there must be a better way to sell computers. The better way, I thought, would be to provide custom products directly to end users with much better service and support and to take the day-to-day feedback from customers and turn that into better products and services.

That's what our company set out to do. It must be working because we have experienced revenue gains of over $1 billion in a single year. Remember that the PC is the ultimate consumer product because you will likely buy three PC's every ten years. Whatever you buy today will be obsolete in four years. And so this product continually replaces itself, which makes for an interesting market.

Focus on Total Value

We recognize that service is very important in this market, along with efficiency and effectiveness in delivery. We started the business with a consumer point of view and with a strategy of mass customization to enable us to tailor our products and services to specific customers. Our company has become a consumer advocate— as opposed to a technology advocate or an advocate of a particular product, strategy, or direction. We interpret the needs of the market and deliver those to customers.

We focus not on the price of the computers we sell, but on the total value—as defined by the product integrity, quality, service, support, brand name, ease of purchase, and the feelings and attitudes that come with buying the product and dealing with the company. We do not introduce technology for its own sake; we introduce technology that meets the needs of customers.

We maintain a direct relationship with our customers. We speak with them every day. We target and segment our customers in an increasingly specialized fashion. Our product strategy is driven by customer input. We've made the customer the most important person in the business; the ideas of satisfying and pleasing customers are the chromosomes of our company. Every part of our company is crafted around serving the customer and being accountable to the customer. This focus enables us to customize hardware, software, peripherals, and services. Every area of our business—manufacturing, finance, services, product development, management, and sales—receives feedback from customers daily and turns that into changes that improve our products and processes.

This strategy has been met enthusiastically. We have grown rapidly, expanding throughout Europe, Mexico, and Japan. Japan has been our fastest growing new subsidiary. The Japanese quickly accepted our direct marketing approach because the distribution systems in Japan are incredibly inefficient. Our computers sell for about half the price of any Japanese PC, and yet our gross margins are highest in Japan. Japanese customers are quality and brand conscious, and so establishing a brand and a service attitude within a Japanese operation is critical. But U.S. companies have a huge opportunity to introduce new approaches that play to the weaknesses of Japanese systems. In the next five years, our Japanese operation may become our second largest.

Database Marketing Model

Because of the efficiency and economy of scale of our database marketing model, we believe the customer satisfaction strategies that we bring to the market will yield a strong long-term business. In the first quarter alone, our company mailed about 15 million catalogs in the United States. In every market we enter, we hire a local business person who can execute our model effectively and ask that person to implement the model with the nuances of a given culture.

By acquiring customers through various distribution channels and then segmenting them by customer type and by application type, we're able to target and focus our marketing in a very specialized way. Of course, we are best known for our direct distribution system. One of our executives once said: "If you wake up every morning at 4 a.m. and do 300 push-ups, you're likely to get a strong upper body." In our business, if you take 25,000 phone calls every day and respond to the customer, your business is likely to change in many ways. Our business listens and responds to those phone calls. Being close to the customer fosters a partnership with our customers. We install many tools to ensure that we maintain a high level of responsiveness. Having this contact with customers allows us to provide follow-on selling opportunities and to contact them at exactly the right point with new offerings.

The best way to segment a business is by customer type. As our business grows, we become increasingly segmented. The ultimate segmentation is a personal phone number for the customer. If you're a large Dell account, you can call us toll free using your own special phone number, type in your company name, and speak directly to the Dell Account Team assigned to serve you 24 hours a day. Such specialization makes us very attractive to large corporations. We're organized to serve the needs of each customer.

While we have been very active in the direct distribution approach, we don't believe that buying directly from Dell is a religious experience, nor do we believe that our channels of distribution are sacred. We believe that we should provide our products and services in the best possible way as defined by the customer. For example, we've signed agreements with super stores and mass merchant companies like the Price Club, Sam's Club, and Walmart to provide products to the growing consumer PC business. While we don't sell that product directly to the customer, we provide them with the services directly, and we have many follow-on selling opportunities to that customer. All customers flow into a huge database; and the more customers we have, the more specialized our marketing gets.

In addition to the 25,000 phone calls a day, we also conduct focus groups, one-on-one interviews, mail-in surveys, advisory groups, and meetings with key customers. In focus groups, we will often expose customers who represent a trend in leading new demand to new product concepts. For example, we will show them Concept A, Concept B, and Concept C, and then get their reaction to the new products. We can't always take the approach of "Well, they haven't asked for it, therefore, they don't want it," because our business technology evolves at such a rate that customers are unaware of what we are likely to have in a year in terms of the art of the possible. So we often have to construct logical alternatives and present those to customers and then receive input and feedback. Our process is validated when we introduce the product and it does well in the market.

This whole customer passion has become so strong that it's like a highway where cars speed along at 120 miles per hour. If you get on the highway at a slower speed, you get run over. Our culture is so strong that if you come into the company and you're not up to speed, it just chews you up and spits you out fast. It doesn't accept a non-customer responsive attitude. In our orientation, we expose new employees to our business strategies, and we reinforce this training after the indoctrination. The incentives, the profit sharing, and the bonus plans are clearly tied to customer responsiveness. All of our communications and all of the company communication efforts are customer centered. We tell stories about service heroes and give risk-taking awards to people who go the extra mile to take care of a customer. Those things become part of the culture of the company, and the culture rewards taking care of the customer.

Even when we sell computers through Walmart, we keep close to the customer by being completely responsible for all the after-sales support to those customers. We also do post-sale surveys; in fact, feedback from customers is more important two years after the initial purchase because current satisfaction levels reflect what they will buy as a replacement PC.

Efficient Distribution

We have, in effect, built a large electronic super store. In some cases, we provide products and services through a virtual (Stealth) warehouse. We sell several products that never sit on our shelves, but are delivered to customers within the next business day by various distribution partners who are more capable at packaging and providing software, peripheral, and accessory products to customers in a rapid deployment fashion. We intend to be the easiest PC company to do business with, easiest to buy from, and we believe we have many advantages in our logistics and distribution system. Our inventory turns are twice that of our major competitors, and our asset utilization is much higher.

We believe more in a vertically connected enterprise than in a vertically integrated enterprise. So we have close relationships with suppliers and partners who are more capable and more specialized in specific areas. Our strategy is to supply customers with products they want to buy—not just with new technology that they find interesting or exciting. Our focus is on taking customer feedback and driving that into the right products and strategies. We focus on value engineering because cost and reliability are very important to our customers.

Service and Support

Service and support have become part of our brand in the sense that customers believe that when they buy a Dell product, the Dell Company takes care of them. Service is the ultimate competitive weapon. Customers delight over the responsiveness and the quality of our replies to their queries. We don't have any particular rules in terms of how many times you can or can't call us or what questions we do or don't answer. We simply say that when you buy one of our products, we take care of you.

Our customer focus has grown with the company from the beginning. As the company grew, the executive team had to make decisions as to how we would treat our customers, and those decisions created an understanding among employees as to how we would collectively deal with our customers. It's been a very positive experience for us because the management team walks its talk about being customer-focused. We have been intent on making sure our customers are satisfied and that our employees are empowered to make changes and do special things for customers. We believe that having a group of passionate employees who care about the customer is a huge competitive advantage.

Many businesses get caught in the trap of having a mission that is confusing to their associates. For example, if in a company meeting, I stand up and say, "The goal of this company is to make a lot of money and run away," few people would be inspired by that vision or mission. They might say to themselves, "I need this job, but if the mission is to make a lot of money and run away, is this the right thing for me to be doing? Are we doing right by our customers?"

Now, if I get up in a meeting and say, "Our job here is to take care of our customers and to make them happy," I think that many people will naturally identify with the goal and become passionate about carrying it out. If you can identify with people's core concerns, and put in place a reward system that focuses on those, you will cultivate a very positive cultural element within the business.

Every Friday at 7:30 a.m., we hold a Customer Advocate Meeting. A group of about 175 people throughout the business get together in Austin, and for 90 minutes we review as a team the key statistics around customer responsiveness. We talk about our abandonment rates, about the time it takes for us to process orders, about how our process works in satisfying the needs of our customers. We then call a customer who has had a difficult problem during the past week and ask that customer to profile for us what went wrong with our process. Every area of the company is represented in this meeting. And we all talk with these customers to understand their concerns and understand what we need to do as a company to improve our processes. On occasion, we call our own phone lines and pretend to be a customer. We time our responsiveness, and track the quality of the telephone call to see how well we are satisfying customer needs.

It's fairly easy for those people on the front lines to be sensitive to customer needs because they talk to customers every day, but it's harder for someone in manufacturing or product development to understand customer needs. Tools like the Customer Advocate Meeting involve everyone in the company in the process of satisfying customers.

Adapt and Grow

We continue to make adjustments based on what we understand from customers and based on the evolution of the business and technology. We approach service as a product, and we focus on continuously improving it. In our company, the things that are average are considered messed up or in need of great improvement by our employees—and that's why we enjoy great success. To instill that continuous improvement culture within the business, we have made the customer the most important person in our business and made our obsession and essential goal to satisfy our customers.

We take the approach that one size does not fit all and that one size fits one. Our mass customization system allows us to build computers one at a time and to segment our marketing finely and to approach customers in ways that are targeted to their specific needs.

We assign our business leaders the role and responsibility of both strategy development and implementation. As an executive team, we meet for two days about every three months to talk about the key success factors of our business. We talk about what we believe the key strategic elements of our company need to be in five years and in ten years. We then assemble cross-functional teams to drive major projects throughout the company.

We want to be the best place to buy computer products and services. Our company is well positioned because we are a pure play on delivering the right products and services to customers. We also have the technology capability to adapt those products. We have a huge opportunity to be the leading supplier of computers by the year 2000.

I don't think our company has any silver bullets, myself included, that are the answer to all the issues. What we have is a unique culture and way of doing business. We don't sprinkle pixie dust on our employees to make them customer oriented. We don't give them customer-responsiveness injections. This is the just the way the company operates.

Companies like IBM, Sears, and General Motors have found that it's tough to turn around the culture of a well-established company to cope with the challenge of an aggressive fast player. To stay fast and aggressive, we are committed to change. There are signs hanging up in our offices that say, "We're Changing Everything." We change everything all the time. We like to change things. Change is good, and everybody knows that. At least, everybody at our company knows that change is good.

Chapter 43

Strategy for Service, Disney Style

**By Terry Brinkoetter,
Senior Seminar Representative,
Walt Disney World Seminar Productions**

*T*he culture and the environment communicate to people all the time, either reinforcing their perception of quality service or detracting from it.

Many executives want to improve their level of service, but few recognize the importance of the corporate culture in the process. Disney believes strongly that the culture, environment, and performance of people lie at the heart of quality service.

We define quality service as a series of behaviors performed by Cast Members in the presence of Guests. These behaviors include smiling, making eye contact, using pleasant phrases, performing their role functions, and the many other details that add up to the "personal touch."

Guests at the Walt Disney World Resort typically comment on three aspects of quality service: the cleanliness of the place, the show itself, and the friendliness of the employees (Cast Members). These reactions—compiled through comment forms, surveys, focus groups, and letters—reflect the business philosophy of Walt Disney, who said: "Quality will win out! Give the people everything you can give them. Keep the place as clean as you can keep it. Keep it friendly. Make it a fun place to be."

This applies to any service organization. What brings this philosophy to life at Disney is a well-structured, fast-moving organization composed of Cast Members who are committed to creating happiness for Guests (not customers).

After visiting our parks, resorts, and recreational facilities, many people ask, "How does Disney do it? How do they get over 35,000 Cast Members to perform more than 1,500 roles (not jobs) and deliver quality service with a smile for millions of Guests, 365 days a year, often in high heat and humidity? How do they maintain such a quality service standard?"

The secret to the Disney approach is that there is no secret! We attain quality service by developing, refining, and living a business strategy based on hard work, attention to detail, and exceeding Guest expectations. The key is to make Guests happy. If Guests are happy, they'll return. Repeat visitation is the name of the game. We have a loyal audience with high expectations. Many people travel great distances in search of their happiness. We can't disappoint a Guest, even once. Each Cast Member serves each Guest one at a time. This series of "magic moments" adds up to the overall experience. With each Cast Member, Disney knows its name and image are on the line; the show is that fragile. Guests remember the best and the worst experiences; the rest fall into a standard. To raise that standard, Disney works hard to recognize and reward Cast Members who do it right. Cast Members who do not meet the standard are coached and, as a last resort, disciplined. We strive for perfection, knowing we'll never be perfect, but that we'll reach a higher standard for the effort.

Culture Is the Key

The key to "how Disney does it" is the corporate culture. We believe that to the degree that an environment can be controlled, the appropriate reactions of people within that environment can be predicted. Disney strives to control, within good business sense, much of the environment. The experience of the Guest and Cast are orchestrated to be positive.

The Disney philosophy of Guest service was established by Walt Disney at Disneyland in 1955. Walt took his greatest film endeavors and translated them into a form of three-dimensional "reality." Walt took a theater audience and lifted them onto the stage, surrounded them with sets and props, and had them interact with actors and actresses (the Cast Members). He put Guests in the middle of the action, engaging all five senses and enabling them to experience the show, scene by scene. Disney views its show like a live performance and the physical setting like a movie set. Everything must be carefully designed and constructed to bring home the feeling of theme and service to the Guest. Each day, the set must be perfect, restored to its shiny luster so it always looks like "opening day."

The concept of show business permeates the culture and helps attain the "buy in" of Cast Members who are not hired for jobs, but cast for roles. They wear costumes, not uniforms. They play before an audience of Guests, not a crowd of customers. When they are in a Guest environment, they are "on stage." And when they are in a

Cast environment, they are "backstage." When on stage, they are not necessarily to be themselves, but rather to play a role. The role calls for an aggressively friendly approach—one that incorporates smiles, enthusiasm, sincerity, high energy and concern for the happiness of the Guest. In short, a Cast Member is a host or hostess who tries to exceed the expectations of the Guests.

Knowing the Audience

To exceed expectations, Disney conducts "Guestology" studies to understand who the Guests are and what they want. Ongoing surveys help us keep a finger on the Guest pulse. In addition, we receive tens of thousands of Guest letters and comment forms annually, and we respond to each one as quickly as possible. To close the information loop and provide valuable feedback to management, Guest Comment Reports, abbreviating the essence of all Guest comments, are distributed weekly to management. These reports list all compliments and complaints, bringing problems to light quickly so they can be dealt with and reoccurrences prevented. Focus groups are also conducted to gather qualitative information concerning the open-ended impressions of Guests and their reactions to future projects. Daily inspections, show-quality reports, wait-time studies, maintenance punchlists, and utilization studies all contribute to a safe and efficient operation.

But the most important feedback system is "management by walking around" when managers get out to observe and talk to Guests and Cast Members at the point of service delivery. While top executives commit many hours to this process, line supervisors spend 60 to 70 percent of their time observing Cast Members serving each Guest one at a time. These firsthand experiences develop a sense of urgency to react quickly in service recovery when things go wrong.

With so much data concerning Guests, Disney has learned to focus on what matters most. We quantify data, for example, including it in proformas on future projects which include Guest satisfaction and value factors. As much as possible, business decisions are based on facts. Through Guestology, Guests help design the future Walt Disney World Resort. As Walt once said: "You don't build it for yourself. You know what the people want, and you build it for them."

Uniqueness is part of the Disney strategy. Michael Eisner, Chairman and CEO of The Walt Disney Company, likes to get involved in the creative process. He continually challenges Team Disney with questions like, "Where's the Disney Difference?" and "What makes it Disney?" He does this to find or create something unique that will fit within the well-defined Disney culture. The culture fosters creativity and innovation within everyone's role. It also instills a desire for continuous refinement.

Empowering the Cast

Empowering Cast Members begins with leaders who create a vision of the future, sell the vision to each member, and ensure that each milestone is reached. Empowerment begins at the top with a strong commitment and willingness to "walk the talk!"

The Disney show is fragile, requiring hard work and discipline. The people involved have to want to do it. The autocratic method doesn't work for Disney, nor have we written everything down and structured the process to the finest detail. A Strategic Planning team helps develop five- and ten-year plans. These are updated annually with corporate executives. The resort management develops an annual budget and plan. Together, these tools help keep Disney on track. Once given an assignment, the people responsible for results are provided with the necessary resources and authority. This empowerment also holds them accountable for completion of the project.

Empowerment is the key to getting everyone involved. In Disney's view, empowerment is an active process that encourages the Cast to get involved, taking the strategic plan from the corporate boardroom to the point of action on Main Street U.S.A. in the Magic Kingdom Park.

Disney has a positive approach to sharing the vision for the future in a way that creates excitement among Cast Members. We remember the traditions of the past—those things that have brought Disney to where it is today. Disney uses company history to their advantage, telling Cast Members that nearly seventy years of Disney history, along with the Disney name and image, are on the line with each of them. As Cast Members, they can choose to reinforce or tear down that image with each Guest they meet. The reality of Disney's business, and perhaps that of everyone's in the service industry, is that success comes down to each Cast Member making the right decision and providing the right behavior for each Guest situation.

Empowerment of the Disney Cast begins with a service theme of "creating happiness" for people. Disney then provides extensive training, ongoing communication, and dependable support systems to help them make the right decisions in each Guest encounter. Empowering over 36,000 Cast Members requires Disney to establish a framework that supports each person in his or her decision making.

Four service standards—safety, courtesy, show, and efficiency— facilitate decision making in daily operations, particularly when Cast Members are confronted with a situation or variable they have not previously encountered. Disney tells the Cast that the only time courtesy can be sacrificed is in the interest of safety. The safety of the Guest is the first priority and must be built into everything they do. Show will be sacrificed only in the interest of safety or courtesy to Guests. These four standards form the basis of how we measure quality service—a measurement that is included in the Cast Member review process.

Disney takes a positive view of quality, never referring to it as what's left after the defects and problems are removed. They go for the emotions in people and get them excited about what they are doing. This emotional approach also underscores the importance of each member of the Cast in delivering a quality show.

The Disney setting refers to the environment, the objects within the environment, and any system or procedure that affects that environment. The physical environment communicates to people all the time, either reinforcing the perception of quality service or detracting from it. A well-defined environment assists Cast Members in delivering quality service by reinforcing the message.

The environment is viewed as a movie set. The set must be as perfect as possible while communicating a theme or mood to the Guests. Disney attempts to involve the five senses to reinforce the message. We also try to build into the setting the four service standards: safety, courtesy, show, and efficiency.

Creating the best balance between "good show" and business goals is always a challenge. Disney believes that it is possible to create so much quality that the Guest can't sense it. The Guest ultimately determines what is quality. Quality needs to be where the Guest can touch it, feel it, or sense it. We put real gold leaf on the carousel horses, for example. We do have limits to quality, but at Disney that line is a bit beyond the expectations of most Guests.

Delivering Quality Service

Numerous support systems enable employees to perform assigned functions and maintain positive attitudes. If an attraction is inoperable, Disney is not supporting its Cast Members. Support systems can also be as mundane as a telephone, stapler, or user-friendly computers. They also include procedures that must work for Cast Members in the delivery of quality service.

The Walt Disney World Resort was designed to have strong support systems, including the resort's own telephone and energy services companies, as well as attractions designed for reliability and show appeal. Support teams—such as horticulture, art and design, human resources, central shops, and maintenance—assist line managers by providing services that free them to concentrate on their assigned role and to spend more time coaching their Cast Members and obtaining feedback from Guests.

In delivering quality service, there are two parts to every Cast Member's role: the mechanical and the personal touch. The mechanical is the Cast Member's job function—serve food, sell merchandise, drive a monorail, or help people on or off an attraction. This must be done in a manner that exceeds Guests' expectations.

More important, however, is the personal touch—the eye-to-eye contact, the smiles, the pleasant, courteous tone, the sincere caring that comes through the transaction. This is the competitive edge that companies strive for in the service business. Disney has found they can't force the personal touch. To obtain it, we must get Cast Members to "buy in" and play their role in the show.

Management must set the example and influence the tone of the work environment. To the degree that management is positive and supportive, Cast Members will emulate them. For example, a system known as "cross-utilization" is in place for the resort's peak times when demand outstrips the number of Cast Members for a short interval. As a part of cross-utilization, members of management and support teams put their paperwork aside and work short shifts in custodial, food service, or any number of onstage positions. In this way, the Guests are served, Cast Members are supported, and management and support personnel gain a renewed respect and empathy for the frontline Cast Member.

The Disney approach is more than just the corporate culture—it's a way of life. Not reliant on campaigns or gimmicks to motivate the people, this approach is hard work. We keep it simple so that all members of the team will not only understand the mission and strategy, but most important, carry it out.

Dick Wools, Chairman of Walt Disney Attractions, once said: "It all boils down to two words: Quality and Pride. If you design it, build it, operate it, and maintain it with quality, people will take pride in it."

Once Cast Members take pride in the organization and their role, they will give an extra effort of themselves that usually translates into the personal touch.

Chapter 44

Corporate Commitment to Customer Satisfaction

 By John J. Shields,
Senior Vice President of Sales,
Services, Marketing, and International,
Digital Equipment Corporation

When I began working at Digital, the computer industry was very different from what we know today. To most people, computers were large, expansive, and mysterious machines that sat in glass rooms, far removed from the day-to-day work.

Today, computers are used by people in all kinds of jobs to do many different things. The computer that once filled a room is now no bigger than a match head—and its cost has similarly been reduced. Computer networks are making it possible for people and computers to work together more effectively and across long distances.

Tomorrow promises more dramatic changes, not only for the computer industry, but, in part, because of the computer, for every industry. Changes in product and services. Changes in the ways products are created, manufactured, and delivered. Changes in government regulations, competition, and markets.

Change in any one of these areas dramatically impacts an organization's plans and its ability to succeed. Yet change is inevitable— and largely unpredictable. How, then, can we develop long-term business strategies? How do we organize, motivate, and measure people? How do we make the right day-to-day operational decisions?

The good sailor works with, not against, changing wind and wave conditions, yet he sets a course. In business, as in sailing, navigation means pursuing a constant in a sea of change. In my experience there is one constant in every successful business which does not change: an unflagging commitment to the customer's satisfaction. The customer is the star by which to plot the course.

When executives put the customer at the center of their operation, their course is true. When the customer's opinion is respected, respect flows back to the organization. The opinion of the service and sales people who deal with customers day-to-day is listened to. People feel they are making a contribution. They think of their jobs in terms of "how does what I do benefit the customer?"

The priorities of the organization are driven from the outside in, rather than from the inside out—from service to sales, distribution, manufacturing, engineering, and marketing. You begin to think of building a product to fill a customer need, instead of "creating a customer need" to buy the product that you have built.

With its inception, every enterprise is customer-centered. Everyone is very aware that without the customer, there is no business. Everyone feels that pressure to get and keep satisfied customers—and each person applies pressure to the other.

The real challenge comes with success. How do you maintain a corporate commitment to customer satisfaction? As an organization grows larger and more complex, it becomes easier for people to lose sight of the connection between what they do and how it benefits the customer. The work they do becomes "just a job." The rewarding feeling of making a contribution fades, and with it, the quality of the work.

When quality and service slip, management often compounds the problem. Rather than making people more directly responsible to the customer's satisfaction, the tendency is to add more internal controls or hire more "experts" to check on the work done by the people in the organization who deal with the customer. Then, when that doesn't work, more checkers begin to check the checkers. When, in this way, an organization centers on itself, it loses its star to steer by, and it flounders.

The interactive nature of Digital's computing solutions helps keep us focused on our customers. To succeed long-term in a rapidly changing industry, we must do more than meet our customers' immediate computing needs: we must understand how computers help our customers succeed long-term. We must help make sure the right person has the right information at the right time to make the right decision in the customer's unique competitive situation. It's an ongoing job, and it's a two-way street. As we work with customers to help them implement the information technology to support their business objectives, we learn how to make better products, and our customers benefit from our increased expertise.

One of the things we learn from our customers is what problem needs to be solved. For example, we learned some time ago that a real problem for our customers was the significant investment in software applications and training they lost each time the computer hardware changed. To succeed, our customers needed to protect this investment.

In response, Digital developed a completely compatible range of computers called VAX that allows customers to use the same application on all sizes of computers—and on every generation of computers over time. Applications developed to run on a VAX system ten years ago will run today, without change, on any size VAX computer—from small desktop systems to large mainframe-like cluster systems in the data center.

We learned, too, that the ability to network computers, enabling the people who use them to work together simply and easily, is crucial to the success of our customers. Digital applied vast resources to develop the technology to network computers from many different vendors, throughout the organization.

The success Digital enjoys today is based largely on how well our family of computers and our networking products help our customers be more successful.

Our commitment to customer satisfaction begins with listening to the customer. Marketing studies, financial projections, internal organization goals, and competitive analyses are all important—but all are as changeable as the weather. I believe that the best way to learn what customers want is simply to ask them. The benefits of direct and ongoing communications with customers on every level has led us to implement a number of formal programs to interact with our customers, in addition to day-to-day sales and service.

We sponsor conferences for users of our products to meet to share ideas and concerns. We have dedicated organizations to understanding and responding to the unique needs of our customers, both from an industry perspective and an individual company perspective. We regularly host customer visits and technology reviews for customers to share product direction and ideas—and to elicit our customers' guidance. We host a forum for corporate leaders to meet with each other and with industry consultants to discuss the issues they face. We have set up Applications Centers for Technology throughout the world, placing technical expertise and corporate resources near our customers to help develop customized solutions to meet their needs. And every year we invite our customers to DECWORLD, an event where they can see the full range of our solutions, working together, all in one place.

I don't mean to imply by these examples that Digital does not need continually to improve in listening and responding to our customers. Learning how to improve is something we take very seriously. Every year, in addition to relying on information from independent researchers, we conduct our own extensive survey of our customers' satisfaction. We want to know, directly from our customer, how to get better at listening, responding, meeting their needs, supporting their goals, making and keeping commitments, and servicing them for the lifetime of their system—in other words, how can we make it easier for them to do business with us?

When my managers review an employee's performance, in addition to revenue goals, I insist that each person is measured on the results of the customer satisfaction survey for their area of responsibility. Executives, too, are measured directly on the satisfaction of our customers. I spend as much time as possible out of the office, with customers. People listen to what you say, but they believe what you do.

Twenty-seven years ago, I installed the third computer Digital built. As young field service engineers in a young company, my colleagues and I were in a position to learn firsthand what our customers wanted.

Some of our customers were very knowledgeable about and comfortable with computers. They required little in the way of support from Digital. Other customers wanted us to take full responsibility for managing their computer operations for them. We decided the best way to meet the needs of both customers was to charge them for service they needed. This decision was pure heresy at the time. The prevailing wisdom was that service was "free"—that is, the cost of supporting your product was rolled into the price of the product itself. Yet our customers told us otherwise. They would prefer to pay outright for service. In that way they could purchase only the level of service they required—and they would know how much service was costing them.

The idea was controversial even at Digital, yet in the end, we listened to our customers. We set up our service organization as a profit and loss business. The result was innovative, very comprehensive, and very flexible service. We learned that not just a product's performance, but how easy it is to install, to maintain, and learn to use determines our customer's success. Today our customer service organization is often rated the best in the industry and remains a profitable business for our company.

As the world gets more interdependent, satisfying the customer becomes more complex. Sometimes your customer is also your supplier—or even your competitor. In the end, a corporate commitment to customer satisfaction comes down to the relationship between individuals, and an honest respect for the individuals who build those relationships. Today, every business faces rough seas of inevitable, unpredictable change. Those organizations who commit themselves to customer satisfaction gain a perspective as useful in setting their course as is a compass, pointing always in one direction.

Chapter 45

Owning the Service Problem

**By Joseph V. Vittoria,
CEO, Avis, Inc.**

*W*hen the employees own the company, they tend to take better care of their customers. Avis has always been employee- and customer-oriented. We've had to be. Our people have much direct contact with the customer. Many of our long-term people consider themselves to be part of the Avis family. The creation of an employee stock ownership plan (ESOP) in 1987 took this to a much higher level.

Since Avis was established 50 years ago, we have had eleven different owners. When ownership was transferred to employees, they seemed to take a special interest in interfacing with our customers. Anytime you rent a car from Avis, ask the person you're dealing with—whether he or she is a rental agent or a bus driver—what it's like to be an owner. You'll get an intelligent answer. It's not something they take lightly. Ownership definitely affects their service performance.

Beyond a formal plan, the key to employee ownership is open dialogue. We have initiated Employee Participation Groups (EPG) that meet regularly to discuss how to serve our customers better. Employee representatives are elected by their coworkers to attend meetings, supply input, and give management the chance to review objectives. One key objective is to improve the quality of service; and it's amazing how our people have achieved new standards since they became employee-owners. They were good to begin with, but now they're even better.

We're trying to make our quality program even more effective by empowering our people to make the decisions needed to solve a customer's problem on the spot without having to go to a supervisor. Our goal is to provide customer satisfaction, and frequently that can be accomplished by employees taking some action on their own. One of our slogans is "Owners try harder," and we encourage that by giving our people down the line the ability to make decisions. And if they make a mistake, we'll put our arms around their shoulders later on and explain how it could be done better the next time. Part of our management training program is to get managers in line with this new concept of having their people take some actions on their own.

When we began the EPG process, employees started coming up with wonderful solutions to certain problems. Sometimes their managers would get nervous that their superiors might wonder why they hadn't thought of those solutions. So we had to point out that we did that job years ago, and we didn't think of it either. We tell them just to welcome the suggestion and to recognize the person who made it.

I want our customers to feel that our people care about them as individuals and not just credit card numbers. If you make employees feel appreciated, if you treat them properly and correctly, they'll give you a good day's work, and more. Our employees convey the image that we're a warm and friendly company that's also very efficient.

We keep emphasizing the importance of their roles, and we keep in touch by meeting with our people regularly. I devote one week every two months to meeting with them—flying to two cities a day— to fill them in on how we're doing and to listen to their views on how to make things better. Keeping communication lines simple and direct has been a goal of senior management at Avis for many years. Employee ownership gives new importance to this management style.

One way to restore a loss of loyalty or a lack of pride in the company is to give people a piece of the action. Our people are motivated. They feel they're participants, that they can make the company better and their own positions better. They're now players, and they know that to be an effective player, they have to provide added value. And we know that rubs off in their role as ambassadors of the corporate image. Outsiders are often overwhelmed by the activities of our people. Many of our employees are supercharged. What we want to do now is take those supercharged people and use them to charge others.

We're also using computers to supercharge our operations. Our Wizard system—a global, real-time information system—enables us to process car rentals faster and to enhance the service for our customers. We want technology and people to complement each other. Instead of hiring computer experts and teaching them manners, we like to hire friendly people and teach them computers. We want our customers to recognize that quality is worth something. Then it becomes a value relationship rather than just a price relationship.

Rarely will you see a line at an Avis counter backed up because the technology is so fast and because our people care. After all, they're owners, and they take pride in their work.

Chapter 46

Treating People Right

By Dave Thomas,
Founder of Wendy's International

*S*uccess starts inside, but it doesn't mean much until you draw others in. The key is to be fair—to treat people right. To treat people right, you have to master three fundamentals: caring, teamwork, and support.

Caring. Caring is feeling what another person feels. Some people call it empathy. Genuinely caring about people usually leads to success. And successful people widen the circle of people they care about more and more as they grow older. Mary Kay Ash of Mary Kay Cosmetics once told me something that helps her: "Pretend that every person you meet has a sign around his or her neck that says, 'Make me feel important.'"

Just before Christmas one year, I went to a Wendy's restaurant in Albuquerque, New Mexico, to film a TV adoption segment with two youngsters. The little girl, who was about seven, had a fresh scar where her father had walloped her with a beer bottle. As we ate lunch, the girl and her older brother, who was about nine, finally started to look me and an old friend who was with me in the eyes. We talked about how important it is to stick together when you don't have other family. And then the boy said something I'll never forget: "I don't want to be adopted with her. Just look at her ugly scar!" The boy knew his sister's appearance would turn off many possible adoptive parents.

My friend—who is smart in a low-key way and who made it big-time building a business over the years—reached into his wallet and pulled out two crisp $100 bills. "You kids," he said in a quiet voice, "don't have any money to buy Christmas presents. So I want you to buy some Christmas presents, but there is a catch. You can't buy anything for yourself. Think hard about what your brother or sister might like or need and buy that instead. Write me a letter about what you got each other." That one-minute course in caring outdid the best universities anywhere. The kids made up. In January my friend received a letter about what they bought each other, and he sent a copy to me. The kids got adopted. As I hear it, they're quite a team, and their new parents are proud of them—because of the way that they care for each other.

Teamwork. Teamwork is the starting point for treating people right. Most people think that teamwork is only important when competing against other teams. I don't. Competition is only part of the teamwork picture. In most things we do in life, people have to work together rather than against each other to get something done. So, I think win-win situations and partnerships are the most important part of teamwork. The best teams in the world are the ones that help people become better and achieve more than they ever thought they could on their own, so it's no mystery that teamwork is such a big part of success.

One place people learn teamwork is in families. Children get their first teamwork lesson from the way they watch their parents behave toward each other. If you're a parent, you are also a teacher of teamwork—good or bad—every day. Your offspring learn from what you do.

The people I work with have become my family, too. Throughout my career, these "second families" have taught me a lot about teamwork. For example, on Monday morning August 24, 1992, Hurricane Andrew slammed into South Florida. And yet, all but three of our 21 restaurants in the area were open for business by Friday of that week.

We had employees who lost homes and cars, but nearly all of them came to work. Yes, they were loyal employees, but there's another reason that they came to work. When your life has turned into chaos, people like the stability of a job and being part of a team. This experience drove home the importance of teamwork. A hurricane may rob you of your home, but it can feel good on the dreary, lonely morning after a catastrophe to come home to a team.

Support. Caring is what you give people who can help themselves but who need a partner to open a window or to push aside a roadblock. Support is real help, commitment, and effort. Support is "teamwork plus." Support is also sharing feelings and insights with other people. The best way to get support is to give it. It is amazing what can be done when you treat people with respect.

Support is also easier if things aren't too complicated. The simpler you keep it, the better you can execute it. If you want to give and get support, it's a lot more likely to come and keep coming if the rules are simple and clear than if they're fuzzy and complicated.

We have all heard of "vicious circles," and most of us have been trapped in a few of them. But what if we get the arrow pointed in the other direction and start putting some "virtuous circles" into motion? Think of others and never let them repay you, but ask that they anonymously repay their debt to you to someone else.

Section 5:

Special Cases

Chapter 47

Serving Disabled Customers

**By Frank Navran
and Penny Zibula,
Navran Associates**

You will miss golden opportunities if you fail to serve your disabled customers well.

Physically disabled people are a significant segment of the buying public. One American in six has a physical disability, and many of these 43 million people are part of that fast-growing segment of the population, WOOFs (well-off older folks). As the total population ages, the number of customers with hearing, speech, vision, or mobility limitations continues to grow.

High tech and higher education are giving people with physical disabilities more spending power than ever before. Only a high level of service quality will ensure their repeat business. When disabled people (regardless of age) are not treated with dignity and respect, they are just as capable as anyone else of taking their business elsewhere.

If learning new skills for servicing the disabled seems like an overwhelming task, relax. It isn't. All it takes is a little accurate information and a lot of common sense.

Debunking Three Myths

Myths about disabled customers influence our preconceptions and guide our actions and decisions in the absence of other information. When myths are inaccurate, they lead us to behave in inappropriate, counterproductive, or offensive ways.

Myth One: People with disabilities are incompetent, incapable of making decisions, or just plain stupid. Well-functioning disabled customers are often treated as though they are incompetent. If their ability to function effectively is discounted, their reaction is to feel disrespected or hurt, and that feeling greatly diminishes their enjoyment of a purchasing experience. That hurt is associated with a product or service provider whom they will likely choose to avoid in the future. They become lost customers for those businesses.

The common sense alternative to this myth is to address the disabled customer as you would any other customer in similar circumstances. If the disabled customer is truly incompetent, you will know by the responses. As a service provider, you risk less by assuming the disabled customer can perform effectively than by assuming they cannot. Trust them to ask for additional help, or allow their companion to act on their behalf, as needed. It is presumptuous and insulting for you to assume otherwise.

Myth Two: People with disabilities are oversensitive, and so I have to watch everything I say and do around them. Often when a person fails to acknowledge and confront a customer's disability, it results in decisions or actions that make matters worse. The disabled customer feels less cared for and respected than if their disability were acknowledged and dealt with. It is more offensive to many disabled people to have their reality ignored or have someone walking on eggs to avoid offending them than it is to have their reality dealt with directly, with dignity and care.

Service people often confess to being confused about if and when they should help a disabled customer. What is the right answer?

In dealing with any customer, no more or less so with a disabled customer, the first rule of quality service is, "Be yourself." By being comfortable yourself, you help make the customer you are serving more comfortable. We often work with organizations where respect for customers or employees is cited as a key corporate value. Invariably, when these clients articulate the behaviors that communicate such respect, the single most respectful behavior they identify is listening.

The second rule of quality service is, "Listen to your customers." Listen carefully to the customer's choice of language. Take their lead. Use their preferred references and/or euphemisms in conversations—if you can do so comfortably. Again that rule applies equally to able bodied and disabled customers. If a customer refers to a product or service in a particular way, you communicate a degree of respect for that customer (showing that you have listened and that their word usage is appropriate) by using that same language rather than imposing your jargon on the customer. Of course, when the customer's language is imprecise and ambiguous, you should ask questions to clarify the language and/or educate the customer. If you "reach out and touch" an unsuspecting blind person you may receive an unexpected rebuff to your advance.

The third rule is, "When in doubt, ask." You can respectfully ask a customer how you might be helpful. You do it all the time. Simple phrases like, "How may I help you?" "Would you like me to get that for you?" "What else might I do for you?" give your disabled customer an easy opening to ask for whatever help they require or to politely decline help if they so choose. It is the opportunity to accept or reject assistance that empowers the customer. Unsolicited help can be resented if it is interpreted as a reaction to perceived incompetence. Offering assistance lets the customer decide what is required. An offer to help clearly communicates that while help is available, it is the customer's option to determine if that help is required.

At some level those of us who serve others eventually realize that all we can do is the best we can do. If our best-faith effort does not satisfy the idiosyncratic needs of an individual customer, it might just be their problem, not ours. Of course not every customer, disabled or able-bodied, is as polite, friendly, and courteous as you are trained to be.

Myth Three: People with disabilities are more courteous, honest, appreciative, or trustworthy than able-bodied people. There are disabled people who will use their disability to their advantage. They will make unreasonable demands, insist on preferential treatment, and generally prey on the sensitivities and guilt of their able-bodied servers. Your disabled customers are very much like your able-bodied customers in this respect. Most are honorable and fair. Some are looking for any advantage. Those who are seeking an advantage are not above using their disabilities to gain the upper hand in a simple business transaction.

So what do you do if you are in the service role and a disabled customer tries to gain the edge by misusing their disability? First of all, you do not have to take it. Lying, cheating, stealing, or verbal abuse are not more acceptable because the liar, cheat, thief, or abuser has a physical handicap. Neither does that handicap entitle you to treat the person more harshly than you would an able-bodied liar or thief.

We recommend that you apply the same standards of courtesy and consideration regardless of the physical condition of the customer. If normal policy is to confront a shoplifter and threaten them with a report to the police, then apply it equally. If you routinely call security when a customer gets obnoxious or disorderly, then do so consistently. The exception is if the handicapped person is making a best-faith effort to function appropriately and their disability is hampering that effort.

Maintaining a Polite Distance

In addition to their physical burdens, many of your disabled customers must cope with a social burden as well. Many people assume that a person's physical disability is an invitation to intimacy. Your handicapped customers often resent those curious (even if well-intended) inquiries and intrusions into their personal lives. They resent that you and others expect them to answer questions of a personal nature that one would not think to ask an able-bodied stranger.

As a representative of your organization, you risk alienating a disabled customer by assuming that their disability entitles you to a degree of intimacy that the customer might find offensive.

The most appropriate position you can take as a service provider is to be open, friendly, and courteous. Be respectful, listen to your customers, and take their lead. Only be as intimate as they indicate is comfortable for them. If the rule of business in your case is to call customers Mr. or Ms., you are not entitled to call your disabled customers by their given names, unless invited to do so. Let your customers set the tone. Give your customers the power to control the degree of intimacy in their transactions. If you are uncertain, it is better to err on the conservative side. To paraphrase an old saw, when dealing with (disabled) customers, overfamiliarity breeds contempt.

Meeting Customer Expectations

When a customer enters your place of business, or contacts you by phone, fax, or mail, they are engaging in a business transaction. They are looking to engage in an exchange of consideration; your product or service for their money.

It is in your best interest and theirs for that transaction to be prompt, efficient, and courteous. It is in your best interest for it to result in that customer feeling disposed to continue to do business with you on an ongoing basis and to recommend you, your products, and/or services to others.

Fundamental to a customer's level of satisfaction with a given transaction is the degree to which their positive service expectations are met and/or exceeded. If a customer feels entitled to treatment that is polite, courteous, friendly, and respectful, their expectations will reflect that feeling.

Many disabled customers have grown resentfully accustomed to less-than-polite, friendly, courteous, and respectful treatment in the service they receive. They have been victimized by service people who fall prey to their own ignorance concerning the most effective way to serve those whose physical disabilities mark them as different.

If and when these customers encounter polite, friendly, courteous, and respectful service (especially where their experience has prepared them to expect less), you can win a customer for life. You can earn the loyalty of a customer whose pocket or purse contains cash, checks, and credit cards, and whose money spends just as well as that earned by their able-bodied counterparts.

Chapter 48

Angry Customers

By Albert J. Bernstein,
author, *Dinosaur Brains*
and *Neanderthals at Work*

*Y*our goal with the ordinary angry customer is to move him or her from anger to problem solving quickly and effectively.

The "ordinary" angry customer is not very ordinary, in the sense of usual, normal, or everyday. The angry customer has a reason to be angry. Both you and the customer know what the reason is, but you may disagree as to the validity of the complaint and as to whose fault it is.

The most destructive thing that happens to people confronting angry customers is the blanking out of mental faculties. They don't think about the effect of what they say might be, and they come back with a preprogrammed response (fighting back or running away) to anger, and this usually makes the situation worse.

The secret to handling angry customers is thinking about what you will do before you do it. There is no need to believe that you have to respond immediately or answer every question as soon as it is asked. If you say, for example, "Wait a minute, I'd like to think about this," not only are you modeling the behavior you want from the customer, you are also demonstrating that you are taking the situation seriously. You are apt to handle the situation better if you are thinking and not merely responding.

Best and Worst

I have discovered four things that will only make customers angrier: fighting back, running away, explaining, and operating with mixed goals. Both fighting back and running away will tap into the customer's preprogrammed response to anger and augment it. If you fight back, the customer will fight harder. If you begin to back down or run away, the customer will notice and press the advantage with a stronger effort.

What about explaining? The purpose of explaining is to acquaint the customer with your understanding of the situation. In most cases, it is of little interest to the customer how or why the problem occurred. He or she only wants it corrected. Explanations, at best, serve your needs over those of the customer. At worst, explaining is far too often a disguised form of fighting back and running away. Explaining can be helpful, but the dangers of making the situation worse far outweigh the possible benefits.

Having mixed goals doesn't work either: you can't "get the customer back" and calm him or her down at the same time. When dealing with angry customers, you need to calm them as quickly as possible so that they can solve the problem rationally. If at any time you give in to the impulse to add a little dig of your own, you can be sure that the customer will respond to that. You must forget about sarcastic counterattacking. Avoid acerbic or sharp comments, no matter how adept or appropriate.

What does work? I suggest you try the following five techniques with angry customers.

1. *Make a process request coupled with your intention to help* ("Please talk more slowly; I can help you better if I know what the problem is"). If the customer is yelling, you must stop the yelling before you do anything else. A customer who is yelling will not listen to you and process what you are saying. I recommend using the words "Please speak more slowly" because they are less apt to be resisted by the customer than requests like "Please don't yell" because the customer, in order to comply with the request not to yell, must make the tacit admission that he or she is in fact yelling. Yelling is considered inappropriate or wrong by most people, and so the customer may feel that he or she loses face by complying with a request not to yell.

So, ask them to speak more slowly. Rapid speech and yelling tend to occur together. If the customer slows down his or her rate of speech, this will almost automatically lower the volume as well. When making this process request, it helps to lower your own voice level, and perhaps gesture with your hands. Making process requests is so effective because the customer does not expect it—and so it makes him or her stop and think.

2. *If the customer starts yelling again, make another process request.* When a customer is yelling, you can assume that he or she will not process information well. Sometimes it takes several requests for a customer to calm down and listen. However many requests it takes, it is still the best idea to ask the customer to stop yelling or to speak more slowly rather than trying to solve the problem while the customer is still yelling. If you do anything other than ask a customer who is yelling to stop yelling, you run the risk of rewarding him or her for inappropriate behavior; and also, you run the risk of having anything you might say distorted to fit the angry customer's perception of the world.

3. *Validate the person and/or the problem.* When customers lower the volume of their speech, reward them through validation, making them feel that they have been heard and their feelings are respected. Validation is achieved by first acknowledging the existence of a problem, paraphrasing the customer's statement of the problem, giving verbal permission for the customer to feel whatever he or she is feeling ("I can see how you would be upset about that"), and making a verbal statement of your own concern with the customer's feelings ("I'm sorry you feel that way").

4. *Ask the customer what he or she would like you to do.* This question is usually not expected by the customer and will often cause him or her to stop and think. The emphasis in the sentence, "What would you like me to do?" should definitely be on the words "like" or "do" and not on the word "me." Once the customer answers the question, "What would you like me to do?" you are at the threshold of negotiation. The customer has been effectively moved from anger to problem solving.

5. *Now present alternatives and, if you must, explanations.* Only after you have completed the early steps will the customer evaluate your alternatives and explanations. Bringing them up earlier would only be a waste of time.

Chapter 49

Excess Service

By Emil Bohn, Executive Vice President,
and W. A. Adams, President and CEO,
Maxcomm Associates, Inc.

*T*he law of reciprocity governs relations between suppliers and customers; service excess works against both.

Imagine a family in which the children could do anything they wanted, anytime they wanted, and mom and dad would continue to love, nurture, and support them. Imagine a company where the employees could show up any time they wanted and work at their leisure, and the company would continue to pay and promote them. Imagine a religion where the "faithful" could believe and practice anything they wanted, and the church would continue to embrace them. Initially, it might be fun, but eventually, the children, the employees, and the faithful would lose respect for their parents, their company, and their church.

Relationships demand reciprocity. Both parties must know and meet each other's needs and expectations so there is balance in the relationship. When it is one-way, the relationship simply doesn't work. Without reciprocity, one party soon loses respect, and the other gets resentful.

Customer-Supplier Relationships

Many customers and suppliers are locked into relationships that are neither productive nor satisfying. This is true for both internal customers and their suppliers and external customers and their suppliers. In some cases, the suppliers are doing all the giving and the customers all the taking. In other cases, the roles are reversed—the customer gives and gives, and the supplier takes and takes. Either way, the relationship frustrates both parties and yields few long-term results.

For example, once a month for one year, a local store sent their loyal customers a box full of the latest fashions to try on as a special service. At first, customers welcomed the convenience. As time passed, however, more of their purchases were out of obligation. Many sent the boxes back without even opening them.

Yes, customer service can be excessive. As more is written about exceeding customer expectations, more companies jump on the bandwagon and spare no expense in acquiring and keeping customers. Few companies bother to assess their customer's true needs and expectations. They assume they know, or they adopt a strategy of out-doing the competition. A customer service feeding frenzy ensues, but the frenzy eventually ends in frustration as conspicuous consumption dies out or as companies cut back on lavish and extravagant service.

Customers are no longer willing or able to spend the money for non-value-added service. They want quality and value. Suppliers are trying to figure out how to cut back service without alienating long-time customers accustomed to getting everything they ask for and then some. At the same time, they need to remain competitive in attracting new customers.

The key to developing a satisfying customer-supplier relationship is aligning customer needs and expectations with supplier capabilities. This requires an honest assessment of the sustainable capabilities of the supplier. A supplier may provide an unmatched level of service as a one-time offer or for a short time, but if the supplier can't sustain it, such service may do more harm than good.

Begin that assessment by looking at the corporate mission and values. The mission statement should clearly state what business you are in and concisely lay out the business strategies you intend to use. If either of these is missing, employees will be confused, and their confusion will negatively impact the customer. For example, the employees of one company saw the skiing public as an imposition on "their" private mountain. As a result, the guests were often treated more like trespassers than paying customers. Not until the resort clearly stated that their purpose was to cater to the desires of the customers did service improve.

Corporate values articulate the ethical code of conduct. They state how employees will treat each other and how they will treat customers. If value statements are vague or are not modeled by leadership, customers will be negatively impacted. And if management does not allow frontline employees to make decisions on their own, customer requests outside corporate policy won't be met.

Assess employees' willingness and ability to provide service in alignment with customer needs and expectations and corporate mission and values. Some employees may know what service the company wants to offer customers to meet their needs and expectations, but they can't provide it because they lack the skills to carry out their jobs. Other employees have the skills, but they choose to treat customers inappropriately.

Don't design and implement a customer service strategy around assumptions based on previous knowledge and experience with the customers. And don't rely on customer service surveys and market research to learn what customers think, need, and expect.

Meeting with customers face-to-face provides a better way to determine their needs and expectations. When meeting with customers, ask them: 1) What do you need from me? 2) What do you do with what I give you? 3) Are there any gaps between what I give you and what you need? and 4) Are you getting anything from me that you don't need?

To align customers and suppliers, the assessment of supplier capabilities and customer needs and expectations must be ongoing. Internal and external assessment needs to become the way we do business. And, once we have the information, we need to act on it.

Change Masters or Avoiders

Acting on new information and data is not automatic because few leaders and employees actively seek change; in fact, they tend to look for support in doing the same thing in the same way. Over time, they become change avoiders, and their organizations become closed systems.

A closed system leads to non-adaptive cultures characterized by bureaucracy; reactive, risk-averse employees; restricted flow of information; and an emphasis on control that dampens motivation and enthusiasm. Such cultures increasingly become impervious to feedback, customer input, employee suggestions, and new ideas. Leaders then tell each another what a wonderful job they are doing and then dictate what should be done and how it should be carried out. Reward and recognition systems reinforce the old way of doing things, killing incentive for employees to change anything.

Such organizations are operations-driven; they make it easy on themselves to do business and are slow to respond to changing customer needs and expectations. They only react to major changes in the market that force them to pay attention and change. They don't anticipate change, and they can't create a demand for their products and services.

Change master companies make it a priority to gather, analyze, and act on a continuous stream of internal and external information. This strategy becomes a competitive advantage as they not only anticipate market changes but also create needs and then fill them with their own products and services. These companies are constantly fine-tuning their internal capabilities and continually assessing customer needs and expectations.

Such companies have "adaptive" cultures built on high trust, a proactive approach to life, and open systems. A constant stream of information and data flow in, and leaders use this information to interrupt, confront, and challenge thinking about the market, internal capabilities, current modes of operation, and customers' needs and expectations.

The next step is doing whatever is necessary to stay ahead of the competition. One way is to clearly articulate a compelling, desired future state in the form of a vision, statement of purpose, mission, or core values. This process begins with the leadership team and then involves all other members to enlist ownership of and commitment to the desired state.

Once a compelling future is articulated, some "unfreezing" is required. Unfreezing is about telling the truth, letting go, and moving on to something better. People need to know which attitudes, behaviors, and practices are not in alignment with the desired state. They then need to abandon attitudes, behaviors, and practices that no longer serve them, the organization, or the customer—and commit to new behaviors to move forward.

Replication is about getting employees to try out the new, long enough to replace the old. This requires ongoing reinforcement, coaching, and modeling by leaders. If they do not set the new standard by example, everyone else has an excuse for not changing. Systems and procedures also need to reinforce the new attitudes, behaviors, and practices. Finally, we may need to restructure the organization. Anything that restricts the natural flow of goods and services to the end customer consumes huge amounts of unnecessary time, energy, and resources.

Customer-driven companies make it easy for people to do business with them. They try to align their capabilities with customer needs and expectations. Adaptive cultures out-perform non-adaptive cultures by huge margins in revenues, growth of the workforce, growth in stock prices, and net income.

Suppliers must communicate what services they can provide and what responsibilities the customer has. For customers who are used to getting what they want and demanding more services, this may come as a shock: the customer is not always right! Customers who violate corporate values should become non-customers. Either the rules and values apply to everyone, customers included, or they become a joke. Leaders can't allow the integrity of the operation to be violated by the behavior of a few.

The days of customer service excess are over. But, customer service remains the competitive advantage for those companies willing to assess their customers' needs and expectations, assess their internal capabilities, and then bring the two into alignment based on corporate values, goals, and objectives.

Chapter 50

Responsiveness: One Size Does Not Fit All

**By Karl Albrecht, Chairman,
Karl Albrecht & Associates**

*M*any service organizations talk a good game about responsiveness to their customers, but far too many are unwilling to go to any real lengths to make it happen.

Real customer responsiveness is a highly developed art form. Is a service business being customer responsive when it forces you to sit through an agonizing "voice menu" every time you place a telephone call? It may be a case of false efficiency to cut costs at this all-critical moment of truth when the customer first contacts the business.

But speed is only one factor in responsiveness. Sometimes "fast" is best, but sometimes fast is not good at all. Sometimes "just in time" or "just on time" is best. There's no "one size fits all" when it comes to making a service responsive to the customer's values.

When Fast Is Best

Probably the quintessential example of fast is best is in the fast-food business. In a consumer society, a response time of 60 to 90 seconds represents high performance. Americans are such spoiled consumers that a wait of two minutes for a hamburger seems like an atrocity. Yet a McDonald's customer in Moscow thinks a wait of two hours is reasonable in view of the total value he or she perceives in the experience.

If the customer only has 15 minutes for lunch, fast is critically important. On the other hand, a total fine-dining experience in a quality restaurant might take two hours or more and still be comfortable for the couple or group that wants to relax and chat.

When Fast Is Not Best

One morning I called room service in my hotel and ordered breakfast. When I asked the person taking the order how long it would take for the food to arrive, she gave me an estimate of 25 minutes. For me, that was perfectly suitable, because it allowed me enough time for a shower and shave. I could enjoy breakfast and still be out the door in good time.

However, about 10 minutes after I had placed the call, I was in the shower when there was a knock at the door. The delivery person had arrived with my breakfast. I was soaking wet and faced with an interesting trade-off. I could either finish the shower and let breakfast get cold, or I could eat breakfast right away while still wet with a robe wrapped around me. Under those circumstances, fast was not good for me. Yes, they had exceeded the promised delivery speed, but that created no additional value. For me, the value was "when promised."

George Bernard Shaw noted that the "golden rule" may not be precise enough to serve as a quality guide. "Do not do unto others as you would have them do unto you," he cautioned. "Their tastes may not be the same."

Value the Customer's Time

Some businesses misuse and abuse the customer's time. Some have so little regard for the customer's time that they take for granted that waiting is satisfactory. Hospitals, clinics, and doctor's offices, for example, are notorious for their cavalier attitude about their customers' time. They consider the time of the medical professionals as valuable, not to be wasted, but they assign no intrinsic value to the customer's time. After all, consider the very name they give to the customer: the patient. Just think of the connotations, and you see how the mindset operates.

An associate of mine reports on the operation of a medical clinic in Kochi, Japan, that is designed from end to end to make the most efficient use of its customers' time. Kochi Medical Center manages to get almost all of its patients through their outpatient treatments or tests and on their way within a two-hour period. The people there have designed the flow and sequence of activities for time efficiency, and have integrated a total information system that enables them to manage the customer's experience without wasting his or her time.

We are entering a new age of customer performance that will make unprecedented demands on all of us to invent ways to individualize our customer value packages. Phrases like "mass customization" and "a segment of one" are beginning to take on real meaning as terms of art. We've got to win customers one by one, and hold on to them the same way.

Chapter 51

Retaining Your Most Profitable Customers

**By Richard R. Shapiro,
President, M. J. Rich Associates**

*T*he key to increasing your profits is retaining your best customers. Let them tell you how by asking the right questions.

In response to competition, customer demands, and the need to reduce costs and increase profits, executives are launching many initiatives designed to gain or retain market share. Unfortunately, these programs rarely focus on retaining their best customers who supply the bulk of their profits. The costs of bringing in new customers are high, and the sales cycle is long. By targeting key customers, you will more likely achieve your profit objectives.

A proactive program to retain key customers 1) meets or exceeds customer expectations through an effective measurement and communication program; 2) improves service delivery based on in-depth and direct customer feedback; and 3) builds strong customer relationships by involving employees directly in developing performance improvement plans that turn dissatisfied users into satisfied customers, tell customers that they are being heard, and thank customers.

Customer Life Cycle

Four stages make up the customer cycle.

Stage 1. Everyone is excited about sales landing a new account. The customer is impressed with all the attention from sales and senior management. Customers are told that their business is appreciated and that their needs will be given constant attention until they become familiar with the services.

Stage 2. The original sales person or sales team is now focusing on winning other new accounts. The initial excitement is gone. Sales commissions are reduced. The account management function takes over. The customer feels comfortable with using the services and seems satisfied with the buying decision.

Stage 3. With turnover inside both customer and supplier companies, everyone forgets the time and effort that went into winning the account. The customer requires less attention and has become more profitable. Original parties to the buying decision have changed, and the supplier is communicating only with the user. The competition is reaching the customer, informing them of newer technologies, better approaches, or more cost-effective ways of providing services.

Stage 4. The customer decides to review their suppliers. The customer now wants even more effective communication, stronger partnerships, and key contacts within supplier companies. The supplier must now resell their "own" customers on why they should continue to buy services from them and not use someone else.

The most important question in the customer life cycle is: At what stage are your customers?

Customer Retention Programs

Retention programs are frequently reactive, emphasizing "fire fighting" rather than "fire prevention" and featuring measures to "save" customers after they threaten to end the relationship. Sales and service people are given incentives to recapture business only after it has left, not to retain current business.

Most retention programs are merely "stop gap" measures, rarely resulting in long-term results. When one customer problem is resolved, management moves on to the next, never analyzing situations to ensure they do not happen again.

Senior managers may be required to visit key customers, but these "key account programs" are seldom effective because managers are not trained in interviewing, communications, or interpersonal skills. They seldom know what questions to ask or what to do with the information they receive. And so future customer visits become rare, leaving the customer with unmet expectations.

Few executives place enough emphasis on servicing new customers. First-year attrition rates are often double those of older accounts. By doing extensive "exit" interviews, we learned that early attrition occurs for four reasons: 1) if a problem develops during the first few months, customers assume these situations will occur frequently and feel buyer's remorse; 2) the original sales person doesn't speak with customers regularly; 3) an account management or customer service function is not set up with the customer; and 4) the customer still does some business with a former supplier, making it easy to return to them.

Organizations are more vulnerable to competition if they fail to track when original decision makers leave and new ones take over. In fact, service organizations rarely communicate with decision makers. They end up talking with users or technical buyers. Even if these individuals were involved in the purchasing cycle, they are not responsible for retaining an organization as a supplier.

And then, there are "imaginary" customers, who still appear on the billing files as active accounts, but who decided months ago to stop using an organization as a supplier. Nobody wants to admit that these customers have left.

Customers start purchasing less from you for one of three reasons: 1) the customers' business has been reduced, and so they need fewer services; 2) they have decided to provide the service in-house; and 3) they have gone to the competition because they are not satisfied with the quality of your services, communication, technology, cost, etc. These situations afford chances not only to gain back market share, but also to obtain an even larger share of the customer's business. But this will only happen if the company can turn unhappy users into satisfied customers.

Customer Feedback

Customer satisfaction surveys may be effective in measuring overall satisfaction, but don't send your best customers a "standard" mail-in survey. Often they will not take the time to complete the survey. Even if they do, key customer contacts frequently delegate the survey to people who are not decision makers. Moreover, a mail-in survey sent to your best customers may send the unintended message that the customer is not important because of the impersonal nature of the instrument. And by the time the surveys have been tabulated, they rarely provide the timely or detailed information needed to develop an effective performance improvement strategy.

The best sources to articulate expectations and make recommendations to increase customer satisfaction are your best customers. Take better advantage of these relationships. Know what your most profitable customers expect in the way of communications, both written and verbal skills, and technical abilities from each person they interface with. This information provides the basis for a detailed customer satisfaction measurement system that can be implemented through either in-person or phone interviews. Determining customer expectations will provide you with "job descriptions." Your employees will know exactly what is expected of them by their customers. When you focus on delivering service excellence to your most profitable customers, all your customers will benefit.

Quality improvement teams often work in a vacuum, reviewing reports generated from internal data or analyzing outdated and summary information from customer satisfaction surveys.

When some members of the quality improvement team are involved in collecting detailed feedback through direct communication with customers, the entire team becomes more effective. The information tends to be more accurate and up-to-date. The most profitable customers often provide recommendations that offer the best solutions. Members of the team are more motivated to develop performance improvement strategies. Managers hear directly from the customers what works well and what needs improvement. The people responsible for the work can ask detailed questions about what needs to be improved. And customers feel that they are appreciated.

Before you ask your people to communicate directly with your most profitable customers, train them and supply them with the right questions to ask customers in interviews to receive valuable information for creating strong customer partnerships. Involve managers in sales, service, and other key areas in gathering direct customer feedback. This provides them with useful information and helps them build better relationships with customers. Coordinate the effort internally to avoid duplication of effort and customer confusion.

After the Sale

Typically, several people are involved in the final decision to purchase services. These professionals form a "buying center" that includes the user of the service: the person who determines the specifications; the person who selects the vendor; the decision maker who has final authority for vendor selection and terms; and the gatekeeper who controls the information into the buying center.

Most organizations fail to develop or maintain their relationship with the initial members of the buying center, leaving themselves vulnerable to competition. This occurs because sales and service personnel and even senior management often end up dealing with the day-to-day users in a customer's organization, not the decision makers. The chances of this occurring increases the longer a company has a customer. When relationships are built with users—not decision makers—employees feel uncomfortable approaching senior managers within the customer's organization. They feel insecure approaching people they don't know well. When you fail to communicate with the members of the buying center regularly, you see high levels of customer attention.

Direct communication with decision makers increases retention of your profitable accounts and creates chances to "cross sell" additional services. Collect direct feedback through a process that 1) provides sales or service reps with a legitimate reason to review with the decision maker how well their needs are being met; 2) collects information using a set of questions and makes it easier to analyze the information gathered; and 3) enhances communication between the customer and the company reps.

When you effectively communicate with key customers and ask the right questions, you improve your chances of discovering dissatisfied users and turning them into satisfied customers. A formal process shows concern and interest for customer input, provides a chance to communicate improvements, explain new policies or procedures, and express appreciation for a customer's business.

Most customers simply want service providers to deliver on what they promise and not to take their business for granted. Rarely do customers hear the words, "Thank you" and "We appreciate your business," except perhaps in form letters addressed "Dear Valued Customer." Sending your best customers these letters may be worse than not sending any communication at all. If a customer is worth having, all written communication should be personalized.

Having a customer database that contains an updated address, correct spelling, and current title is essential. And even more important is periodically saying "thank you" in person. When you collect direct customer feedback, you have many chances to thank customers.

Chapter 52

Service Recovery

**By Ron Zemke, President,
Performance Research Associates, Inc.**

You need every customer you have. And you'll need them tomorrow as well, if you intend to be in business for long.

Good friends of ours recently celebrated their 25th anniversary. We called to congratulate them, and to check on the flowers we'd ordered for their big party. To our chagrin, what arrived was not what we envisioned—it was, instead, a puny potted plant.

It was after 6 p.m., and their party was set for 7:30. We caught our neighborhood florist on his way out the door, and explained the situation. "Don't say another word," he advised, "I'll fix this right now." At 7:10 p.m., our friends called to tell us that a truck has just delivered two magnificent arrangements and a center piece for their buffet table.

Did I mention that our friends live in North Carolina, and we—and our florist—live in Minneapolis, one time zone away?

When the bill arrived, it was for the cost of our original order only and was hand delivered by the florist with a small flower arrangement, an apology, and assurance it would not happen again.

The true test of a company's commitment to service quality isn't in the pledge it makes in its literature; it's in the way the company responds when things go wrong for the customer.

Customers who complain and have their complaint satisfied are more likely to purchase additional products than are customers who have experienced no problems with the organization or its products and services. When it comes to service recovery—solving customers' problems—the message is very clear: "Do it right the first time. If you don't, be sure you do it right the second time."

The impact of poor recovery goes far beyond the loss of a single customer. Only 4 to 10 percent of dissatisfied customers even give you a chance to make things right. Most disappointed customers would rather switch than fight. But they will bad-mouth you to every one who mentions your company within ear shot. And if one of those few who do complain to you is dismissed with some perfunctory line such as "I can't help you—that's our policy," the spurned complainer often will set out with an almost religious zeal to assassinate your character.

Customer Expectations

What do customers want you to do after you've done something wrong? When you fail to meet their expectations? When you break a promise to them? What do they think ought to happen then?

Customers expect five things when problems arise.

1. To receive an apology. An apology goes a long way toward calming an aggravated customer. And though a simple apology costs nothing to deliver, the customer is likely to get one in only 48 percent of the cases where there is a problem with a product or service. The two most frequently remembered elements of a positive recovery experience are "they acknowledged and dealt with my upset" (79 percent), and "They apologized for my inconvenience" (69 percent).

An apology is most powerful when delivered in person. A corporate form letter lacks the sincerity and authenticity of a personal, verbal acknowledgment. A sincere, "I'm sorry for any inconvenience this late arrival may have caused you" suggests that the pilot or lead cabin attendant is taking a personal, professional interest in the situation.

2. To be offered a "fair fix" for the problem. The typical customer does not expect a pound of flesh for every snafu. Most customers bring a sense of fair play to the table when service breakdowns occur. If the service provider offers a rational explanation, and demonstrates sensitivity and concern, the customer will respond in kind.

It's revealing to ask customers what they think a fair fix might be for a problem. When we asked telephone subscribers what they expected from the phone company when service failures occurred, we found that they made a clear distinction between a service failure that happened on a weekend and one that occurred on a weekday. They figured that phone company employees like to spend weekends with their families, as do the customers themselves. One caution: every situation has special handling potential. A teenage telephone user reporting a problem with the family's second line, the one in his/her bedroom, can have recovery expectations dramatically different from those of a 75-year-old shut in with a heart condition.

3. To be treated in a way that suggests the company cares about the problem, about fixing the problem, and about the customer's inconvenience. Customers experience every service as both an outcome and a process. Outcome is the culmination of getting a service need met: the customer got the loan, the car was properly repaired, the meal tasted great, the right blend of coffee was ground and packaged. Process is what the customer experiences while the need is being met: the waiting time, the paperwork, the courtesy of the salesperson, and so on.

Likewise, service recovery involves an outcome and a process. The outcome is the solution the customer finds satisfactory. Often, however, the process is equally important to the customer's satisfaction. Customers generally do not expect service providers to be perfect (doctors, nurses, and dentists are exceptions here), but they do expect providers to care about the work they are doing and the customer's satisfaction with it. How that care is demonstrated during the recovery process separates the service-recovery stars from the also-rans.

4. To be offered some value-added atonement for their inconvenience. Atonement is not necessary for every breakdown. However, if the customer has been "injured" in the process—if she feels victimized, greatly inconvenienced, or somehow demeaned by the problem—then atonement becomes critical.

Atonement is a gesture that says, "We want to make it up to you." Atonement can take the form of "The next one will be on us" or "Please accept a free drink," or "Naturally, we'll tear up the bill." It's a demonstration of goodwill.

And though it may cost the organization real money, the act of atonement is essentially symbolic. Little things, sincerely done, mean a lot to the customer. Customers do not expect you to shoot the franchisee or give them a free family vacation trip to Walt Disney World for keeping them waiting in the reception area an extra 10 minutes.

There are times, however, when a custom-tailored or highly aggressive act of atonement might be necessary to keep the customer. And there are times when a determined, proactive effort can really "wow" the customer. When L. L. Bean Co. learned that a sport shirt it was selling had a tendency to fray at the collar after only a few washings, the catalog retailer sent letters to every customer who had purchased the shirt, explaining the problem and urging that the shirts be returned. The letter went on to say that should the customer find it inconvenient to return the shirt, the Bean customer service unit would be pleased to arrange a personal pick up.

5. Keep your promises. Make sure customers can rely on your organization to deliver what it promises. If a flight will be 90 minutes late, but the airline announces a 15 minute delay—and then another and another—it has proven unreliable. Customers would rather be given bad news than be lied to.

The Hidden Factor

The hidden factor in making service recovery work is the spirit in which the recovery is carried out. A customer who has to threaten and cajole to get reparation from you doesn't walk away feeling good about you or about herself. That's a customer who sees you and the incident as yet more proof of the way life is in the commercial jungle—only the meanest animals survive. Not living up to that expectation, making it easy and even pleasant to have a problem solved, is what impresses the customer. At Hardee's they tell frontline employees "Don't Fight, Make It Right." It's an important rule for making your service recovery memorable and noteworthy.

Today, shrugging your shoulders and accepting errors and mess ups as inevitable, is an unacceptable risk. Solving customer problems adroitly is more than a strategy or a set of skills. It is a way of life. It is part of the culture of organizations that serve customers well.

Chapter 53

Customers for Life

**By Lynda R. Paulson,
President of Success Strategies, Inc.**

To keep me as your customer, greet me every time; treat me special sometimes; and never complain, explain, or be a pain.

In one week, I became a lifelong customer of one business and I walked out of another business forever. These personal experiences of customer service are examples of why some companies thrive and others dive.

The horror story. Looking into the mirror at my formerly auburn hair, I wondered if the large audience I was scheduled to address the next day would notice the three dazzling colors on my head—light red, dark red, and an electric shade of purple. Somehow my $100-a-pop-plus-tip beauty salon in San Francisco had turned me out with a badly done color job.

So I arranged another appointment with Mimi, the colorist, at the salon, which is an hour's drive from my home. In discussing my tri-colors, Mimi became defensive and informed me that I "didn't understand hair" and that the purple didn't look that purple to her. This really rubbed me the wrong way.

I was left sitting like a little kid while she fussed over another customer. By now, I was angry, embarrassed, and feeling intimidated. When Mimi began her work on my hair, I was scared. What would she do next? Could I trust her?

Well, my hair turned out okay. But, why was I, the customer, made to feel wrong? Why was I the one suffering from embarrassment and discomfort?

Mimi's assistant told me, "Mimi never makes mistakes." I admire anyone at the top of her trade. However, we all make mistakes, and we only compound them when we won't admit them.

The hat trick. A few days later, I experienced the ultimate hat trick. Wearing a great new hat (to cover my hair), I attended a wine-tasting event. My enthusiastic friend waved his glass in my direction and knocked off my hat, drenching it with red wine. It was ruined, or so I thought.

After the wine tasting, I took my hat to several cleaners. None would try to clean it. I thought of Greene's, a local cleaners that had sent me a card when I stopped taking them my clothing. I went to Greene's with my hat. They took the hat and cleaned it beautifully—at no charge!

I asked, "Why no charge?" and the owner, Pete Smith said, "Because we want you for a customer, and we'll do just about anything to keep you." The freebie made me feel like someone special.

Pete's staff are unfailingly cheerful and friendly, no matter how busy and no matter what I ask them to do. Besides, they call me by name. I love it.

Greene's is it for me forever. And the beauty salon? I'll never go back.

Freebies won't get customers for life, but creating good feelings will. Make your customers feel good, and they'll come back. People want to believe that you care about them. Empathy works; personal attention works; extra effort works.

Your customers will never return if you intimidate or ignore them. If you're defensive and angry, your customer feels uncomfortable and embarrassed—too embarrassed to come back.

Research shows that 74 percent of all shoppers will buy something at the first store they go into if they are just treated right. Shoppers may forget what they purchase, but they do remember how they were treated, how they were made to feel. Nordstrom manager Peter Devin tells me that his salespeople like to "shock customers with how far we will go to please them." And, The Limited chain of sportswear stores promises, "No sale is ever final."

More than price, more than location, more than merchandise, people buy your products and use your services because it makes them feel good to do so.

Chapter 54

Invisible Customers

By Mark J. Warner,
Assistant Professor of Health Services,
James Madison University

*N*o one needs our service more than our invisible customers—employees who are taken for granted. Unfortunately, if they are not satisfied with the service they are getting, they have fewer options than their external counterparts who can vote with their feet, meaning they can go get their services elsewhere. Invisible customers often don't have this luxury; however, they may express their dissatisfaction in other ways. Their morale becomes lower, they become cynical, and productivity drops off. They also "talk down" the organization, which spreads the disease of discontent from department to department.

Progressive leaders realize the potential danger of the invisible customer syndrome, so they focus on the "internal customer." These leaders understand that employees within an organization have been taken for granted and that it is time to recognize them as customers. This heightened awareness acknowledges that employees receive services and focuses attention on improving the services. Morale is improved to an adequate level and productivity is enhanced. Unfortunately though, when employees are labeled "internal customers," the individuals and the organization are limited. In fact, I heard one employee say, "I'm offended to be called a customer in my own organization; we should be much more than that to each other." So it is that we need to advance to the highest level of the customer continuum, which is "partner."

Enlightened leaders create organizations based on partnerships. These organizations have moved beyond the paralyzing boundaries of "invisibility," have stretched the restricting parameters of "internal customer" labels, and embraced the philosophy of partnership power. When partnership philosophies are adopted, the organization evolves into a state of excellence characterized by increased morale and improved productivity and synergy.

Where on the continuum is your organization? How can you move to the "partner" dimension of the continuum?

Stop, Look, Listen, and Grow

To create partnerships, let me suggest that you stop, look, listen, and grow!

Stop. Stop only considering external customers in decision making, evaluating, and goal setting. Assess who all the customers are and identify needs, evaluate satisfaction, and solicit feedback for improvement.

Look. Look for ways to enhance services for colleagues. Look for opportunities to exceed their expectations. Look for chances to collaborate with co-workers to achieve common goals.

Listen. Listen to what fellow employees are saying, both overtly and those important messages between the lines. Listen to the concerns. Listen to the successes. Listen to gather the vital data that can be used to improve services for everyone.

Grow. Grow partnerships by acknowledging that fellow employees are more than colleagues, more than service providers, and more than customers.

By stopping, looking, and listening, we position ourselves to cultivate true partnerships. However, the only way to be successful is to follow through with action. We need to set specific goals and follow-up evaluations regarding "partner growth."

Spirit of Volunteerism

By creating an organization based on partnerships, you move toward productivity, synergy, and service excellence.

Winston Churchill once said, "We make a living by what we get, we make a life by what we give." By translating his words into action, we can make a difference in the lives of those we touch and make the world a better place.

Recently, I saw the name of a sermon to be preached at a country church. The title was, "Service is love in action."

Since we receive from our community every day, we also need to return something to the community. What better way than through volunteering? We need to put our "love into action."

Too often we hide behind the excuse that we don't have time. We need to make time. As volunteers, we not only give of our time and talents, but we give of ourselves. For society to thrive, we need to give unselfishly. Throughout history the major social changes have been brought about through the dedicated work of volunteers.

Volunteers give another very important gift to others, the gift of comfort and strength. Think of a time when you were lonely, depressed, or ill—and someone comforted you. Remember that magic feeling? You were strengthened, given hope that you would make it through that trying period in your life. This is precisely how the people feel that you help.

Great leaders know of the significance of these gifts. The most successful and admired companies encourage their employees to volunteer. Both employee and company benefit.

Volunteering is buttressed by the spirit of generosity. This spirit characterizes the true essence of volunteerism—giving unselfishly to others. Generosity restores our faith in the goodness of people.

As leaders we have to not only create a climate for volunteering, but we have to model gracious acts as well. There is an incredible amount of potential in people, and unleashing it will make a profound difference in our communities.

Service is not a convenience, but a necessary sacrifice which not only enriches the lives of others, but our own lives as well. Service is the life-blood of the soul.

Chapter 55

Customer Candor in Times of Emergency

By Chip R. Bell, Partner,
Performance Research Associates, Inc.

*C*ustomer candor, mixed with five principles of forward-thinking prevention, can save your reputation and your customers in times of genuine emergency.

"One of the surest signs of a bad or declining relationship with a customer is the absence of complaints. Nobody is ever that satisfied, especially over time. The customer is either not being candid or not being contacted." These words of Harvard professor Ted Levitt worried me for days after I first read them! Here I was striving to minimize customer irritation and ire only to hear Levitt tell me that having no complaints was something to be avoided—and that it was my fault for not getting any! I was confused! Weren't we supposed to be seeking zero defects, 100 percent "you-walk-on-water" happy sheets, a perfect ten, five-stars, a hole-in-one?

How can "getting more customer complaints" be a virtue? Can you imagine marching into the division head with the "good news" that complaints were up to 23 percent, and therefore you needed a bigger budget, more personnel, and a larger salary increase?

Then, I had one of those significant emotional experiences with my wife of 25 years. We were attending a weekend retreat—sort of a family enrichment workshop—associated with our son's high school. One assignment was for each of us to list the strengths and limitations of other members of the immediate family.

My wife and I enjoy a very open, honest relationship. And yet, the pace of managing dual, fast-paced professional careers with typical family challenges can work counter to the late-at-night, no-kid-gloves honesty which we desire. Let me tell you, reading one's limitations out loud sobered me and provoked a high level of candor.

I began to appreciate why Levitt compared a quality customer relationship with a marriage. "The sale consummates the courtship at which point the marriage begins. The quality of the marriage depends on how well the seller manages the relationship," wrote Levitt. "The absence of candor reflects the decline of trust and the deterioration of the relationship."

My weekend encounter prompted me to examine other pearls of service wisdom. Customers, like spouses, do not expect us to be perfect; they just expect us to demonstrate that we care. When we demonstrate caring, customers reciprocate by caring enough to offer their suggestions. My wife's listing of my improvement opportunities was not an act of critical judgment, but rather an act of caring and love.

Customer service research directed by John Goodman, president of the TARP Institute in Washington, D.C., has unearthed several findings consistent with Levitt's pronouncement. The average business only receives complaints from about 5 percent of its less-than-satisfied customers. The others are out there wimpishly answering "fine" when restaurant cashiers ask "How was everything?" Customers would rather privately register their disapproval with their feet than to publicly deliver their disdain directly to the front line.

Why aren't customers straight with us? TARP Institute found three major reasons: 1) customers don't know how to register complaints; 2) they believe it won't really do any good; and 3) they fear some retaliation might be levied by the service provider.

Why do service organizations or internal service-providing units avoid assertively soliciting complaints? Perhaps some lull themselves into thinking "no news is good news," or "let sleeping dogs lie." Some fear that if they seek and receive customer complaints and no corrective action ensues, they might be perceived worse than if they had left well enough alone. The research, however, does not support such an assumption. Better to have asked and not acted, than to not have asked at all. Some have not figured out how to effectively ask for complaints without sounding almost masochistic. Some have asked incorrectly, failed to get helpful information, and simply given up asking.

The "better to have loved and lost" orientation is one consistent with solid service wisdom. Those customers who have been directly asked for feedback are much more likely to give that service organization favorable reviews than those who have not. Customers who have had a service problem and had it elegantly corrected are more loyal than those who have never had a problem. Only 9 to 37 percent of irate customers (depending on the dollar value of their problems) who don't complain will return to a service provider if nothing happens after they have been aggrieved. However, if there is a legitimate outlet for their ire, that 30 percent return business jumps to almost 50 percent—without correction of the service problem. Add up all those facts and figures and you get a convincing argument to go out and plead with your customers to "tell us how it really is."

How do you get customers to level with you? My wife skillfully enticed me to deliver a more honest cataloguing of her improvement opportunities. Her approach may offer guidance for soliciting customer candor. When I first attempted to offer candid critique, she thanked me! "That is very helpful," she said, "tell me more about that." Plus, she gave undivided attention during my stammerings. She never once got defensive, even as I got more bold in my critique. She reiterated what she heard to let me know my feedback was understood. She never once tried to "set me straight" by explaining her actions. And, she even occasionally "primed the pump" by putting on the table frustrations she already knew I had. "I know it sometimes bothers you when I . . . What else like that bugs you?"

Here is the best part! She actually changed some of her actions based on my critique! Not everything, mind you! But, certainly enough to let me know that my critique made a difference. So, the next time she queried, "How can I improve?" I was much more assertive and complete in my candor.

Acting on much of what customers suggest shows them not only that you care, but allows them to share more. A primary example of a company putting this into practice is Stew Leonard's Dairy in Norwalk, Connecticut. Stew Leonard's was listed the *Guinness Book of World Records* for having the largest dollar volume per square foot on any retail establishment in the world. "We do it by listening to our customers," Stew explains. "Customers tell us what they don't like . . . and, they tell us because we react to it." This is not to say Stew does exactly what every single customer suggests. But, he acts on much of it. Most of his customers are convinced that Stew values their input—enough convinced to give the store gross receipts of almost $2 million a week.

No customer relationship is likely to be perfect all the time. The healthy customer relationship, like the healthy marriage, is one marked by candor and welcomed critique. Honesty begets more honesty if defensiveness is absent. As the relationship improves, the service provider-to-receiver relationship evolves into a true partnership. And as candor triggers improvement, those who serve feel responsive, those served feel heard, and the partnership feels healthy. "Now, customer, tell me what you really, truly, no-holds-barred, honestly think of our service!"

There are times when you have to provide emergency service to your customers. This is when your candor can really kick in. Customers are more forgiving if you work as hard when things go wrong as you do to make service distinctive in normal times.

As a service management consultant, I am challenged to "practice what I preach." I got an opportunity to do so after Hurricane Hugo struck. I happened to be a hurricane victim! Fortunately, I was not one of those victim's who, after no electricity for two weeks, sported a lapel button which read, "Don't mess with me; I still don't have power!" But, with hours of chain-saw duty required for backyard clean-up, I was "forced" to neglect the close customer encounter I try to practice. Certain clients could hear the strain in my voice as they made unique service requests.

This frustrating emergency situation invited me to be particularly attuned to other service providers who struggled to maintain high service standards in the face of an unexpected, service break down.

I interviewed a few "service winners"—those companies we mention in the same sentence with *service excellence*. I also practiced closer-than-usual observation of "the best" at their worst. They showed their capacity to maintain a reputation for customer pleasure despite the pain of an emergency. There was amazing consistency in their adherence to several principles.

Five Proven Principles

Line or staff executives can face the unexpected "we-never-dreamed-this-would-happen" situation with panic or principle; with frantic hand wringing or forward-thinking wisdom. I recommend the following five principles.

1. When an unexpected service breakdown results in customer disappointment, fix the customer, then the problem. When major snow storm stranded airlines in Richmond, passengers became increasingly irritated as they discovered that they would be remaining overnight in the wrong city and that all nearby hotels were filled to capacity. As gate attendants struggled with the long lines to make early morning flight reservations, Delta Airlines had their grounded flight attendants serve passengers from the stock previously loaded on the now grounded aircraft. Hot coffee, warm blankets, milk for infants, snacks, playing cards, and magazines quickly were transferred from plane to terminal.

Customer research for a major telephone company revealed an intriguing discrepancy between customer expectation and actual practice. When the telephone repair technicians arrived at a residence to restore service, they invariably began their requested repair work by going to the side of the customer's house or up a nearby pole. Yet, customer interviews and surveys strongly indicated a customer expectation ("What ought to happen") that the repair person first knock on the front door to announce his or her presence and intention. "After all," customers said, "the phone company did require me to take the day off to be there for the phone to be repaired." Fix the customer, then fix the customer's service problem.

2. *Make customers your partners rather than end-users—frequent customers can sometimes be made "quasi-employees."* Hugo resulted in an unexpected overload of customers at Myers Park Hardware in Charlotte, North Carolina, as customers "mobbed" to purchase candles, propane gas, camping stoves, flashlight batteries, etc. The store turned to patrons for help. As three frequent customers were recruited by the store manager to assist in bagging merchandise and ringing up sales, the crowd of formerly frustrated customers suddenly broke out in applause. These "volunteers" also registered their pleasure with the scene by offering to give up their "helper" slot to the highest bidder. It became a bit like Tom Sawyer's convincing his skeptical on-lookers that whitewashing the fence was an honor only for the carefully chosen and lucky few!

3. *Be completely honest about the situation and sincerely solicit customer patience.* An American Airlines flight from Dallas to Denver was loaded and ready to depart when airline maintenance noticed that the signal light for the windshield heater was not working properly. The plane had arrived in Dallas from Minneapolis having been forced to fly through a major rain storm. The pilot's explanation for the delay got very technical, as if passengers were all aeronautical engineers. Yet, customers appeared relieved and settled in for a lengthy delay. "I don't know what he said," commented one passenger, "but he sounds like he knows what he's doing."

At moments of service anxiety and instability, customers need demonstrations of confidence and competence from service providers. This is one reason why frontline empowerment is important. Give more details not fewer; data overload (normally a negative) can be a boon to bolstering customers' confidence by assuring them they are in good hands.

4. *Find ways to authentically lower customers' expectations.* Four Seasons Hotels has new front desk clerks wear name badges with "trainee" under the clerk's name. They find it encourages guests to be less demanding and more forgiving of mistakes. It also enables novices to take more risks as they transform shaky skills into confident mastery. Similarly, an emergency, if honestly addressed, can prepare customers for less service quality than they might normally expect.

Vision Cable of Charlotte, North Carolina, was a hard hit victim of Hugo. A company known for excellent service, they ran radio ads with the general manager, Milton Moore, saying: "Many of our customers have been hard hit by Hurricane Hugo, and so was Vision Cable. Miles of cable have been destroyed. Vision Cable has restored service to half of the service area. We are continuing our night-and-day effort to restore service to 100 percent of our customers. We sincerely appreciate your patience. You can help us by only calling our office to report service lines to your home which are down. Please be assured that adjustments will be made on your bill for the period you were without service."

Commenting on the company's service philosophy, Moore said, "We try to treat all our customers like neighbors. We believe if you are honest with customers, they will treat you like a neighbor when circumstances beyond your control put you in a tough position."

5. *Create a "this is very unusual" perspective to prevent adversity-driven service heroics from becoming a routine customer expectation.* Despite my having a guaranteed reservation at the Marriott Long Wharf Hotel in Boston, I found "no room at the inn" when I arrived very late one evening. Their recovery response to me was impressive, but I still had to sleep in another hotel some distance away. The following week I again arrived late at the Long Wharf, and the same front desk manager, Jan Blum, was about to "walk" me again. An earlier power outage nearby had caused several hotels to divert their arriving guests to the Marriott. Realizing my past patience would likely turn into present ire if walked again, Blum said with a twinkle in his eye, "I have a surprise for you! We never use Room 200 in overbooked situations like this. But, you are a special guest, it's very late, and you are only here for one evening. I want you to get Room 200. The mystery room turned out to be a gigantic two bedroom penthouse suite complete with panoramic view of the Boston harbor, a sunken living room with fireplace, grand piano, library—the works! I immediately regretted it was midnight, and I was staying only for one evening. However, I would never expect such a delightful offering to reoccur. Jan had carefully and sincerely positioned his heroic gesture as a "once-in-a-lifetime" occurrence.

These five principles can be practical guidance for escaping emergency experiences with an excellent evaluation. But remember that perceived culpability can play an important part in the customer's expectations during service quality deterioration or break down. If the flight is late departing because a flight attendant failed to arrive on time, the airline may get little customer sympathy. However, if customers perceive the "less-than-expected" service to be due to a situation beyond the control of the service provider, they will be more reluctant to register low marks on their mental service report cards.

The service provider which considers itself "off the hook" during adversarial times, however, is asking for trouble. Customers are more forgiving if service providers work as hard when things go wrong as they do to make service distinctive in normal times. The superstars of service all understand that unless extraordinary service actions accompany unusual emergency times, patrons will register their disappointment by silently taking their service business elsewhere.

ABOUT THE AUTHOR

Ken Shelton is chairman and editor-in-chief of *Executive Excellence* Publishing, publishers of newsletters, magazines, books, audio books, and CD-ROMs on personal and organizational development. The mission of *Executive Excellence* is to "help you find a wiser, better way to live your life and lead your organization."

Since 1984, Ken has served as editor of *Executive Excellence*, the world's leading executive advisory newsletter, and more recently *Personal Excellence*, a digest of the best thinking on personal and professional development. He is the editor of several books, including *In Search of Quality, A New Paradigm of Leadership*, and *The Best of Personal Excellence*.

For many years, he has enjoyed a close association with Stephen R. Covey, primarily as a writer and editor on various projects, including *The 7 Habits of Highly Effective People, Principle-Centered Leadership*, and *First Things First*. He is a former editor of *Utah Business* and *BYU Today* and a contributing writer to several other magazines.

Ken has a master's degree in mass and organizational communications from Brigham Young University and San Diego State University. In San Diego, California, he worked four years as a marketing communications specialist for General Dynamics Aerospace. He now lives in Provo, Utah, with his wife, Pam, and their three sons.

His book, *Beyond Counterfeit Leadership*, represents a creative synopsis of his writing and teaching, based on 30 years of professional experience, observation, and global travel.

EXECUTIVEllence

Personal Excellence

The Magazine of Life Enrichment

Our newest publication, *Personal Excellence*, is the magazine of life enrichment. As a value-based newsletter dedicated to personal and professional development, *Personal Excellence* focuses on such broad themes as Life-Career Balance, Spirit-Soul Enrichment, Health and Fitness, Relationships, Motivation, Mentoring, and Self-Esteem.

"I appreciate the quality and content . . ."

—John Naisbitt, author of *Megatrends* and *Megatrends 2000*

Contributing editors to *Personal Excellence* include:

Stephen R. Covey, author of *7 Habits of Highly Effective Families*
Ruth Stafford Peale, chairman of Guideposts, Inc.
Denis Waitley, author of *The Psychology of Winning*
Lou Tice, founder of the Winner's Circle Network
Dianna Booher, prolific author and motivational speaker
Ken Blanchard, co-author of *Everyone's a Coach*
Hyrum W. Smith, chairman of FranklinCovey Co.
Brian Tracy, author of *Maximum Achievement*

"Personal Excellence is a very interesting and worthwhile publication that provides its readers with positive and beneficial reading material."

—Tipper Gore, mental health policy advisor to President Clinton

Books of Related Interest from Executive Excellence Publishing

 **KEN SHELTON
A New Paradigm
of Leadership**

This compilation of perspectives on leadership from top CEOs and consultants such as Jack Welch (GE), Ross Perot, Stephen R. Covey, and others, offers informative advice on transition to the new paradigm of continuous change, learning and quality improvement, increased teamwork and empowerment, as well as bolder, more accurate decision making.

 **ROBERT E. STAUB
The Heart of
Leadership**

Robert "Dusty" Staub tells us that those who purport to lead often fail because they don't understand who it is they're trying to be. Thus, they don't know how to lead. Dusty gets to the heart of the matter by teaching us about the four chambers that make up the heart of a true leader: competency, intimacy, integrity, and passion.

 **THOMAS RISKAS
Working Beneath
the Surface**

Riskas's book challenges popular thinking in human development and provides a new perspective for realizing the soul's "hidden agenda" and deep need for wholeness and fulfillment. This book helps you perform the deep, inner work necessary to empower the soul to find greater wholeness and meaning in life.

 **WARREN BENNIS
Managing People Is
Like Herding Cats**

This book spells out the dilemma facing our leaderless society, details the qualities that successful leaders must have, and explores the challenges that today's leaders must face as they move toward change. Along the way, Bennis challenges our complacency and asks some serious questions.

 **KEN SHELTON
Beyond Counterfeit
Leadership**

In this book, Shelton explores the causes, cures, and outcomes of both counterfeit and authentic leadership. He reveals the elements of counterfeit in the conception and implementation of several models of leadership.

**Executive Excellence
Magazine on
CD-ROM**

This new "Instant Consultant" 12-year archive of Executive Excellence is an essential upgrade from the original 10-year edition. You also receive the 1996 issues of Personal Excellence FREE on the CD. You'll have indispensable research capabilities at the click of your mouse. Includes Mac and PC formats.

To order any of these books, call 1-800-304-9782.

Executive Excellence
publications are perfect:

- *As personal or professional vitamin pills.* Executive Excellence is an enriching monthly supplement to an executive's current diet of management and leadership training. *Personal Excellence* enhances the on-going personal and professional development programs of people at any age and stage in life.

- *As in-house management or personal development newsletters.* The magazines can be customized and received under an organization's own cover sheet.

- *As thought pieces for focus groups and management meetings.* The magazines can be analyzed and applied to help with current organizational dilemmas.

- *As a public relations gesture.* The magazines can be sent to favored suppliers and customers or displayed in reception and reading areas.

- *As gifts.* Executive Excellence may be given to newly promoted managers or to a management segment of the company. *Personal Excellence* may be given to all employees as a benefit.

Custom Corporate Editions
Corporate editions of both magazines are available. The magazine may be wrapped with a "false cover" with messages and announcements from the company, printed with the company logo, enhanced with articles by prominent company officers, or a combination.

Custom Reprints
Order custom reprints of your favorite articles (or chapters in this book)—in black & white or color—for use in your corporate training and development programs and seminars.

Foreign Language Editions
Executive Excellence is available in Korean, Japanese, and Turkish, editions. English-language editions for Australia, Ireland,and India are also available. *Personal Excellence* is available in Japanese and Turkish languages.

Executive Excellence Publishing has other publications in a variety of languages. For more information on other special editions, please call 1-800-304-9782.